BYRON

a poet before his public

BYRON
a poet before his public

PHILIP W. MARTIN

Lecturer in English,
King Alfred's College, Winchester

CAMBRIDGE UNIVERSITY PRESS

Cambridge

London   New York   New Rochelle
Melbourne   Sydney

Published by the Press Syndicate of the University of Cambridge
The Pitt Building, Trumpington Street, Cambridge CB2 1RP
32 East 57th Street, New York, NY 10022, USA
296 Beaconsfield Parade, Middle Park, Melbourne 3206, Australia

© Cambridge University Press 1982

First published 1982

Printed in Great Britain at the Pitman Press, Bath

Library of Congress catalogue card number: 81–21598

British Library cataloguing in publication data
Martin, Philip W.
Byron: a poet before his public.
1. Byron, George Gordon Byron, *Baron*
– Criticism and interpretation
I. Title
821′.7   PR4388

ISBN 0 521 24186 3 hard covers
ISBN 0 521 28766 9 paperback

Contents

Illustrations

Preface

This is not a survey of Byron's verse, whatever the conventional arrangement of its chapters may suggest. Certain works are untouched, and I have not discussed *The Vision of Judgement*, because I believe it to be a poem justly appreciated, and I have little to contribute to the current evaluation. Neither has this study any pretensions to conclusiveness. Although it challenges many of the current readings of Byron, I am attempting to open, rather than close, an argument offering a new perspective. Perhaps this is the place to say that in developing my view of Byron, my greatest critical debt is to W. W. Robson's 'Byron as Poet', and in the early stages of my thinking, Paul West's *Byron and the Spoiler's Art* forced me to consider some essential questions. The argument developed here differs from those of these two studies as much as they differ from each other, and there is no attempt to preclude them. Here the emphasis is on the poetry and the influences which shaped it. I have tried to see Byron not simply as a Romantic, but as a Romantic poet of the second generation, whose sense of his historical position heightened his consciousness of his modernity and his anxiety about his relation to those of his contemporaries (Wordsworth, Shelley, and Goethe, in particular) in whom he thought he recognized the new spirit of the age.

Acknowledgements

This book originated in a doctoral thesis submitted at the University of Exeter, and I wish to thank my supervisor, Professor Peter Thomson, for his guidance and encouragement, and Mr Charles Page for his numerous suggestions, sustained interest, and patient discussions. My thanks are also due to Dr Roberto Bruni of the Department of French and Italian Studies, Exeter University, for his help with Italian texts and translations; to all my friends and ex-colleagues at Exeter who took an interest in my studies; and to Mrs Melba Chapman for her typing and her cheerful acceptance of so many alterations.

A note on the text

Quotations from Byron's poetry outside of *Don Juan* are taken from Coleridge's edition; those from *Don Juan* are taken from the edition edited by Steffan, Steffan, and Pratt. References are given in brackets after each quotation. For Byron's letters and journals, Marchand's edition has been cited wherever possible, supplemented by Prothero's. All these works are listed in full in the Bibliography, section I. For quotations from contemporary reviews and recorded conversations I have cited the most readily available source.

Works in a language other than English are usually quoted in the original. Translations have been used when it seems likely that Byron did not read these works in the original.

This book was researched before McGann's new edition of Byron's poetry was produced.

Abbreviations

The following abbreviations for Byron sources are used in the notes:

CC: Lovell's *Collected Conversations*
CH: Rutherford's *Critical Heritage*
LJ: Marchand's letters and journals
Medwin: Medwin's *Conversations*
Prothero: Prothero's letters and journals
PW: Coleridge's edition of the poetry

These works are listed in full in the Bibliography.

Introduction

Despite an abundance of contemporary critical material, the modern reader is unlikely to find a more stimulating comment with which to begin his study of Byron than the following, written by Macaulay in 1831:

[Voltaire], like Lord Byron, put himself at the head of an intellectual revolution, dreading it all the time, murmering at it, sneering at it, yet choosing rather to move before his age in any direction than to be left behind and forgotten.[1]

Although we may be disturbed by Macaulay's comparison of Byron to Voltaire, as well as by his use of the word 'intellectual', his description of Byron's relation to his age can be usefully placed alongside an interesting yet puzzling observation made by W. W. Robson in his penetrating 'Byron as Poet':

He is a poet not only in that (to use a convenient vulgarism) he 'gets across' his egoistic passions; he conveys along with them, though doubtless unwittingly, a sense that his vehement indulgence in them is, deep down, against the grain. And our recognition of this ultimate probity is allied to our pleasure in Byron's vitality.[2]

The attraction of this is that it encourages us to see a rebellion within the bombast and emotional generosity of the early poetry, but even the most sympathetic reader is likely to wonder how this can be achieved, and the current state of Byron criticism offers no means of assistance. This is where Macaulay is of use. His description of Byron's relation to his period demands that we recognize the significance of his relation to his public. It is this, Macaulay implies, that in turn determines his competitive and anxious relation to his contemporaries, and governs the nature of his poetry.[3] If we take the force of this, we are compelled to look at the manner of Byron's presentation of himself to a public whose applause was alluring and simultaneously the subject of his contempt: we are forced to study a performance in which the performer exhibits himself in a way that he resents, and in which, therefore, there may exist indications of his distaste.

If we are to approach Byron in this way, then we must first evolve a more satisfactory view of his motivation for writing than that which is usually offered. Obviously the answer is going to be radically different from those produced in the cases of Wordsworth, Coleridge, and Shelley, but not because of anything that is to be explained in his own terms: his much-exhibited views of himself as an erupting volcano or a man seeking relief from the tortures of his ennui. And in thinking of the distinctive nature of Byron's relation to his public, we are reminded that the history of his poetry is also the history of a relatively new public, the nature of which his verse proved uniquely capable of revealing. If this pushes us away from comparisons with the major Romantic poets and towards Scott, it is only to notice that the effects of this public's existence on Byron are not merely to be explained in terms of its constituting a demand. That might be all that one would wish to conclude about Scott's relation to his readers, but Byron's case is different, both in terms of what he offered his audience, and in terms of their expectations. In *Childe Harold I & II*, Byron invited his reader to equate the emotions of his verse with the real emotions of the poet, the experience alluded to in the poem with the real experience of Lord Byron of Newstead. I shall argue that he did this – at least in part – facetiously, but his public chose not to recognize the disclaimers. Herein lies the difference between Scott's reception and Byron's. The blindness, and one is tempted to say wilful blindness, of Byron's readers testified to the extent of their control over his product, but his loss of artistic independence was compensated for by the attractions of the image they had fashioned for him. Thus at the beginning of his career Byron was confronted by an unsophisticated reading public that was tempting him to produce material through which this image could be sustained or strengthened. This, obviously, makes the critic's task an awkward one.

Indeed, what makes the poetry from *Childe Harold I & II* onwards so difficult to approach is its instability as textual material. So much of it is evidently being used by the poet as a means of creating fantasies about himself, fantasies which are not self-sufficient, but require the reinforcement provided by the public's willingness to participate in them. What Byron includes in these fantasies, therefore, is governed by what his audience is prepared to believe about him. Further, it is not simply a case of Byron imagining that he is, or could have been, the Giaour or Lara. He is involved in larger, more consequential fantasies: at the centre of his entire achievement lies the illusion that a wealth of worldly experience, or at least a huge capacity for worldly experience, provides him with the essential qualifications of a great poet. This is an illusion partly presented to him by the circumstances of his success, by his readers' responses, by his critics' claims, and Byron naturally finds it seductive. It also derives from his strong sense of belonging (after his introduction to the Holland House circle in 1812) to a metropolitan literary milieu that felt its tastes threatened by the distinctly provincial verse of the Lake poets:

They are a set of the most despicable imposters – that is my opinion of them. They know nothing of the world; and what is poetry, but the reflection of the world? What sympathy have this people with the spirit of this stirring age? . . . They are mere old wives. Look at their beastly vulgarity, when they wish to be homely; and their exquisite stuff, when they clap on sail, and aim at fancy. Coleridge is the best of the trio – but bad is the best. Southey ought to have been a parish-clerk, and Wordsworth a man-midwife – both in darkness. I doubt if either of them ever got drunk.[4]

The fantasy of poetic greatness is structured around a fantasy of his experience of life, whether received or expected: he is prepared to believe in himself as a great poet because he is prepared to believe in his capacity for the kind of experience upon which he thinks great poetry is founded. But to perpetuate the illusion of his capacity for life, Byron needs his poetry. Paradoxically, it becomes the surrogate for the life he has not had, or for the life that he has not *felt* as intensely as he considered himself bound to feel.

The circumstances are made more complex by another paradox, the paradox of Byron's success; his discovery of public (and social) acceptance by his presentation of himself as an isolate. This, one senses, was not merely the employment of a popular motif, but received its initial impulse from the resentment of an aristocratic poet whose historical circumstances denied him an elite audience, an audience whose habits and tastes complemented his own. By presenting himself as a social outcast, he was able to persuade himself that he was preserving his artistic and aristocratic independence, although his resentment, and thereby his assumed posture, became more extreme as the applause of the usurping middle-class audience rang louder in his ears. Once again, a vicious circle was established, for to Byron that applause represented a form of support for his private vision of himself. 'He is', wrote Hazlitt, 'that anomaly in letters and in society, a Noble Poet',[5] and the nature of his verse, as we shall see, suggests that he felt it too.

These, I suggest, are the forces acting upon Byron's verse of which we have to be aware. It is insufficient simply to pronounce the poetry to be good or bad – we have to consider its determinants. And charting the nature of Byron's relation to his art and audience need not be a guessing game. There are indications within the verse suggesting much about his attitudes, and these can be clearly apprehended if we are prepared to see the poetry not as a mysterious autonomous text, but as a consciously produced artefact designed for the appeasement of a particular audience, a performance conducted under special conditions, the nature of which I have outlined above. And the significance of this performance, I suggest, inheres not in its script, nor in the manner of its presentation, but ultimately in the degree of conviction with which it is conducted. Here I am in disagreement with Robson, who has called attention to the usefulness of seeing Byron's poetry as a performing art:

On that question of Byron's sincerity . . . the comparison with a dramatic performer throws some light. It is possible, in watching a great actor, to respond simultaneously in two ways: 'How moving!' and 'How well he plays his part!' And we should not feel the actor's greatness less, were we to infer a corresponding duality of consciousness in him. There is no question of insincerity; the performance is successful or unsuccessful, good or bad, but it is not sincere or insincere. Success is a matter of being able to mobilize emotions which one has either had, or can imagine having, without necessarily having them at the moment.[6]

The difficulty is that so frequently we cannot 'infer a corresponding duality of consciousness' in Byron of this kind. The most awkward and persistent worry that confronts his readers is that which grows out of the recognition that his being seduced by the attractions of a particular role (be it that of *Childe Harold* or *Don Juan*) is of such a

4

nature that it impedes the manifestation of a controlling self-awareness in the poetry. The creation of a figure of the poet, an image of a man behind the verse, is apparently his primary concern, and where he stands in relation to this fiction, and in relation to the performance which created it, is frequently obscure or ambiguous. It ought to be said here that this is as true of *Don Juan* as it is of *Childe Harold*. The later poem succeeds in postponing the question by its repeated warnings against taking its poet's stances seriously, but the mask which Byron adopts so that he may claim his right of access to this kind of mobility – that of a man grown old before his time, numbed by the excesses of his experience – is one which we are apparently required to accept without questioning whether it belongs to the mechanism of the performance. He may occasionally utilize this posture whilst expanding his repertoire of burlesque gestures, but elsewhere, both inside and outside the poem in contemporaneous pieces, we are asked to defer to it, to make the concession by which the Byronic myth is to be sustained. The sense received when reading much of Byron's verse is not so much 'How well he plays his part!' nor even (conversely) 'He doesn't mean it really and of that he is aware' as 'He fails to convince me and himself that he means it here, but he thinks he might, he thinks he could do.' And within this kind of response, we may concern ourselves with the degree of Byron's conviction.

In determining this, and in attempting to understand how Byron conceived of his verse, I have found it useful to examine its constitution (or perhaps in this case 'chemistry' is a better word). For within the instability of much of Byron's poetry may be seen the strong traces of a productive process that has no real equivalent elsewhere in English Romanticism, a process wherein disparate and eclectic elements are taken and mixed together in such a way as to deny the reader the impression of there being a single controlling idea, or clearly envisaged purpose, behind the experiment. The presence within a single work of such oddly sorting elements as Rousseau, Young, and Wordsworth, or the *Lyrical Ballads*, Dante, Sterne, and Philips (see Chapter 3), alerts us to the complexity and peculiarity of Byron's methods. It is not that his handling of, say, Rousseau, can be taken simply as a matter of 'source' or 'influence'. Rousseau's presence in *Childe Harold III* suggests the presence of an interference: he is the means by which Byron comes to terms with Wordsworth. This study concerns itself with interferences and interpolations of this kind, for they offer themselves as means of understanding the nature of Byron's relation to his art and his audience. They are, in fact, his literary contexts, and they have remained largely unexplored.

The approach I have adopted may solve two of the most awkward problems that all students of Byron confront. The first is the question of development. Few would deny that *Don Juan* is Byron's finest poem, but the way in which it is commonly related to his earlier works – as a document which undermines them and thereby demonstrates an intellectual transcending of their bombast and limitations – is manifestly unsatisfactory. Not only do we find Byron writing *Mazeppa*, *The Island*, and *Heaven and Earth* at points in his career when, by the implications of this approach, he should be producing much finer things, but also this thesis does nothing to explain the close proximity of *Childe Harold IV* and *Manfred* to *Don Juan*, any more than it is willing to provide a precedent for *Don Juan*'s impressive manoeuvrings. The maturity and quality of *Don Juan* cannot be defined or given precedent by reference to a developing consciousness, but they can be understood as deriving from a shift of mode which permits the dramatization of a kind of performance that had found its skills inhibited by the restrictions of Byron's earlier modes. Looking at Byron in this way may surprise some readers. On the one hand they may be disappointed by the suggestion that *Don Juan* proceeds from the same kind of consciousness that informs the earlier works. On the other, looking at the whole of Byron's achievement, they may be pleased to recognize the earlier works as deriving essentially from the same consciousness that makes *Don Juan* what it is.

The second problem declares itself most clearly in that penetrating remark of Santayana's – 'he did not respect himself, or his art, as much as they deserved' – a remark justly appreciated in Robson's essay. The obstructions for the critic are ostensibly large: how can we approach a poet who, quite apart from his self-mutilating tendencies (both inside and outside *Don Juan*), so frequently displayed scant regard for his craft? Here there are wider issues to be considered. Byron's treatment of his poetry does not derive entirely from a dilemma explicable in psychological terms: the question of his attitude towards his art, and towards himself as artist, demands a consideration of the social conditions which made his poetry possible. We could say that the technical crudity of the

Turkish Tales shows Byron respecting his art as much as it deserves and no more. For art in these lays, and for that matter in most of Byron's poetry, is not to be vaguely defined in terms of a consecrated wider concept, but in terms of the demands that elicited it into being, the demands of popular consumption. These demands, creating a relaxation of critical standards, subsequently resulted in there being no serious resistance to Byron's propensity to use his verse for the purposes of building fantasies about his ego. By not conceiving of his poetry too seriously Byron was able to protect himself against the less acceptable facets of his poetic production; able too, by his subsequently achieved sense of detachment, occasionally to conduct minor internal performances for himself, of which he expects his readers to remain oblivious. Their function is to support his illusion of independence: they may be seen as attempts to persuade himself that he was not committed to a business in which success was necessarily defined in terms of publishers' receipts. Further, this non-serious relation to his verse allowed Byron the possibility of a non-serious relation to his fantasies, of which, we may conjecture, he had need in his more sombre moments of reflection. Again, if we are prepared to approach the poetry by seeing it in terms offered by the analogy of a performance, we need not be coerced into disapproving of Byron's lack of artistic self-respect, but recognize it instead as an inherent part of his production. Apart from being an essential step towards seeing Byron in the context of his age, this is also a means of discovering his 'probity', of understanding how and why we feel that his 'indulgence . . . is . . . deep down, against the grain'.

I have not begun with these hypotheses and attempted to wrench the poetry into a corresponding position. The view of Byron presented here is one which depends almost entirely upon the verse itself. 'The assessment of Byron's poetry . . . must begin and end with the poetry.'[7] Quite so: if we accept the trend of current Byron critics and advocate taking him seriously without a proper examination of the verse, we will find ourselves involved in the same kind of ostentatious critical games, displays which demonstrate that taking Byron seriously is equivalent to not taking the poetry (or indeed the critic's task) seriously. The sincere student of Byron must accept that a large proportion of his time will be spent examining poetry written without serious intent. It may be that when proper acknowledgement of the unstable relationship between poet and public has been made, we are left feeling sceptical about Byron's status as a major poet, particularly when considering the verse not written in *ottava rima*. But we cannot ignore this essential, perhaps unique, dimension of a poet's work simply because it may affect his conventional standing. If we wish to persist in perpetuating the Byronic myth, in seeing the poetry as the issue of single-minded passion, or in registering the reiteration of a limited number of gestures and motifs as an expression of the *Zeitgeist*, and no more, then we must read Byron with our eyes half-closed. To insist that he was a philosophical poet, or even that the verse was written with the earnestness of a Shelley or a Wordsworth, necessitates a perversion of what is before our eyes on the page. Although an approach based on such assumptions may be able to claim superficially that it is a positive appreciation, ultimately it offers us only an impoverished experience of the verse. By not starting from an acceptance of Byron as a great poet, however, we can liberate ourselves from this narrowness. What I wish to argue for here is a fuller, richer experience of the poetry by considering its determinants, a reading which may allow us to recognize and understand the nature of the integrity with which 'our pleasure in Byron's vitality' is closely associated.

1

Experiment in *Childe Harold I & II*

The Preface to *Childe Harold's Pilgrimage* seems to indicate that Byron is unsure of the kind of poem he has written:

The stanza of Spenser, according to one of our most successful poets, admits of every variety. Dr. Beattie makes the following observation:–

'Not long ago I began a poem in the style and stanza of Spenser, in which I propose to give full scope to my inclination, and be either droll or pathetic, descriptive or sentimental, tender or satirical, as the humour strikes me; for, if I mistake not, the measure which I have adopted admits equally of all these kinds of composition.' Strengthened in my opinion by such authority, and by the example of some in the highest order of Italian poets, I shall make no apology for attempts at similar variations in the following composition; satisfied that, if they are unsuccessful, their failure must be in the execution, rather than in the design sanctioned by the practice of Ariosto, Thomson, and Beattie.

If one proceeds from here to the original manuscript, and in particular to the stanzas which Dallas and Murray persuaded Byron to omit, the question of the nature of the poem Byron was writing on his Grand Tour becomes even more awkward and persistent:

> But when Convention sent his handy work
> Pens, tongues, feet, hands combined in wild uproar;
> Mayor, Aldermen, laid down the uplifted fork;
> The bench of Bishops half forgot to snore[1]

This sort of flippancy – the quality which Byron admired in the author from whom he took his poem's epigraph[2] – is capable of being sustained and indulged for its own sake:

> Eftsoons his little heart beat merrily
> With hope of foreign nations to behold,
> And many things right marvellous to see,

9

> Of which our lying voyagers have told,
> In many a tome as true as Mandeville's of old.[3]

It is capable too of anticipating *Beppo* (but perhaps not the more sophisticated games of *Don Juan*) by exploiting a trick probably learnt from Prior:

> In golden characters right well designed
> First on the list appeareth one 'Junot;'
> Then certain other glorious names we find,
> (Which Rhyme compelleth me to place below:)
> Dull victors! baffled by the vanquished foe,
> Wheedled by conynge tongues of laurels due,
> Stand, worthy of each other in a row –
> Sirs Arthur, Harry, and the dizzard Hew
> Dalrymple, seely wight, sore dupe of t'other tew.[4]

How did Byron conceive of *Childe Harold* when he was writing it? The question is one that has troubled few critics: the majority are either irritated by its postures or content to recognize in them a suitable context for the embodiment of a distinctly Romantic *Weltschmerz*. The poem is thus either considered to be of limited interest or conceived of as a confessional piece of occasional rhetorical power and considerable poetic promise.[5] The latter reading seems to me to be the more perverse, but neither takes account of the poem's tonal variety. However much *Childe Harold*'s reception and subsequent criticism have obscured its tonal variation, it is clear from his apology in the Preface that even after the revision of the original manuscript, Byron was only too aware of this quality in his poem.

After a glance at the poem's opening stanzas, it is surprising that this aspect of *Childe Harold's Pilgrimage* should have been so neglected. Only Bernard Blackstone has chosen to comment on the peculiarity of the invocation:

It is a measure of Byron's artistry that this address to the Muse, though couched in terms of Delphi, and though added to the poem as late as July–November 1811, is subtly adapted in its tone to the half-flippant picture of Harold at Newstead which immediately follows. The tone is not disrespectful – Byron could never be that about Delphi – but it is ironical and slightly debunking.[6]

Yet the stanza is devoid of the kind of control and assurance upon which irony depends. Whilst repeating the familiar satiric formula of *English Bards and Scotch Reviewers*, the first four lines also present an impression of the poet's desultory temperament:

> Oh, thou! in Hellas deem'd of heavenly birth,
> Muse! form'd or fabled at the minstrel's will!
> Since shamed full oft by later lyres on earth,
> Mine dares not call thee from thy sacred hill   (I, i)

The modesty is a foil: what is reflected here is a willingness to believe in his superior skills that finds no confirmation in the chosen idiom. Instead, he chooses to present his qualifications in the form of a reference to his experience:

> Yet there I've wander'd by thy vaunted rill;
> Yes! sigh'd o'er Delphi's long deserted shrine,
> Where, save that feeble fountain all is still   (I, i)

Finding himself playing the wandering bard, however, Byron clearly has difficulties in taking himself seriously. The final couplet indicates this: it is a reversion to a mode which happily accommodates his insecurity and ambivalence. Far from being a 'measure of Byron's artistry', this is an extremely uncertain touch:

> Nor mote my shell awake the weary Nine
> To grace so plain a tale – this lowly lay of mine.   (I, i)

Considering the following stanzas (which rather than being 'half-flippant' seem to me to be almost completely so) one wonders at this point whether Byron's claim for the sort of freedom that will allow him to be 'droll or pathetic, descriptive or sentimental, tender or satirical, as the humour strikes' ought not to be regarded with suspicion. Such freedom requires confidence, a type of confidence almost realized in *Don Juan* perhaps, but never to be found in *Childe Harold's Pilgrimage*. It seems more likely that Byron is preoccupied with the problem of manufacturing a figure of the poet that he can come to comfortable terms with. The question with which he was confronted while writing the first two cantos of *Childe Harold* was perhaps not primarily 'How will my public conceive of me and with what sort of regard?' but 'How am I to conceive of myself and my art?' Byron has no real need to be ironic about the muses, as Blackstone implies, but perhaps he did feel a need to be ironic about himself as poet. It is a dilemma which the satirist of *English Bards and Scotch Reviewers* could for the most part afford to ignore.

Childe Harold I & II must be considered in its context. It is a poem written by a man flushed with the success of *English Bards and Scotch Reviewers* and prepared to continue his poetic career by publishing *Hints from Horace*. There seems no good reason to disbelieve Dallas's account:

> He said he believed satire to be his *forte*, and to that he had adhered, having written, during his stay at different places abroad, a paraphrase of Horace's *Art of Poetry*, which would be a good finish to *English Bards and Scotch Reviewers*, forgetting the regret which, in his last letter, he had expressed to me for having written it. He seemed to promise himself additional fame from it . . .
>
> In not disparaging this poem however, next day, I could not refrain from expressing some surprise that he had written nothing else: upon which he told me that he had occasionally written short poems, besides a great many stanzas in Spenser's measure, relative to the countries he had visited. 'They are not worth troubling you with, but you shall have them all with you if you like.' So came I by *Childe Harold's Pilgrimage*. . .
>
> . . . I was surprised to learn that I could not obtain credit with Lord Byron for my judgement on *Childe Harold's Pilgrimage*. 'It was anything but poetry – it had been condemned by a good critic – had I not myself seen the sentences on the margins of the manuscript?' He dwelt upon the paraphrase of the *Art of Poetry* with pleasure; and the manuscript of that was given to Cawthorn, the publisher of the Satire, to be brought forth without delay.[7]

Little credence, I think, can be given to those authors who insist that Byron's primary intention was to publish *Childe Harold*, and that his coy manoeuvres with its manuscript were the schematic tactics of a man already involved in the process of building myths about himself. In many ways *Hints from Horace* is a better poem than the 'Romaunt', and certainly it guaranteed a moderate success, whereas *Childe Harold* was undoubtedly a risk. Nevertheless it is almost certain that Byron took a real interest in his Spenserian poem. It is both too lengthy and highly worked to be conceived of as the consequence of completely idle scribbling. His hesitation in publishing, I believe, is symptomatic of an artistic equivocation that is far deeper and more intriguing than the not

unreasonable fears of a man still smarting from the unprecedented spite of the *Edinburgh Review*. The inception of *Childe
Harold* was an experiment; an experiment not so much upon the
public, but conducted more for Byron's own purposes, to discover
just how seriously he was prepared to take himself and his art. I
hope to be able to show that this equivocation is clearly recognizable in the text of the poem itself.

As presented to Byron through its eighteenth-century usage, the
Spenserian stanza was peculiarly well qualified to accommodate
this kind of ambivalence. Before discussing this usage, however, it
is necessary to dispense with the notion that *Childe Harold* is
modelled on, inspired by, or even usefully comparable to Spenser's
poetry. Robert Gleckner makes the comparison (apparently in
order to conclude that 'Byron's technique, then, is not so much that
of Spenser and Du Bellay as it is that of Eliot and Yeats, Joyce and
Faulkner')[8] and Leslie Marchand rather weakly explains Byron's
use of the stanza form by suggesting that 'he had been reading some
extracts from Spenser and so began his "fictitious" poem of the
wandering pilgrim in the Spenserian stanza'.[9] No supporting
reference is given, and Marchand takes no account of Leigh Hunt's
claim that Byron knew very little of Spenser in 1822:

Spenser he could not read; at least he said so. I lent him a volume of the
'Fairy Queen', and he said he would try to like it. Next day he brought it to
my study-window, and said, 'Here, Hunt, here is your Spenser. I cannot
see anything in him:' and he seemed anxious that I should take it out of his
hands. That he saw nothing in Spenser is not very likely; but I really do not
think that he saw much. Spenser was too much out of the world, and he too
much in it.[10]

Byron obviously knew of Spenser when he began *Childe Harold* in
1809, and perhaps he had read some extracts, but it is unlikely that
Spenser was in any way his model. The stanza had received liberal
attention in the eighteenth century from (amongst others) Collins,
Shenstone, Thomson, and Beattie – poets with whom Byron
would have been well acquainted. Although Byron mentions
Beattie in his Preface, *Childe Harold* bears few similarities to *The
Minstrel*. After reading Beattie's claims for the flexibility of the
stanza form, one is disappointed by the tameness of his poem.
Occasionally, however, one is struck by the verse's drollery:

> There lived in Gothic days, as legends tell,
> A shepherd-swain, a man of low degree;

> Whose sires, perchance, in Fairyland might dwell,
> Sicilian groves, or vales of Arcady;
> But he, I ween, was of the north countrie;
> A nation famed for song and beauty's charms;
> Zealous, yet modest; innocent, though free;
> Patient of toil; serene amidst alarms;
> Inflexible in faith; invincible in arms.[11]

One senses that Beattie is smiling at himself here, and this is confirmed by a footnote he appended to the fifth line of this stanza which reads 'There is hardly an ancient ballad, or romance wherein a minstrel or harper appears, but he is characterized, by way of eminence, to have been "of the north countrie."'[12] The slightly sardonic narrative manner recalls another eighteenth-century Spenserian poem, Shenstone's *The Schoolmistress*:

> O ruthful scene! when from the nook obscure
> His little sister doth his peril see:
> All playful as she sate, she grows demure;
> She finds full soon her wonted spirits flee,
> She meditates a prayer to set him free:
> Nor gentle pardon could this dame deny
> (If gentle pardon could with dames agree)
> To her sad grief that swells in either eye
> And wrings her so that all for pity she could dye.[13]

A comment by Shenstone on the relative insobriety of his poem discloses a point of reference that is perhaps unexpected: Pope's 'The Alley', an early imitation of Spenser:

my Schoolmistress, I suppose, is much more in Spenser's way than any one wou'd chuse to write in that writes quite *gravely*: in which Case The Dialect & stanza of Spenser is hardly preferable to modern Heroic. I look upon my Poem as somewhat more grave than Pope's Alley, & a good deal less yⁿ Mr Thomson's Castle etc.[14]

Shenstone's enjoyment of 'The Alley' probably derived from Pope's burlesque of Spenser's allegorizing:

> Hard by a Sty, beneath a Roof of Thatch,
> Dwelt *Obloquy*, who in her early Days
> Baskets of Fish at Billingsgate did watch,
> Cod, Whiting, Oyster, Mackrel, Sprat, or Plaice:
> There learn'd she Speech from Tongues that never cease.
> *Slander* beside her, like a Magpye, chatters,

With *Envy*, (spitting Cat,) dread Foe to Peace:
Like a curs'd Cur, *Malice* before her clatters,
And vexing ev'ry Wight, tears Cloaths and all to Tatters.
(Pope, 'Spenser: The Alley', 28–36)[15]

It is a technique that Shenstone does not employ, preferring instead to exploit the sardonic narrative manner of the Spenserian stanza, a manner which Pope, perhaps, was responsible for discovering in his parody. Shenstone's peculiar judgement of *The Castle of Indolence* as a 'grave' poem is easily explained, for at the time of this remark he had not read the work. His conjectures were probably governed by his acquaintance with *The Seasons* and *Liberty*, and he was pleasantly surprised upon reading the poem at a later date.[16]

It seems that the quaintness of the Spenserian stanza, and the way in which its fourth rhyme can appear to be just a little over-extravagant, lent itself to a self-consciously quaint style of narration. Pope and Shenstone seem to be capable of exploiting this, whereas Beattie, whilst recognizing the stanza's possibilities, fails to capitalize on them. However, it is Thomson's *The Castle of Indolence*, more than any other significant work of the eighteenth century, which exploits the kind of quizzical energy to be found in 'The Alley' and *The Schoolmistress* with assurance and consistency. It is emphasized partly by Thomson's retention of the archaisms which Shenstone and Beattie, for the most part, rejected. The 'imitation' is a piece of affectation undertaken by Thomson with his tongue in his cheek:

This poem being writ in the manner of Spenser, the obsolete words, and a simplicity of diction in some of the lines which borders on the ludicrous, were necessary to make the imitation more perfect.
(Advertisement to *The Castle of Indolence*)[17]

It would be a mistake to suggest that Byron was unaware of the absurdity of the simple and archaic diction employed in *Childe Harold*. He knew *The Castle of Indolence* very well, and the style and techniques particularly of the early parts of *Childe Harold* make use of this intimacy.[18] How conscious Byron was of following Thomson is an issue that defies resolution, and ultimately it is an issue of little consequence. What is important is that the poet of *Childe Harold I & II*, consciously or unconsciously, finds the attractions of the mode of *The Castle of Indolence* alluring.

The salient feature of *The Castle of Indolence* is that its poet is unwilling to take himself seriously. According to Sir Harris Nicholas, who published the first memoir of Thomson in 1831, the poem 'was originally intended to consist of a few stanzas ridiculing his own want of energy and that of some of his friends'.[19] Its beginnings are only too evident in the apologetic yet confident irony in which the poem's 'moralizing' is couched:

> O mortal man, who livest here by toil,
> Do not complain of this thy hard estate:
> That like an emmet thou must ever moil,
> It is a sad sentence of an ancient date;
> And, certes, there is for it reason great;
> For, though sometimes it makes thee weep and wail,
> And curse thy star, and early drudge and late,
> Withouten that would come an heavier bale, –
> Loose life, unruly passions, and diseases pale.
>
> (I, i)

The burlesque consists not merely of mocking an assumed style, but in the way in which the poet amuses himself by regarding his posture with a sardonic eye. The fifth line exploits the inevitability of the couplet by assuming all the resignation of the tired, head-shaking, and sagacious moralist. A similar pattern and gesture can be seen here in *Childe Harold*:

> Oh, Christ! It is a goodly sight to see
> What Heaven hath done for this delicious land:
> What fruits of fragrance blush on every tree!
> What goodly prospects o'er the hills expand!
> But man would mar them with an impious hand
>
> (I, xv)

Both poets are playing upon a Miltonic cliché. Thomson's reference is only vague; Byron's more precise, echoing Milton's

> By him first
> Men also, and by his suggestion taught,
> Ransacked the centre, and with impious hands
> Rifled the bowels of their mother earth . . .
>
> (*Paradise Lost*, I, 684–7)[20]

A more obvious result of Thomson's influence is to be found in the opening stanzas of *Childe Harold*:

> Whilome in Albion's isle there dwelt a youth,
> Who ne in virtue's ways did take delight;
> But spent his days in riot most uncouth,
> And vex'd with mirth the drowsy ear of Night.
> Ah me! in sooth he was a shameless wight,
> Sore given to revel and ungodly glee;
> Few earthly things found favour in his sight
> Save concubines and carnal companie,
> And flaunting wassailers of high and low degree.
>
> (I, ii)

Again that gesture appears in the fifth line, and the irony here is closer to Thomson's; the emphasis given to the flippancy of the final line by the alexandrine is particularly telling too. The Bacchanalia of the first canto's early stanzas is the equivalent of Thomson's indolent scenes, regarded in the same ironic light, and described in terms which include a strong element of self-caricature. Just as we see Thomson and his friends lolling around his castle, so we recognize Byron and his circle imitating Churchill and the hell-fire club at Newstead:

> The Childe departed from his father's hall:
> It was a vast and venerable pile;
> So old, it seemed only not to fall,
> Yet strength was pillar'd in each massy aisle.
> Monastic dome! condemn'd to uses vile!
> Where Superstition once had made her den
> Now Paphian girls were known to sing and smile;
> And monks might deem their time was come agen,
> If ancient tales say true, nor wrong these holy men.
>
> (I, vii)

Recent critics have been reluctant to recognize *Childe Harold* as a caricature of Byron himself.[21] And yet this is made so obvious in the poem's early stanzas that it would seem to be beyond question. The issue of the purpose and style of the caricature, however, is worth consideration. Clearly Byron's caricature is not of the same ilk as that picture of himself which Thomson included in *The Castle of Indolence:*

> A bard here dwelt, more fat than bard beseems;
> Who, void of envy, guile, and lust of gain,
> On Virtue still, and Nature's pleasing themes,
> Pour'd forth his unpremeditated strain.

The world forsaking with a calm disdain,
Here laugh'd he careless in his easy seat;
Here quaff'd encircled with the joyous train,
Oft moralizing sage: his ditty sweet
He loathed much to write, ne cared to repeat.

(I, lxviii)

The idea of self-caricature in *Childe Harold* almost certainly derives from Thomson, but both its manner and motive are different. Thomson is putting on a show for his friends, and we necessarily feel that we are largely excluded from the poem's convivial intimacy when reading it. Those contemporaries of Thomson who constituted the wider audience of *The Castle of Indolence* may have felt compelled to be amused by it, but could not possibly have regarded themselves as anything other than distanced spectators. The interesting aspect of *Childe Harold*'s caricature is that it is addressed to no particular audience, wide or narrow. Hobhouse and the 'fellow Bacchanals' may have appreciated it, and in this very limited sense *Childe Harold*'s audience is comparable to that of *The Castle of Indolence*. But in no sense is Byron's poem a poem written for an exclusive set, a fashionable clique in the fashionable public's eye. At the time he wrote *Childe Harold* Byron was a lord with no lordly friends, a gentleman of fashion without a coterie. Unlike Thomson, therefore, Byron had no claims to make, and indeed the idea of having to display his credentials for being regarded as a gentleman with exclusive friends was no doubt repugnant to him. Whilst Thomson's reference is in no sense ignominious, the deferential qualities of his poem, and therefore of his caricature, would thus have had few attractions for Byron, although the mode of casual flippancy in which Thomson presents his self-portrait may well have drawn his admiration.

At its simplest Byron's caricature can be seen as a piece of self-amusement, a consequence of the same extravagant whimsy that manifests itself in his letters. If this is so, then it is also symptomatic of a deeply rooted indifference towards an undefined prospective audience who are thus forced to accept this facet of the poem along with the rest. At a more complex level it can perhaps be regarded as an experimental exploration of a version of himself that he later chose to adopt with more confidence and panache, without necessarily respecting it any the more:

Yet oft-times in his maddest mirthful mood
Strange pangs would flash along Childe Harold's brow,
As if the memory of some deadly feud
Or disappointed passion lurked below:
But this none knew, nor haply cared to know;
For his was not that open, artless soul
That feels relief by bidding sorrow flow,
Nor sought he friend to counsel or condole,
Whate'er this grief mote be, which he could not control.

(I, viii)

This bears an obvious relation to the later stances that are commonly regarded as 'Byronic' (a dreadfully misleading and over-used term).

However distinct Byron's caricature may be from Thomson's in most respects, there is one important similarity. Thomson's portrait of himself crystallizes a hazily defined figure of the poet that the reader has been attempting to bring into focus from the poem's early stanzas. For we are constantly aware not merely of the opulence of Thomson's verse, but also of the fact that he is making an exhibition of this opulence. His moralizing gestures, therefore, can only be regarded as the dicta of a man who can afford to make presents of them to his friends and patrons. The image of Thomson 'carelessly laughing in his easy seat', 'oft moralizing' over his claret, is thus entirely consistent with the outline of the poet which the verse has succeeded in conveying (if not defining) before we arrive at the caricaturing stanza. As Johnson noted, the poem's 'lazy luxury' is apparent from its very beginning.[22] The stanza therefore is precedented; it confirms our opinion that the mode is exaggerated and affords its poet continual ironic amusement. In a similar way, Byron's caricature is not confined to its immediate context. Working the other way round to Thomson, he toys with an image of himself that amuses him at the beginning, and then proceeds to play upon it throughout. It is a cruder technique, and ultimately proves to be far less successful. Byron lacks Thomson's poise and assurance. Whilst the poem's opening makes us aware of the fact that the mode of Byron's poem amuses him, and whilst his ambiguous use of the stanza consistently reasserts this fact, we are not always certain of the level at which Byron is being entertained. Is he watching himself perform with ironic self-regard, or is he playing the ham in defiant contempt of an unsophisticated audience? Or is he sometimes tempted to play the part with sufficient conviction to make us suspicious? These are questions which recur again and again when we are reading *Childe Harold*, and they present problems that are perhaps beyond complete resolution, but which nevertheless demand to be investigated.

There is evidence to suggest that Byron, following Thomson, conceives of his poetry as something that is essentially staged. This is an impression of *Childe Harold* that one is perhaps only fully prepared to recognize in its latter half when Byron is prepared to play the part of the leading actor without equivocation. It can be seen, for instance, in the famous stanzas beginning

> I have not loved the world, nor the world me;
> I have not flatter'd its rank breath, nor bow'd
> To its idolatries a patient knee

> (III, cxiii)

The Shakespearean flavour is strong; the influence of the kind of theatre behind Kean's extravagant gesturing clearly discernible. But one is aware of a similar attitude earlier in the poem. The most obvious advantage of the device of the Childe is that it allows Byron to remain at one stage removed from his more 'impassioned' pieces of rhetoric:

> And ever since that martial synod met
> Britannia sickens, Cintra! at thy name;
> And folks in office at the mention fret,
> And fain would blush, if blush they could, for shame.
> How will posterity the deed proclaim!
> Will not our own and fellow nations sneer,
> To view these champions cheated of their fame,
> By foes in fight o'erthrown, yet victors here,
> Where scorn her fingers points through many a coming year?

> So deem'd the Childe, as o'er the mountains he
> Did take his way in solitary guise

> (I, xxvi–xxvii)

'So deem'd the Childe', and since we have not been encouraged to take the Childe seriously, the passage remains suspended in its own ambiguity. The quaintness of the third, fourth, and final lines undermines the stanza's sonority, yet there is no controlling irony here, nothing to suggest that Byron is burlesquing either the style

20

or the utterance. Thomson's 'bad lines', his quaint padding and his cumbersome allegorizing, were the jokes of a poet who placed a deal of value on his own sophistication, jokes deferentially intended for an exclusive readership that liked to conceive of itself as equally sophisticated. Byron has none of these motives and yet all of Thomson's self-consciousness. He cannot rely on any audience, least of all a sophisticated one. He therefore puts on the show for anyone who is prepared to sit through it, whilst abdicating his responsibility for the quality of the production by placing a caricature in the leading role. The difficulty for the reader of *Childe Harold* is that, with the exception of the opening stanzas, this caricature is so imperfectly and inconsistently sketched that neither the distinctions from Byron nor the similarities to him are made sufficiently clear. As the poem proceeds, so this difficulty becomes more awkward. Finally we are left with the impression that the Childe has been used as a device by which Byron can watch himself perform. Sometimes his antics make him laugh, occasionally he finds them irresistibly attractive, but most of the time he is unsure what to think of this image with which he is experimenting; his response is thus a mixture of attraction and repulsion.

This kind of ambivalence can also be recognized in Byron's framing of the Childe's 'Good Night' and 'To Inez', and the Suliotes' 'Tambourgi!' This perhaps is the most obvious manifestation of Byron's staging, and almost certainly was learnt from Thomson. Thomson introduces the songs of his enchanter and bard in a remarkably similar way:

> Thither continual pilgrims crowded still,
> From all the roads of earth that pass there by:
> For, as they chanced to breathe on neighbouring hill,
> The freshness of this valley smote their eye,
> And drew them ever and anon more nigh;
> Till clustering round th' enchanter false they hung,
> Ymolten with his syren melody;
> While o'er th' enfeebling lute his hand he flung,
> And to the trembling chords these tempting verses sung
>
> (I, viii)

> The bard obey'd; and, taking from his side,
> Where it in seemly sort depending hung,
> His British harp, its speaking strings he tried;
> The which with skilful touch he deftly strung,

21

> Till tinkling in clear symphony they rung.
> Then, as he felt the Muses come along,
> Light o'er the chords his raptured hand he flung,
> And play'd a prelude to his rising song:
> The whilst, like midnight mute, ten thousands round him throng.
> Thus, ardent, burst his strain
>
> (II, xlvi–xlvii)

The introduction to the 'Good Night' follows Thomson fairly closely, Byron preferring 'string' and 'fling' to 'strung' and 'flung':

> But when the sun was sinking in the sea
> He seized his harp, which he at times could string,
> And strike, albeit with untaught melody,
> When deem'd he no strange ear was listening:
> And now his fingers o'er it he did fling,
> And tuned his farewell in the dim twilight.
> While flew the vessel on her snowy wing,
> And fleeting shores receded from his sight,
> Thus to the elements he pour'd his last 'Good Night.'
>
> (I, xiii)

The Miltonic echo of Thomson's introduction is picked up by Byron in the framing of 'To Inez':

> And as in Beauty's bower he pensive sate,
> Pour'd forth his unpremeditated lay,
> To charms as fair as those that soothed his happier day.
>
> (I, lxxxiv)

More precisely, this recalls Thomson's caricature of himself –

> On Virtue still, and Nature's pleasing themes,
> Pour'd forth his unpremeditated strain.
>
> (I, lxviii)

To Thomson the 'unpremeditated strain' was simply one of those jokes that he could afford to make within the extravagant precincts of his verse.[23] Apart from the obvious ironic application to himself (*The Castle of Indolence* took him fifteen years to write), it was an aspect of Milton's style that in a contemporary context elicited more amusement than admiration in the circles in which he moved. It is a joke in the same category as 'Then, as he felt the muses come along'. Because Byron lacked the kind of audience for which Thomson was performing, the jest cannot possibly have the same application. Yet it would be a mistake to suppose that he was completely unaware of Thomson's ironic use of Milton in the framing of the bardic songs in *The Castle of Indolence*, and that he was merely copying the mode because he liked it. Byron has no need to be ironic about using Milton, and no exclusive readership to appreciate the irony. But because his verse, unlike Thomson's, has intermittent bursts of a strong 'unpremeditated' flavour, it is distinctly possible that he felt a need to identify with the kind of detachment that he detected in Thomson. For Byron's acting is sometimes infused with a kind of enthusiasm which we do not find in *The Castle of Indolence*:

> And must they fall? the young, the proud, the brave,
> To swell one bloated Chief's unwholesome reign?
> No step between submission and a grave?
> And rise of rapine and the fall of Spain?
> And doth the power that man adores ordain
> Their doom, nor heed the suppliants appeal?
> Is all that desperate Valour acts in vain?
> And Counsel sage, and patriotic Zeal,
> The Veteran's skill, Youth's fire, and Manhood's heart of steel?
>
> (I, liii)

It is important to realize that this is acting still; the enthusiasm is an enthusiasm for style and not for subject-matter. It is the same kind of enthusiasm which informed his speeches in the House of Lords:

Are these the remedies for a starving and desperate populace? Will the famished wretch who has braved your bayonets be appalled by your gibbets? When death is a relief, and the only relief it appears that you afford him, will he be dragooned into tranquillity? Will that which could not be effected by your grenadiers be accomplished by your executioners? . . . suppose this man, and there are ten thousand such from whom you may select your victims, dragged into court, to be tried for this new offence, by this new law; still, there are two things wanting to convict and condemn him; and these are, in my opinion – twelve butchers for a jury, and a Jefferies for a judge![24]

We may be assisted in reading this by Moore's account of Byron's behaviour after a later speech:

He was, I recollect, in a state of most humorous exaltation after his display, and, while I hastily went on with my task in the dressing-room, continued to walk up and down the adjoining chamber, spouting forth for me, in a sort of mock-heroic voice, detached sentences of the speech he had just been delivering. 'I told them', he said, 'that it was almost flagrant violation of the Constitution – that, if such things were permitted, there was an end of English freedom –' – 'But what was this dreadful grievance?' I asked, interrupting him in his eloquence. – 'The grievance?' he repeated, pausing as if to consider – 'Oh, *that* I forget.'[25]

Just as Byron felt free to parody his dramatic speech in the House of Lords, so in the stanza which follows the one quoted above he chooses to present his rhetoric in a different light:

> Is it for this the Spanish maid, aroused,
> Hangs on the willow her unstrung guitar,
> And, all unsex'd, the Anlace hath espoused,
> Sung the loud song, and dared the deed of war?
>
> (I, liv)

The rhetorician is transformed into the quaint poet; the pause which the novel gesture of the second line enforces, the echo of Lady Macbeth, and the oddity of the 'espousal' of the 'Anlace' all combine to emasculate the force of the rhetorical questioning. It is as if Byron, slightly amused at the amount of wind in his own sails, tacks around, and steers a safer course.

The framing of the 'unpremeditated lays' is one means by which Byron indulges his enthusiasm for style whilst retaining the kind of detached 'innocence' which he found in Thomson. As the poem proceeds, however, he becomes more confident in playing the *improvvisatore*, moving quickly from one style to another, making no apologies for the sudden shifts of tone. This was perhaps more obvious in the original draft, but the extant text provides numerous examples. Byron still finds room, for instance, for schoolboy-like asides alongside his rhetoric:

> Of brains (if brains they had) he then beguiled
>
> (I, xxv)

> Soon as the matin bell proclaimeth nine,
> The saint adorers count the rosary:
> Much is the VIRGIN teased to shrive them free
> (Well do I ween the only virgin there)
>
> (I, lxxi)

And even within *Childe Harold*, there is a place for the kind of advice found more frequently in *Don Juan*:

'Tis an old lesson; Time approves it true,
And those who know it best deplore it most;
When all is won that all desire to woo,
The paltry prize is hardly worth the cost:
Youth wasted, minds degraded, honour lost

(II, xxxv)

Occasionally, too, one detects the same kind of ironic self-regard
that is found in the bathetic final couplet of the *ottava rima* poems
in the last couplet of the Spenserian stanza:

While strangers only not regardless pass,
Lingering like me, perchance, to gaze, and sigh 'Alas!'

(II, lxxxvi)

And had he doted on those eyes so blue,
Yet never would he join the lover's whining crew.

(II, xxxiii)

Pluto! if this be hell I look upon,
Close shamed Elysium's gates, my shade shall seek for none.

(II, li)

One could suggest at this point that it is the stanza form that is
preventing these shifts of tone from succeeding artistically, and
then perhaps proceed to diagnose the failure of *Childe Harold I &
II* as the failure of an artist who finds himself unable to create the
right kind of context for turning his chimerical temperament into
poetry.[26] But this is to identify the poem's purpose as the expression of such a temperament, to conceive of it, perhaps, as an unsuccessful *Don Juan*. This would be a mistake. Byron clearly feels no
need to resolve the paradoxes of his poem, neither is he
embarrassed by its cacophonies. Indeed, at this stage of his career it
is doubtful that he conceived of his poetry as being *obliged* to
achieve anything. This is particularly conspicuous at the end of the
first canto:

Oh, known the earliest, and esteem'd the most!
Dear to a heart where nought was left so dear!
Though to my hopeless days for ever lost,
In dreams deny me not to see thee here!
And morn in secret shall renew the tear
Of Consciousness awaking to her woes,
And Fancy hover o'er thy bloodless bier,
Till my frail frame return to whence it rose,
And mourn'd and mourner lie united in response.

25

Here is one fytte of Harold's pilgrimage:
Ye who of him may further seek to know,
Shall find some tidings in a future page,
If he that rhymeth now may scribble moe.
Is this too much? stern Critic! say not so:
Patience!

(I, xcii–xciii)

Any relationship there may be between these modes is certainly not under the controlling influence of a mind that is artistically self-aware, a mind that understands poetry to be an appropriate medium for the resolution of its antitheses. The freedom to be 'droll or pathetic, descriptive or sentimental, tender or satirical' as he pleases may be the explanation of his poem's anomalies that Byron expects his readership to accept, but such a contrast as this is far more a deliberate abandonment of decorum than an exhibition of whimsy. The juxtaposition of these two stanzas thus betrays Byron's fundamental indifference towards his art and also evinces an equal lack of regard for his readership. The problem of accommodating the discord is firmly transferred to an audience which he implies is unlikely to be seriously disturbed by it.

As the second canto proceeds, so we begin to witness the predominance of one of these modes over the other, as Byron seemingly commits himself to the development of an attitude that owed more to Rousseau than to Thomson:

To sit on rocks, to muse o'er flood and fell,
To slowly trace the forest's shady scene,
Where things that own not man's dominion dwell,
And mortal foot hath ne'er or rarely been;
To climb the trackless mountain all unseen,
With the wild flock that never needs a fold;
Alone o'er steeps and foaming falls to lean;
This is not solitude; 'tis but to hold
Converse with Nature's charms, and view her stores unroll'd.

But midst the crowd, the hum, the shock of men,
To hear, to see, to feel, and to possess,
And roam along, the world's tired denizen,
With none who bless us, none whom we can bless;
Minions of splendour shrinking from distress!
None that, with kindred consciousness endued,
If we were not, would seem to smile the less,

> Of all that flatter'd, follow'd, sought, and sued;
> This is to be alone; this, this is solitude!
>
> (II, xxv–xxvi)

Whether or not we are convinced by this is not the appropriate question. On the precedent of the first canto, one wonders rather whether Byron has succeeded in convincing himself. His employment of the phrase 'all unseen', which may be considered suspect after Johnson's decidedly ambiguous isolation of it in his discussion of *Il Penseroso*,[27] perhaps suggests that he had not, although obviously an argument of any strength could not be built upon such a fragile basis. The ambiguity of the second canto is far less obvious than that of the first; the archaisms are there but used with more restraint, the gestures of the verse are equally arbitrary but indulged with more panache than irony, and the rhetoric similarly 'staged' but more sustained. Yet we cannot conclude from this that *Childe Harold* develops into a serious Romantic poem wherein the poet's moods and emotions are given free expression.[28] Whilst Byron may have given up tempering his acting with the kind of self-regarding irony that pervades the first canto, we are only too aware that it is acting still, acting undertaken with an exaggerated amount of stylized flair:

> Then must I plunge again into the crowd,
> And follow all that Peace disdains to seek?
> Where Revel calls, and Laughter, vainly loud,
> False to the heart, distorts the hollow cheek,
> To leave the flagging spirit doubly weak;
> Still o'er the features, which perforce they cheer,
> To feign the pleasure or conceal the pique:
> Smiles form the channel of a future tear,
> Or raise the writhing lip with ill-dissembled sneer.
>
> (II, xcvii)

This is Byron's exit from a stage which in the second canto he has trodden with increasing confidence, and, as such, it is one of the more assured gestures of the poem. The actor who previously felt compelled to stand back from his antics and regard them with a smirk is now prepared to remain on stage longer, replacing the detached ironic contemplation of himself with the kind of exaggerated and ambiguous swagger that is clearly recognizable in the last line of this stanza. It is as if the equivocatory self-regarding interludes of the first canto have served as a precondition for a more confident assumption of style; a style which here is indulged with sufficient ostentation to allow Byron to incorporate his awareness of the contrivance involved into the act itself.

Although there is no evidence to suggest that Byron has discovered how seriously he is prepared to take his art in the first two cantos of *Childe Harold*, he clearly has discovered that he can enjoy the indulgence of certain gestures within the poetry, and that this enjoyment is sufficiently engrossing to postpone the question. At the same time we cannot help but see in this indulgence and postponement a certain uneasiness that perhaps bears some relation to the kind of restless satiety that provided the first canto with its predominant motif. For however conscious we are of the acting of *Childe Harold*, we might reasonably expect to be moved by it at some point. Yet even in those elegies for the deaths of Byron's friends and mother, one is struck by just how extensively destructive the compulsive self-dramatization has become, and despite the allowances made for the necessary formality of these passages, their emotional content is almost entirely consumed by the poet's preoccupation with the gestures the dramatic situation permits him to make:

> What is my being? thou hast ceased to be!
> Nor staid to welcome here thy wanderer home,
> Who mourns o'er hours which we no more shall see –
> Would they had never been, or were to come!
> Would he had ne'er return'd to find fresh cause to roam!
>
> Oh! ever loving, lovely, and beloved!
> How selfish Sorrow ponders on the past,
> And clings to thoughts now better far removed!
> But Time shall tear thy shadow from me last.
> All thou couldst have of mine, stern Death! thou hast;
> The parent, friend, and now the more than friend;
> Ne'er yet for one thine arrows flew so fast,
> And grief with grief continuing still to blend,
> Hath snatch'd the little joy that life had yet to lend.
>
> (II, xcv–xcvi)

Self-dramatization here stands between Byron and the world of real emotions. Yet however distant this world may remain, the pageant wherein its actions are mimicked is perhaps his only link with it. For it is not that the ambivalence of the poem is a consequence of Byron's desire to make a display of disowning the poetry and its emotional antecedents: he is not the fastidious gentleman embarrassed by his own feelings. On the contrary, as a child of his time who knows all about St Preux and Werther even if he knows nothing about Wordsworth, he feels compelled to provide his poetry with an emotional dimension. The ambivalence involved in the attempt to create this dimension, however, causes us to wonder whether Byron is capable of feeling any of the emotions which form a part of his act. The poetry of *Childe Harold I & II* is therefore not the medium for the expression or incorporation of Byron's feelings, but the medium wherein he searches for the kind of emotional excitement that he thinks a poet of his age should offer. It is an exploration undertaken with little method or assurance, and one which seems rather to offer its desultory poet a distracting kind of amusement. However diverted we may be by the spectacle of the poem, we are finally left with a somewhat disturbing impression of the gulf between the gestures of the self-dramatizing poet and the world which provided the models for those gestures.

By the end of the second canto the attractions of Thomson's mode have been replaced by the attractions of the repertoire of dramatic gestures Byron has discovered, a repertoire defined for him by his assumption of the role of a social outcast. In playing the role of the Childe with more confidence, Byron has evidently dispelled his anxieties about his independence as a poet. If the early stanzas represent his building of a fictional situation in which he may delude himself into believing in his independence as a poet writing for an exclusive audience, then the latter parts suggest that the fiction of his independence has been transferred to, and sustained by, his representation of himself as the Childe, the exile relieved of his social responsibilities.

2

The discovery of an audience:
the Turkish Tales

Together with the narrative poems of Sir Walter Scott, the tales
Byron wrote between 1813 and 1816 occupy a unique position in the
history of English literature. The distinction shared by the two
poets, that of bringing the popular poem to the apex of its tran-
sitory circulation, is perhaps a dubious one, and one which also
depends on the fortuitous state of social circumstances rather than
on an artistic impulse to create or cater for a democratized reading
public. The kind of irresponsibility of which Scott and Byron were
both guilty (freely acknowledged by Byron in 1821)[1] can be fully
realized by a consideration of their verse narratives alongside the
diagnosis of the malaise of metropolitan society made by Wordsworth in 1800:

For a multitude of causes, unknown to former times, are now acting with a
combined force to blunt the discriminating powers of the mind, and, unfit-
ting it for all voluntary exertion, to reduce it to a state of almost savage
torpor. The most effective of these causes are the great national events
which are daily taking place, and the increasing accumulation of men in
cities, where the uniformity of their occupations produces a craving for
extraordinary incident, which the rapid communication of hourly intelligence hourly gratifies. To this tendency of life and manners the literature
and theatrical exhibitions of the country have conformed themselves. The
invaluable works of our elder writers, I had almost said the works of
Shakespeare and Milton, are driven into neglect by frantic novels, sickly
and stupid German Tragedies, and deluges of idle and extravagant stories
in verse.[2]

Unlike Wordsworth, neither Scott nor Byron had any desire to use
his art as an instrument for the improvement of the spiritual health
or literary taste of the reading public. This is patently obvious.
Both 'conformed themselves' to the tastes Wordsworth describes

here, exploiting the reading public for their own ends. The significance of Wordsworth's diagnosis, however, is not merely that it casts a shadow of moral irresponsibility over Byron and Scott, but that it emphasizes the unique social conditions that governed their successes. Wordsworth was only too aware of the perenniality of popular literature;[3] his point here is that the reading public of his time were subject to new influences creating the kind of habits and expectations that were liable to protect and foster popular literature more than ever before. This class of art, exhibiting, as he later argued, 'qualities . . . such as startle the world into attention by their audacity and extravagance', keeping 'the mind . . . upon the stretch of curiosity, and the fancy amused without the trouble of thought',[4] thus found its appeal intensified in the early years of the nineteenth century. The reader, Wordsworth implies, found himself pushed into a non-creative role, whereupon he increased his demands for external and cruder stimuli. Writing on Scott's fame some twenty years later, Coleridge makes some similar observations:

I occasioned you to misconceive me respecting Sir Walter Scott. My purpose was to bring proofs of the energetic or inenergetic state of the minds of men, induced by the excess and unintermitted action of stimulating events and circumstances, – revolutions, battles, *newspapers*, mobs, sedition and treason trials, public harangues, meetings, dinners; the necessity in every individual of ever increasing activity and anxiety in the improvement of his estate, trade, &c., in proportion to the decrease of the actual value of money, to the multiplication of competitors, and to the almost compulsory expedience of expense, and prominence, even as the means of obtaining or retaining competence; the consequent craving after amusement as proper *relaxation*, as *rest* freed from the tedium of vacancy; and again, after such knowledge and such acquirements as are *ready coin*, that will pass *at once*, unweighed and unassayed; to the unexampled facilities afforded for this end by reviews, magazines, &c., &c.[5]

The reading world of the eighteenth century, Coleridge continues, was at once 'less stimulated, and, therefore, less languid' than that of his own time.[6] We will perhaps find no better descriptions of the immediate effects of the 'multitude of causes unknown to former times' than these, and they can therefore be used as a basis for an examination of Byron's reading public during his years of fame.

The particular emphasis laid by Wordsworth and Coleridge on newspapers as a pernicious force is perhaps a little mystifying at first sight, but I believe it to be of some significance. Whilst I would not necessarily suggest that the extensive reading of newspapers bred a pattern of reading habits that was easily transferred to the reading of literature, I wish to argue that their important place in the ritual of daily life was responsible for eliciting an attitude towards print that is of relevance when considering the success of Byron's tales. According to Southey, in 1807 there were some 250,000 'people in England who read the news every day and converse upon it'.[7] Newspapers were thus firmly established as part of a respectable middle-class way of life by the Regency, and perhaps one of the most important consequences of the widening circulation of newsprint was the inculcation upon the minds of the reading public of the value and status society granted to the informed reader. To be well informed upon all the most recent happenings in fashionable society was a guarantee of access to formal conversation (one recalls, for example, the status assumed by the Miss Steels in *Sense and Sensibility*). Reading newspapers was also one means by which an individual could confirm his claims upon a place in the social hierarchy. By reading, for instance, of the departure from London of a certain member of the landed aristocracy, the middle-class reader could in some way feel that his access to this information ratified his status in society as one of privilege. That such trivia did appear in the papers Byron makes clear:

> A paragraph in every paper told
> Of their departure. Such is modern fame.
> 'Tis pity that it takes no further hold
> Than an advertisement, or much the same,
> When ere the ink be dry, the sound grows cold.
> The *Morning Post* was foremost to proclaim:
> 'Departure for his country seat today
> Lord H. Amundeville and Lady A. . . .'
>
> (*Don Juan*, XIII, 51)

And perhaps the inroads cut by the increase in communication across social and geographical barriers is nowhere better illustrated than in the passage in which Mr Price relates to his daughter a newspaper account of Henry Crawford's elopement in *Mansfield Park*.

The availability of newspapers, and the way in which they could be speedily converted into conversational currency in metropolitan society, may well have elicited certain expectations and demands in the reader for similar qualities of novelty and utility in other forms of literature. Whether or not this is true, the newspaper certainly played an important role in the establishment of the fashionable world of the Regency.

> The newspaper of the day, the favourite magazine of the month, the review of the quarter, the tour, the novel, and the poem which are the most recent in date and most fashionable in name, furnish forth the morning table of the literary dilettante.[8]

Thus wrote Peacock in *An Essay on Fashionable Literature*, and his point emphasizes just how much the fashionable excesses of Byron's era depended upon the expansions in journalism. 'All fashionable people read', Peacock wrote, '(gentlemen who have been at college excepted), yet as the soul of fashion is novelty, the books and the dress of the season go out of date together; and to be amused this year by that which amused others twelve months ago would be to plead guilty to the heinous charge of having lived out of the world.'[9]

Another important factor in the history of the expanding reading public in Byron's time, and perhaps the most important factor in terms of its direct influence, was the rapid growth of the reviewing periodicals. The influence of critical journalism in the early nineteenth century has been amply stressed elsewhere, and is commonly acknowledged,[10] but what I wish to concern myself with here is the relationship of the reviewing phenomenon to the composition of the reading public, and thereby to the spectacular successes of Scott and Byron. The facts, as far as they can be established, are these. In 1802 the *Edinburgh Review* was begun with a printing of 800 copies. By 1818 it had reached its apex with a circulation of 14,000. By 1817 the *Quarterly Review* (founded in 1809) had a circulation of 10,000.[11] Halévy estimates that in 1815 the joint circulation of the reviews was 20,000.[12] In 1814 Jeffrey estimated that 50,000 people read 13,000 copies of the *Edinburgh*, that is, approximately four readers for every copy,[13] but by 1820 he had revised his estimate, calculating that the *Edinburgh* reached some 500,000 readers within a month of its publication. This estimate of thirty-five readers or more per copy is closer to Southey's claim, made in 1817, of 500,000 readers for 10,000 sold copies of the *Quarterly*.[14] In 1807 Southey guessed that each newspaper sold found five readers,[15] and whilst one would expect each single copy of a review to have more readers than each single copy of a newspaper (making Jeffrey's estimate of 1814 absurdly low) fifty readers per copy sounds a little excessive. In addition to these major periodicals, there were in circulation between 1802 and 1824 sixty other journals which included literary reviews within their pages.[16] Amongst these were the reputable *Monthly Review* and *Monthly Magazine* (each with a circulation of 5,000 in 1797), *The Gentleman's Magazine* (with a circulation of 4,500 in 1797), *The British Critic* and *The Critical Review* (each with a circulation of 3,500 in 1797), and *The Examiner* (with a circulation of 2,200 in 1807).[17]

This gives some idea of the increase in the size of the reading public in Byron's time. More significant, perhaps, these figures make it clear that this readership was no longer to be exclusively located within the upper classes. Certainly the rise in the popularity of reviews may partly be accounted for by fashionable demands for the most recent opinions on the most recent books. But it probably also depended upon subscription from a large proportion of the middle classes whose educational limitations encouraged them to regard the reviews as providing them with an assured basis for their reading, a basis protected by what was imagined to be the public consensus. This protection would have been of particular importance to those anxious to have their new place in the fashionable hierarchy confirmed. The reviews not only told them what to read, but told them what to think as well. Conducted from within the precincts of fashionable society, they represented the dictates and values of that milieu, values that were unlikely to be challenged by a group of people who naturally preferred that their social mobility might allow them to be regarded as genteel conformers rather than as a source of potential subversion.

The assurance thus guaranteed to the critics that the majority of their readers were bound to accept their judgement frequently allowed them to adopt the tones of pompous condescension that is perhaps the most distinctive aspect of early-nineteenth-century reviewing. These are tones which also remind us that the reviewers were aware of a wide provincial readership as well as a metropolitan one. In a review of Crabbe's *Tales* of 1812, Jeffrey states that the 'middling classes' will appreciate Crabbe more than any other class of reader. His definition of these 'middling classes' is 'all those who are below the sphere of what is called fashionable or public life, and who do not aim at distinction or notoriety beyond the circle of their equals in fortune or situation'. It is perhaps a mark of Jeffrey's own station that he does not care to involve himself in the definition of a lower limit. He estimates the number of readers among this social bracket at 200,000, ten times more than his estimate of 'higher class' readers. It is therefore

wise and meritorious of Mr Crabbe to occupy himself with such beings . . . It is easy to see therefore which a poet should chuse to please for his own glory and emolument, and which he should wish to delight and amend out of mere philanthropy. The fact too we believe is, that a great part of the larger body are to the full as well-educated and as high-minded as the smaller; and, though their taste may not be so correct and fastidious, we are persuaded that their sensibility is greater. The misfortune is, to be sure, that they are extremely apt to affect the taste, and to counterfeit even that absurd disdain of their superiors, of which they are themselves the objects; and that poets have generally thought it safest to invest their interesting characters with all the trappings of splendid fortune, chiefly because those who know least about such matters think it unworthy to sympathise in the adventures of those who are without them.[18]

'Fastidiousness' and 'correctness' were, after all, the means by which the minority in 'fashionable or public life' distinguished themselves from the expanding middle classes. These were also implicitly the qualities which segregated the reviewer from the majority of his readership. This article can leave us in no doubt that reviewers such as Jeffrey envisaged their critical activities as educational and informative as far as the bulk of their readership was concerned. Coleridge, whose criticism of the literary reviews is well known, was nevertheless ready to appreciate this aspect of their function, estimating 'at a high value, the services which the Edinburgh Review, and others formed afterwards on the same plan, have rendered to society in the diffusion of knowledge'.[19] It is, however, also clear from this article that Jeffrey is anxious to preserve the distinctions between his upper and middle classes, to the extent that he is prepared to designate to those outside fashionable life literature which he deems to be peculiarly suited to their position. 'Each to his own place' is of course a particularly pertinent adage for the sympathetic reviewer of Crabbe's *Tales*, and Jeffrey's trust in this sentiment renders his recommendation of Crabbe all the more urgent and patronizing.

This review also demonstrates just how readily literary

gentlemen such as Jeffrey equated the readership of the 'middling classes' with children. Jeffrey apparently saw them as a section of society in want of instruction and development. He roundly asserts that 'It is not only on account of the moral benefit which we think they may derive from them, that we would peculiarly recommend the writings of Mr Crabbe to that great proportion of our readers which must necessarily belong to the middling or humbler classes of the community', and also ranks Crabbe's verse with 'the inimitable tales of Miss Edgeworth . . . calculated to do nearly as much good among that part of the population with which they are principally occupied'.[20] This is almost certainly a reference to the *Moral Tales* of 1801 and the *Popular Tales* of 1804, although the earliest of the volumes of *Tales from Fashionable Life* had been published in 1809. Maria Edgeworth's earlier tales were intended as part of the moral education of a younger readership. This tendency to conceive of a proportion of the new reading public as childlike can also be observed in Scott. When considering the writing of the history of Scotland in story form in 1827, he commented in his Journal: 'I am persuaded both children and the lower class of readers hate books which are written *down* to their capacity and love those that are more composed for their elders and betters.'[21] Clearly Scott is more disposed than Jeffrey to tolerate the tendency of the 'lower class of reader' to use his reading as a claim upon gentility. Scott was apparently particularly conscious of this fact, writing of the *Edinburgh Review* in 1803 that 'no genteel family *can* pretend to be without it'.[22]

It was perhaps partly the early-nineteenth-century reviewer's assumption that the vast majority of his readership derived from the 'middling classes' that permitted him to proclaim his critical judgement without feeling obliged to demonstrate his case, a habit censured by Coleridge in *Biographia Literaria*:

The second point of objection belongs to this review only in common with all other works of periodical criticism; at least, it applies in common to the general system of all, whatever exception there may be in favour of particular articles . . . I am referring to the substitution of assertion for argument; to the frequency of arbitrary and sometimes petulant verdicts, not seldom unsupported even by a single quotation from the work condemned, which might at least have explained the critic's meaning, if it did not prove the justice of his sentence. Even where this is not the case, the extracts are too often made without reference to any general grounds or rules from which the faultiness or inadmissibility of the qualities attributed may be deduced, and without any attempt to show that the qualities are attributable to the passage extracted.[23]

Coleridge's observation indicates the extent to which the skills and techniques of literary criticism were liable to remain a mystery to the average reader. Thus Jeffrey, in his review of Southey's *Thalaba*, instructs that large proportion of his readership without the benefits of a humanistic education such as his own that 'Poetry has this much, at least, in common with religion, that its standards were fixed long ago, by certain inspired writers, whose authority it is no longer lawful to call in question.'[24] His implication, of course, is that he is particularly familiar with the rules of these 'inspired writers', and that those who are not so fortunate will simply have to accept his informed judgements. Commenting on the effects of this manner upon the reading public, Southey wrote:

Many are the readers that do not know, and few are they who will remember, when they are perusing a criticism delivered in the plural language of authority that it is but the opinion of one man upon the work of another. The public are deceived by this style . . . A more lasting mischief is, that they profess to show the reader that short cut to wisdom and knowledge, which is the sure way to conceit and ignorance.[25]

In 1818 Peacock made a similar observation in *An Essay on Fashionable Literature*, claiming that the 'country gentlemen' ('a generic term applied by courtesy to the profoundly ignorant of all classes') were prone to being deceived in this way.[26] It must surely be the case that these readers, if not ignorant, were incapable of recognizing literary distinctions. Looking back upon the majority of the literary reviews published in the *Edinburgh* or the *Quarterly*, it is very hard not to see them as examples of 'cant poetical'. Indeed, they were probably exactly what Byron had in mind when he coined the phrase, and the fact that it is to be found in the famous letter on Bowles's 'Strictures' is, of course, important. For perhaps the most obvious feature of the literary reviews is the way in which third-rate literature is discussed with all the earnestness and airs of sophistication that more properly belong in debates on writers of Pope's stature. Whilst not a comment that is primarily concerned with the quality of contemporary literature, Peacock's remark in *The Four Ages of Poetry* that 'the magazine critics . . . continue to debate and promulgate oracles about poetry, as if it were still what it was in the Homeric age',[27] receives its strength from this very fact.

Who, then, were the readers of Scott and Byron, the readers who were responsible for purchasing 10,000 copies of *The Corsair* on its first day of publication? Undoubtedly they included the aristocracy and the members of the London coteries in which Byron moved after the success of *Childe Harold*. They also almost certainly included some of the 'women and soldier officers' who according to Southey were responsible for the popularity of novels.[28] But it is obvious that the huge sales enjoyed by Scott and Byron cannot be wholly accounted for by these groups. Since books were so expensive that Southey (albeit with a measure of exaggeration) claimed that they were 'chiefly purchased as furniture for the rich',[29] then we can identify a large proportion of Byron's readership as belonging to the *nouveaux riches*, people who, despite the alliance Jeffrey made on his own terms with Maria Edgeworth and Crabbe, were making claims upon a place in fashionable society.

Above all, we can safely say that these readers derived from that proportion of the public that placed such a high value on what was fashionable and novel. The average reader of Scott and Byron may not have had the advantage of the kind of education that might have allowed him to lay claim to an informed and discriminating literary mind, but if he did possess this advantage, it is quite possible that his attitude towards it would have been as dismissive as that of Mr Listless in *Nightmare Abbey*, who, upon receiving a parcel 'sent express' containing a new novel, a new poem, and 'the last number of a popular review', prompting Mr Larynx to venture that he would seem to be 'of a very studious turn', replies:

Studious! You are pleased to be facetious, Mr Larynx. I hope you do not suspect me of being studious. I have finished my education. But there are some fashionable books that one must read, because they are the talk of the day; otherwise I am no fonder of books than I dare say you yourself are, Mr Larynx.[30]

It is difficult to imagine gentlemen of fashion discussing contemporary literature studiously in Byron's day, and, significantly, Byron's own comments on this literature are almost exclusively frivolous or slight. Earnest literary discussions, however, may well have occurred amongst those members of the reading public who made no distinctions between their education and their day-to-day reading. Such readers probably took the serious tones of the reviews to heart in their autodidactic zeal, in the manner perhaps of Captain Benwick in *Persuasion*, who, we remember, talks of the 'richness of the present age', and tries 'to ascertain whether *Marmion* or *The Lady of the Lake* were to be preferred, and how ranked *The Giaour* and *The Bride of Abydos*; and moreover, how *The Giaour* was to be pronounced'.[31] Whilst he is not typical in many respects, Captain Benwick's implicit equation of popular fashionable literature with great literature can nevertheless be seen as a direct consequence of his living in an era of reviews which by their very nature placed an exaggerated emphasis on whatever was new and 'original'.

Although impossible to identify with any precision, the reading public of Byron's time can nevertheless therefore be described in the following terms. First, through the demands of a society obsessed by fashion and under the influence of the newspapers and reviews, it was a public accustomed to granting an implicit value to novelty. Secondly, it was broadly divisible into two classes, and we can accept Jeffrey's estimate of the middle classes as constituting by far the larger proportion, since the influx of mercantile wealth into the country at this time and the consequent rise of the middle classes (in importance if not in size) substantiate this. The proportion of this section of the public who were attempting to establish themselves as part of fashionable society therefore probably used their reading of newspapers, reviews, and books as a claim upon gentility, and also as a means of becoming 'informed'. The authority of the reviews makes it clear that they could rely upon general acquiescence in their readership, for whatever reasons. Thirdly, therefore, we can conclude that this readership was predominantly uninformed, or voluntarily undiscriminating.

In a letter to Holland written in 1812, Byron ironically described his era as 'an age when writing verse is the easiest of all attainments'.[32] An article he wrote for the *Monthly Review* in the same year is similarly sardonic:

The 'mob of gentlemen who write with ease' has indeed of late years (like other mobs) become so importunate, as to threaten an alarming rivalry to the regular body of writers who are not fortunate enough to be either easy or genteel. Hence the jaundiced eye with which the real author regards the red Morocco binding of the presumptuous 'Litterateur;' we say, *the bind-*

ing, for into the book itself he cannot condescend to look, at least not beyond the frontispiece.[33]

However much the cynicism of this passage may demand that it should be considered lightly, one detects more than a degree of malice in the reference to the 'presumptuous "Litterateur"' and the wealthy extravagance of his publisher's editions. An increasingly wealthy and hungry reading public naturally presented greater opportunities to aspiring writers, and the spectacle of occasional verse becoming subsumed into the literature market was one which Byron, by his aristocratic and gentlemanly principles, was bound to find unpleasing. 'Literature is . . . like everything else, a trade in England', wrote Southey in 1807,[34] but even in 1818, after considerable involvement in this trade, Byron was reluctant to grant it the comparatively respectable status of a profession:

Hunt's letter is probably the exact piece of vulgar coxcombry you might expect from his situation. He is a good man, with some poetical elements in his chaos; but spoilt by the Christ-Church Hospital and a Sunday newspaper, – to say nothing of the Surry Jail, which conceited him into a martyr . . . Did you look at the translations of his own which he prefers to Pope and Cowper and says so? – Did you read his skimble-skamble about Wordsworth being at the head of his *profession* in the *eyes* of *those* who followed it? I thought that poetry was an *art*, or an *attribute*, and not a *profession*.[35]

Byron is perhaps at his most spiteful when he turns his attentions to the author he regards as a parvenu, the

> solemn, antique gentleman of rhyme,
> Who having angled all his life for fame,
> And getting but a nibble at a time,
> Still fussily keeps fishing on, the same
> Small 'Triton of the minnows,' the sublime
> Of mediocrity, the furious tame,
> The echo's echo, usher of the school
> Of female wits, boy bards – in short, a fool!
>
> (*Beppo*, lxxiii)

The reference here is to Sotheby, translator of Wieland's *Oberon*, and self-appointed mentor of the bluestockings.[36] Whilst Byron had a personal grudge against Sotheby,[37] the lolling manner and lordly intimacy of *Beppo* convey an animus that obviously has deeper roots:

One hates an author that's *all author*, fellows
In foolscap uniforms turn'd up with ink,
So very anxious, clever, fine, and jealous,
One don't know what to say to them, or think,
Of coxcombry's worst coxcombs e'en the pink
Are preferable to these shreds of paper,
These unquench'd snuffings of the midnight taper.

(*Beppo*, lxxv)

The criterion here is social, not literary.[38] Had Byron not become acquainted with such writers as Lewis and Scott, they too would probably have joined Sotheby in *Beppo*'s pillory. Byron had attacked them both in *English Bards and Scotch Reviewers*, wherein Scott is presented as one of the 'ballad-mongers' referred to in the poem's first epigraph[39] (his muse yielding 'just half-a-crown per line'[40]), and Lewis (crowned with the same laurel as that given to Scott)[41] is dubbed 'spectre-mongering Lewis'.[42] Scott and Lewis, and later Sotheby, were perhaps the most obvious targets for Byron in the literature market. All 'angled' for the public taste and manipulated it to their own advantage, looking first towards Germany as a source of novelty and excitement. It must be remembered that Wordsworth's criticism of the 'idle and extravagant stories in verse' in 1800 was a criticism of taste, devoid of any further reference to the possibilities of the exploitation of this taste by booksellers or authors. It was largely through Scott, Lewis, and Sotheby that tales in verse became a commercial enterprise. For the verse ballads and tales of the last decade of the eighteenth century were largely to be found in periodicals. Alternatively, they were known through their being used as an exclusive form of entertainment at parties and dinners. Some idea of the influence of these entertainments is given by the circumstances of Scott's introduction to Bürger's *Leonore*, an account of which can be found in A. M. Clark's *Walter Scott: The Formative Years*.[43] Scott's own attempt at translating this ballad resulted in his first publication,[44] and his account of its failure discloses something of the competitive nature of the literature market he was attempting to enter:

The fate of this, my first publication, was by no means flattering. I distributed so many copies among my friends as, according to the booksellers, materially to interfere with the sale; and the number of translations which appeared in England about the same time, including that of Mr Taylor, to which I had been so much indebted, and which was published in 'The

41

Monthly Magazine,' were sufficient to exclude a provincial writer from competition. However different my success might have been, had I been fortunate enough to have led the way in the general scramble for precedence, my efforts sunk unnoticed when launched at the same time with those of Mr Taylor . . . In a word my adventure, where so many pushed off to sea, proved a dead loss, and a great part of the edition was condemned to the service of the trunk-maker.[45]

Admist this flurry of competitive activity Sotheby published his translation of Wieland's *Oberon* in 1798, within a year of reading the first English account of this hitherto unknown poem.[46] Lewis published *The Monk*, which included several translated ballads, in 1796, and, undoubtedly, the kind of context this book gave to the German ballad was partly responsible for its continuing popularity. It also provided Lewis with a reputation that ensured the success of *Tales of Terror* (1799) and *Tales of Wonder* (1800).

By the time of Byron's verse tales, therefore, the literature trade was well established, and, largely through Scott's successes, the reading public presented itself as a relatively predictable entity to an astute publisher. In a letter to Murray of September 1812, Byron wrote:

What will you give *me* or *mine* for a poem of 6 Cantos (*when complete – no rhyme – no* recompense) as like the last two as I can make them? – – I have some ideas which one day may be embodied & till winter I shall have much leisure. – Believe me

> *yrs very sincerely*
> BYRON

P.S. – My last question is in the true style of Grub Street, but like Jeremy Diddler I only 'ask for information' . . .[47]

The reference is to a further six cantos of *Childe Harold*, to be completed, apparently, in a matter of two 'leisurely' months. The embarrassment evident in the postscript and the yawning manner in which the proposal is delivered demonstrate the reluctance of a young lord to become involved in the demeaning activities of business. Murray's reply can have left Byron in no doubt that whatever his attitude, his success had involved him in the trade: 'You will readily believe that I am delighted to find you thinking of a new poem, for which I should be proud to give you a thousand guineas, and I should ever gratefully remember the fame it would cast over my new establishment, upon which I enter at the close of this present month.'[48] The figure offered by Murray exceeded that offered to Scott by Constable for *Marmion* in 1807, which had 'startled the literary world' and 'made men's hair stand on end'.[49] Whilst Byron must have known of such figures, his earlier proposal to Dallas that his friend might make a hundred or a hundred and fifty guineas from the gift of the copyright of *Childe Harold I and II*[50] indicates that at the time of this poem's publication he was naively unaware of just how deeply his poetry was to embroil him in the affairs of the literature trade. After reading Murray's letter, it must have occurred to Byron that as a successful poet and a lord his position was unique. It was certainly not the first time that the landed aristocracy had found itself involved in a financial system increasingly dominated by mercantile wealth, but it was probably the first time that the writing of poetry had been the responsible factor.[51] Yet despite the social complexity and latent embarrassment of Byron's circumstances, it is not difficult to find an instance of him acting in a manner more reminiscent of a tradesman than a lord:

stick to the East; – the oracle, Staël, told me it was the only poetical policy. The North, South, and West, have all been exhausted; but from the East, we have nothing but Southey's unsaleables, and these he has contrived to spoil, by adopting only their most outrageous fictions. His personages don't interest us, and yours will. You have no competitor; and, if you had, you ought to be glad of it. The little I have done in that way is merely a 'voice in the wilderness' for you; and, if it has had any success, that also will prove that the public are orientalizing, and pave the path for you.[52]

However flippant this may be, it reminds us that Byron's attitude towards the literature trade is by no means as simple as his arraignment of Hunt, Wordsworth, and Sotheby might suggest. The mistake would be to conclude simply that he shifted ground; that the remarks in *English Bards and Scotch Reviewers* were written jealously, that the consequences of his popularity after the early *Childe Harold* were sufficiently flattering for him to revoke his principles; and that the comments on Hunt, Wordsworth, and Sotheby were the utterances of a splenetic exile whose popularity was declining. There may be a degree of truth in each of these propositions, but the formula in which they combine is an inadequate one for our purposes.

As the tales written between 1813 and 1816 testify, Byron was not so fastidious that he could not bear to involve himself in the literature trade. Yet whilst the simple motive of prolonging his fame and its attendant social advantages can explain the writing of this poetry, Byron's own attitude towards it is unclear. The negligence and carelessness of the tales is more or less widely acknowledged, and his derisive comments on the circumstances of their composition have been frequently quoted. Despite this, they have been subjected to the kind of critical attention that one might reasonably expect to find focussed on any serious and finished work of art.[53] This would seem to indicate either that many critics are willing to assume that Byron was secretly pleased with his tales, or that they find pretensions in the poetry that demand its serious consideration.

Now it appears to me that the general quality of the poetry of the tales is so self-evidently poor that there is no longer any need to demonstrate this fact. In addition, *Childe Harold I & II*, offering so little to suggest that Byron knew how seriously he wished to take his art, provides no alternative precedent for a critically rigorous examination of the poetry which immediately succeeds it. The case for studying the tales rests upon the fact that they rather obviously present themselves as poetical performances conducted for an audience that Byron found himself confronted by after the success of *Childe Harold*. It is only by attending to their poetry that we can attempt to trace Byron's developing attitudes towards the verse itself, attitudes which can be fully understood only by reference to its readership. Whilst such an examination cannot improve the quality of the poetry, it can nevertheless allow us to recognize the tales as an important part of the preconditional exercises upon which *Don Juan* depends.

Perhaps one of the most significant consequences of writing the verse tales was Byron's discovery that the composition of poetry could be a very simple exercise indeed. Compared to *Childe Harold I & II*, the poetry of the tales is far more confident, and this assurance no doubt stems from the guarantee of success that the sales of *Childe Harold* provided. Byron's first major public triumph had proved to him that his readers were willing to acclaim poetry which was defective, and were, moreover, oblivious to the experimental nature of the early *Childe Harold*. The verse tales capitalize on this. Their experimental aspect is far less pronounced, but they nevertheless exploit the kind of licence that poetic experiment presumes to adopt. The phraseology of much of their poetry only too clearly discloses a growing tendency on Byron's part to rely upon facile techniques. As an example, we might consider the opening of *The Siege of Corinth*, a particularly revealing passage:

> In the year since Jesus died for men,
> Eighteen hundred years and ten,
> We were a gallant company,
> Riding o'er land, and sailing o'er sea.
> Oh! but we went merrily!
> We forded the river, and clomb the high hill,
> Never our steeds for a day stood still;
> Whether we lay in the cave or the shed,
> Our sleep fell soft on the hardest bed
>
> (1–9)

The source of the pastiche is obvious, but Byron has divested the ballad mode of the slight antiquarian respectability with which it had been endowed by the attentions of Percy and Scott. Almost exclusively, Byron's verse tales are most unlike ballads, and this passage consequently has a particularly anomalous look. Certainly it exists to very little purpose, and appears to be solely a result of the poet's whimsy; a theory which seems to be substantiated by the ending of this brief proem, which is of such a nature as to cause us to wonder where capriciousness ends and facetiousness begins:

> We were of all tongues and creeds; –
> Some were those who counted beads,
> Some of mosque, and some of church,
> And some, or I mis-say, of neither;
> Yet through the wide world might ye search,
> Nor find a motlier crew nor blither.
>
> (18–23)

This borderline is one which the poetry of the tales consistently calls into question. But what this passage primarily reveals is the impoverished depth to which Byron's inspiration could sink without actually preventing him from writing verse. Here he is openly improvising as a warming-up exercise. Yet rather than improvising upon a theme or subject, Byron improvises upon a mode, and this unpromising choice implies that he is more concerned with manufacturing something which has the appearance of verse than with creating a narrative. *The Corsair* begins similarly, as too does *The Bride of Abydos*, where Byron bases his improvisations upon Mignon's song from Goethe's *Wilhelm Meister*.[54] *Parisina*, similarly, begins in a manner akin to Coleridge's *Christabel*, the narration somewhat coyly moving around its subject, anticipating the reader's questions but never answering them fully. Whereas Coleridge may have had a use for such suspense, the technique probably presented itself to Byron as another readily available rhetorical trick, used for no other purpose than to increase the number of words upon the page.

Byron once wrote to the agonizing poet of *Christabel*, 'surely a little effort would complete the poem'.[55] The diminutive effort which he found necessary for the production of his own verse tales is only too obvious from their openings. Further into his narratives Byron improvises with equal facility but with no more grace. A dependence upon negatives, for example, receives ample use, particularly in *The Corsair*:

> He waits not, looks not – leaps into the wave
>
> (III, 578)

> He turn'd not – spoke not – sunk not – fix'd his look
>
> (III, 599)

This is a typical formulation of the tales, and the fact that it is used in clusters (examples can be found in Canto III at lines 81, 93, 96, 98, and 104) shows that once Byron had discovered what he considered to be an attractive and productive turn of phrase he was liable to use it generously without compunction. There is an obvious irreverence about this, but perhaps the emphasis should be placed upon the productivity of Byron's improvising, the self-propagating nature of the verse. Here, for instance, one verb begets another by the potentially happy equation offered by the affixed negative, 'turn'd not – spoke not – sunk not'. Having found one phrase, another two offer themselves, and the nature of Byron's extempore composition demands that they should not be wasted. It is not, however, that Byron must make full use of limited compositional opportunities, but that he cannot resist the easy freedom which his improvising method presents him with. The poetry of the tales is a prolix poetry, a verse deliberately given its head:

> He lived, he breathed, he moved, he felt;
> He raised the maid from where she knelt;
> His trance was gone, his keen eye shone
> With thoughts that long in darkness dwelt;
> With thoughts that burn – in rays that melt.
>
> *(The Bride of Abydos*, I, 327–31)

The first of these lines finds its verbal content through a momentum that frequently offered itself to Byron's mind;[56] the third is a result of the same kind of frivolous rhyming habits that manifest themselves so frequently in the 'versicles' of the letters. In the fourth and fifth lines of this extract, Byron turns to another of his favourite devices, that of anaphora, but here, rather than yielding its usual facile effect, it produces only awkwardness. The consequence of this is to make Byron turn rapidly to another pattern. It is almost as if he is seeking immediate compensation as, unabashed, he throws off a string of five similes:

> As the stream late conceal'd
> By the fringe of its willows,
> When it rushes reveal'd
> In the light of its billows;
> As the bolt bursts on high
> From the black cloud that bound it,
> Flash'd the soul of that eye
> Through the long lashes round it.
> A war-horse at the trumpet's sound,
> A lion roused by heedless hound,
> A tyrant waked to sudden strife
> By graze of ill-directed knife,
> Starts not to more convulsive life
> Than he
>
> (I, 332–45)

The provision of more than one image for his reader's contemplation is a ploy which Byron frequently implements in the tales. When he cannot find alternative images or similes, he improvises upon just one:

> And to the earth she fell like stone
> Or statue from its base o'erthrown,
> More like a thing that ne'er had life, –
> A monument of Azo's wife
>
> *(Parisina*, 348–51)

This is a kind of prolixity that Byron's dexterity with cheap rhetoric only too easily allowed him. Thus, a passage in *The Bride of Abydos* describing Zuleika as 'fair . . . dazzling . . . soft . . . pure', despite the unpromising nature of its adjectives, becomes:

> Fair, as the first that fell of womankind,
> When on that dread yet lovely serpent smiling,
> Whose image then was stamp'd upon her mind –
> But once beguil'd – and ever more beguiling;
> Dazzling, as that, oh! too transcendent vision
> To Sorrow's phantom-peopled slumber given,
> When heart meets heart again in dreams Elysian,
> And paints the lost on earth revived in Heaven;
> Soft, as the memory of buried love;
> Pure, as the prayer which Childhood wafts above,
> Was she
>
> (I, 158–68)

There is of course a deal of exhibitionism in these examples, but it is an exhibitionism peculiarly spiced with a hint of the kind of offhand frivolity more readily associated with *Don Juan*. The 'similes are gathered in a heap'; the reader must 'pick and choose'.[57] Likewise, the transparent improvisation of this last passage requires the reader to consider the quality not of earnest verse, but of poetic doodling. The implicit attitude is similar to that articulated in *Don Juan*:

> I don't know that there may be much ability
> Shown in this sort of desultory rhyme,
> . . .
> Of this I'm sure at least, there's no servility
> In mine irregularity of chime,
> Which rings what's uppermost of new or hoary,
> Just as I feel the *improvvisatore*.
>
> (XV, 20)

Certainly there is no servility of any kind in Byron's tales. Finding himself governed by the form of his verse, Byron discovers not restriction but freedom. He has no difficulty in finding words to fit the pattern presented to him, and when awkwardnesses do occur, he prefers to shift into another rhetorical programme rather than wrestle with the solecism.

We could perhaps simply conclude that the undemanding

routine of Byron's compositional technique resulted in, or even proceeded from, an unconsciously negligent and insensitive understanding of the nature of poetry and language. Yet it is far more likely that the ease with which Byron wrote consistently demonstrated to him just how flexible and easily manipulated words themselves could be. In the absence of a discerning and informed public, Byron found himself free to toy with words. In his hands they become devalued, losing so much of their intrinsic worth, so many of the special associations and connotations that a serious and sensitive poet is able to exploit. Throughout the tales, one senses that Byron is becoming conscious of the extent to which his verse is semantically and poetically destructive. Frequently the rhyming appears not merely negligent or naive, but consciously flippant:

> And there by night, reclin'd, 'tis said,
> Is seen a ghastly turban'd head:
> And hence extended by the billow,
> 'Tis named the 'Pirate-phantom's pillow!'
> (*The Bride of Abydos*, II, 725–8)

> Since last she visited the spot
> Some change seem'd wrought within the grot:
> It might be only that the night
> Disguised things seen in better light:
> That brazen lamp but dimly threw
> A ray of no celestial hue;
> . . .
> A cup too on the board was set
> That did not seem to hold sherbet.
> What may this mean? She turn'd to see
> Her Selim – 'Oh! can this be he?'
> (*The Bride of Abydos*, II, 114–30)

The superfluity of much of this verse suggests that Byron had found himself involved in a process wherein words have been reduced to the compositional elements of a poetic game. He appears to be more interested in the possibilities of verbal manipulation than in the progress of his plot. The enjoyment of these manipulations becomes obvious where he employs oriental words at the ends of his lines, and by the consequent extra emphasis and juxtaposition induced by the rhyme, he brings the crude shape of his poetry into sharp relief, and reduces the English word used to little more than a cipher:

> Though too remote for sound to wake
> In echoes of the far tophaike
>
> > (*The Giaour*, 224–5)

> There sleeps as true an Osmanlie
> As e'er at Mecca bent the knee
>
> > (*Ibid.*, 729–30)[58]

> Enough that he who comes to woo
> Is kinsman of the Bey Oglou.
>
> > (*The Bride of Abydos*, I, 205–6)

More important, this demonstrates Byron's ironic regard for the kind of exoticism valued by his public. The technique is learnt from Pope:

> And when she sees her Friend in deep despair,
> Observes how much a Chintz exceeds Mohair.
>
> > (*Epistle to a Lady*, 169–70)

> Lets Fops or Fortune fly which way they will;
> Disdains all loss of Tickets, or Codille
>
> > (*Ibid.*, 265–6)

> Nay oft, in Dreams, Invention we bestow,
> To change a *Flounce*, or add a *Furbelow*.
>
> > (*The Rape of the Lock*, II, 99–100)

> Where the gilt *Chariot* never marks the Way,
> Where none learn Ombre, none e'er taste *Bohea*!
>
> > (*Ibid.*, IV, 155–6)

The unusual rhyme upon the final syllable of the fashionable commodities gives them an exaggerated and derisive emphasis. Pope deliberately violates the decorum by which he set so much store as a translator of Homer[59] by introducing words into poetry that have no proper place. Thus 'Codille' is presented as an absurdly specific reference, all the more so because it is anticipated in especially fine focus by the rhyme and the late intervention of the caesura. But perhaps the most skilful example of Pope's ironic use of rhyme given here is that of the poised and quietly acidic 'Observes how much a Chintz exceeds Mohair'. Here Pope exploits the rhyme to play off emotional wretchedness against the absolute sterility of the objects of fashionable interest, and it is his use of peculiar rhyme as a means of demonstrating his mockery and detachment that would have been of interest to Byron. What Pope is doing, in fact, is deliberately exploiting the bathos of the 'art of sinking in poetry' in order (in these cases) to make a satiric point about his female readers. He is using what he calls 'The Alamode Style', that 'which is fine by being *new*, and has this happiness attending it, that it is as durable and extensive as the poem itself'.[60] Two examples given in *The Art of Sinking in Poetry* are relevant here:

> See *Phoebus* now, as once for *Phaeton*,
> Has mask'd his face, and put *deep Mourning* on

> While rich *Burgundian* wine, and bright *Champaign*
> Chase from their minds the terrors of the main.[61]

Whilst before Pope it was possible to write verse such as this without an awareness of its bathetic effect, it was increasingly difficult to do so subsequently. When such breaches of decorum do occur, they are usually presented in a mocking sense which derives from Pope's own practice. We have already seen one example of this percolating through into Byron's poetry in his emulation of Thomson's ironic use of Spenserian expletives. The Turkish Tales offer a parallel case, and here the route between Byron and Pope is more direct. Byron lacks Pope's sophistication, but his circumstances do not demand it. It is because Byron is alive to the relaxed critical demands of his era, and aware, too, of the difference between the attractions of fashion in the eighteenth century and the attractions of the exotic in the early nineteenth century, that he is able to exploit the possibilities of rhyming on peculiar words in a markedly cruder way than Pope. Furbelows and mohair evoked for Pope's reader the world of fashionable dress and behaviour and, by Pope's emphases, a world of trivial indulgence and petty material concerns. Tophaikes and Osmanlies however, were likely to mean nothing to Byron's reader, but were nevertheless liable to inspire vaguely exciting and possibly even erotic feelings about the mysterious East. Having travelled, a tophaike to Byron was nothing more thrilling than a musket. It is therefore with considerable self-amusement that he serves up exoticism as a commodity for his reader, an amusement that can be detected in his deliberate indulgence in the art of sinking after the Popean manner. He does not expect his audience to see the joke; his amusement partly depends upon the fact that he can push the game to its limits without their noticing. Thus he is sometimes prepared to rhyme upon two foreign words, exaggerating the facility of the verse:

> And on that eve had gone to mosque,
> And thence to feast in his kiosk.

> > > (*The Giaour*, 463–4)

This is so whimsical and self-consciously clever that it is reminiscent of *Don Juan*:

> O'er which Lieutenant Colonel Yesouski
> Marched with the brave battalion of Polouzki.

> > > (VIII, 76)

The effect of the rhyme is to transfer our attention from the events of the narrative to the voice of the poet; a voice which thus divests the events of his poem of their heroic associations, and invests them with the sentiments of a mind which amuses itself by realizing the absolute governance of idiom over meaning. The result in this case is grotesque comedy, a comedy depending upon our recognition of the antithesis between the subject described and its mode of expression. The couplet is transformed into a vehicle for a *bon mot*, and its formality is perfectly suited to Byron's pompously casual and gentlemanly tones. The movement from 'mosque' to 'kiosk' is identical; the mode of the verbal quip is utterly dissociated from the imaginary movements of an oriental pacha, and seems more appropriate for the description of a Regency gentleman following a visit to the theatre with dinner at his club. The paraphrasable meaning of the verse is thus undercut by its movement, a movement which embodies all the cool detachment of a man playing with words. Occasionally Byron's extravagance is more sustained, and slightly malicious:

> Whate'er it was the sire forgot:
> Or if remembered, marked it not,
> Thrice clapped his hands, and called his steed,
> Resigned his gem-adorned chibouque,
> And mounting featly for the mead,
> With Maugrabee and Mamaluke,
> His way amid his Delis took,
> To witness many an active deed
> With sabre keen, or blunt jerreed.

> > > (*The Bride of Abydos*, I, 230–8)

What Byron was to call the 'fatal facility of the octo-syllabic verse'[62] here insists upon being read with an emphasis on that facility. The superfluous second line anticipates and encourages the kind of response that pays its principal attentions to metre, but the following lines present a problem – that of fitting the metrical feet into 'chibouque', intensified by the fact that a couplet is expected. Counting the feet more rigorously than usual, therefore, 'With Maugrabee and Mamaluke' is liable to receive an absurd degree of emphasis. The mischief of this extract is difficult to miss, and perhaps is only to be expected of a man who entitles a poem 'The Giaour', which he confessed to be an 'unpronounceable name'. Nevertheless, he offers clues by rhyming it with 'bower', 'hour', 'power', and 'tower', the latter being fondly exploited as late as *Don Juan*.[63] The title of his first verse tale embodied more than a little playful spite, and when Moore subsequently chose 'Lalla Rookh' as a title (probably in all innocence) Byron was delighted: 'your poem is to be announced by the name of Lalla Rookh. I am glad of it, first that we are to have it at last, and next I like a tough title myself – witness *The Giaour* and *Childe Harold*, which choked half the Blues at starting.'[64] Writing to Murray on the same day, Byron claimed that '*The Giaour* has never been pronounced to this day.'[65] It was this problem, we remember, that provided Captain Benwick with one of his main topics of conversation. Throughout the tales Byron is playing with readers whom he knows to be bad judges of poetry, yet the games are private ones for the most part. Occasionally, however, he must have expected at least a few of his readers to recognize an element of frivolity. These lines, for instance, contain an obvious punning reference to the famous antics of Caroline Lamb in 1812:[66]

> 'Twas then she went as to the bath,
> Which Hassan vainly search'd in wrath;
> For she was flown her master's rage
> In likeness of a Georgian page
>
> (*The Giaour*, 453–6)

There may be nothing accomplished about this, but it tells us much about Byron's frame of mind when he was composing his verse tales. It also looks forward to the more successful and sustained allusions to Lady Byron in *Don Juan*. It is at this stage in his career, however, that Byron is beginning to realize the extent to which the boundaries of poetry can be distended to embrace not merely the verbal tricks continued by the linguistic *farceur* of *Don Juan*, but also the kind of unscrupulous personal licence that is one of the most distinctive features of the *ottava rima* poems.

Yet although the reader of Byron's tales may find himself frequently wondering how the poet managed to get away with writing such lines as

> The guest flies the hall, and the vassal from labour,
> Since his turban was cleft by the infidel's sabre.
>
> *(The Giaour, 350–1)*

or

> Was he not bred in Egripo?
> A viler race let Israel show!
>
> *(The Bride of Abydos, I, 375–6)*

he is also liable to be constantly aware of the freedom with which Byron moves from such apparent flippancy to passages in which he seems anxious to display his talents as a poet:

> He who hath bent him o'er the dead
> Ere the first day of death is fled,
> The first dark day of nothingness,
> The last of danger and distress,
> (Before Decay's effacing fingers
> Have swept the lines where beauty lingers,)
> And mark'd the mild angelic air,
> The rapture of repose that's there,
> The fix'd yet tender traits that streak
> The languor of the placid cheek
>
> *(The Giaour, 68–77)*

Such flights are perhaps most common in *The Giaour*, but they occur throughout the other tales, and amongst them can be numbered the opening of the second canto of *The Bride of Abydos*, the opening of the third canto of *The Corsair*, and the descriptions of the night in *Lara* (I, 155) and *The Siege of Corinth* (242). When reading these passages one is only too conscious of the fact that Byron has pushed aside his narrative for a moment so that he may indulge in a poetic display wherein he, as poet, receives exclusively an audience's attention that was previously fixed upon the hero or the narrative line.

We might briefly consider how such passages were received in their time. The extract above was considered 'highly wrought' by Ellis for the *Quarterly*, who praised the 'artful and brilliant metaphors by which the poet has connected these apparently incongruous images'.[67] With uncharacteristic impetuosity, Jeffrey, in the *Edinburgh*, declared its 'image more true, more mournful, and more exquisitely finished, than any other that we can now recollect in the whole compass of poetry'.[68] The greatest attributes of these lines, according to both critics, then, were their 'art' and 'finish'. This is significant, and may help us to discover the nature of Byron's composition during his most successful years. Whilst the extravagance of Jeffrey's comment reveals an astonishing lack of critical acumen, and causes us to wonder how he read (amongst others) Shakespeare, Milton, and Pope, we must remember that together with other influences that can be ascribed to the *Zeitgeist*, the nature of Jeffrey's work as a literary critic in the age of the great reviews almost certainly led to an unnatural and unbalanced preoccupation with the poetry of his own time. In addition, this poetry, as we well know, was being subjected to new and consequential influences of change, influences that were threatening the 'standards . . . fixed long ago, by certain inspired writers, whose authority it is no longer lawful to call into question'[69] upon which Jeffrey placed so much value. Since he never cites the source of these standards or rules, and rarely chooses to refer to their existence, we may conclude that their influence upon his criticism is an implicit one: that is, the standards or rules have no systematic arrangement in Jeffrey's mind or even before him upon his desk, but they play a pervasive and ever-present part in his thinking. Probably they are a consequence of certain habits and techniques of reading and writing that can be traced back to his education. In short, Jeffrey (or Ellis for that matter) has not moved far from the kind of judgement encouraged by the use of his Gradus at school, and perhaps a subsequent reading of Bysshe. When confronted by writing such as that of Wordsworth or Southey, therefore, which demanded a different sort of judgement, Jeffrey felt the standards by which he set so much store threatened. These standards were not merely those which revolve around the aesthetic principles that a humanistic education was liable to produce. They were also the social values of whiggish amateurism which viewed the tide of middle-class professionalism towards fashionable life with some misgiving. We have already seen that to control the middle-class readership's reading was one of Jeffrey's aims; another, doubtless, was to control those whom he considered to be their poets. Viewing 'the whole compass of poetry' through this rather insecure and distorted spectrum, and then turning to *The Giaour*, Jeffrey finds himself confronted with a piece of poetry that for the most part places a similar kind of reliance upon the influence of the Gradus as does his own criticism. Of course I do not wish to suggest that this was a consciously realized fact. The point is that to Jeffrey and Ellis, Byron seems to have a decorum that Wordsworth and Southey lacked, a decorum that bears the stamp of his education. His literary good manners, as it were, make him socially acceptable, because they are of the right sort of pedigree.

The passage isolated by Jeffrey and Ellis shows all the traits of what Lytton was to call 'knack': 'the faculty both of repeating other men's words, and stringing imitations of other men's verses'.[70] The familiarity of 'Fires not, wins not, weeps not, now' at line 79 betrays the nature of its composition, as too, upon scrutiny, do such neat rhetorical packages as 'So fair, so calm, so softly seal'd, / The first, last look by death reveal'd!' (88–9) and 'So coldly sweet, so deadly fair' (92). The eloquence of the passage depends upon its adroit manipulation of the device of antithesis, which here slots neatly into a peculiarly poised octosyllabic couplet. Unlike his eighteenth-century predecessors, or Scott, Byron's octosyllabics here utilize iambics emphasized by pauses, and the occasional caesura.[71] He thus brings a distinctive and largely unprecedented elegance to octosyllabic verse, and it was the effect of this kind of dexterity, no doubt, that gave the passage 'art' and 'finish' in its own day.

At this point in the discussion the most pressing and important question concerns Byron's awareness of what he was doing. Since there is little contemporaneous poetry directly comparable to the tales in terms of rhetorical facility, it is not easy to assert that both Jeffrey's critical blindness and Byron's crude yet dexterously manipulated rhetoric were both consequences of standards sanctioned by habit. We therefore have to ask whether Byron wrote poetry with no conscious registration of the fact that he was exploiting tricks of composition nurtured by his early education. This is a difficult issue, and cannot perhaps be fully resolved. Nevertheless, it must be said that it is extremely unlikely that the 'knack' which Byron learnt at Harrow could become buried in his subconscious so quickly, and yet there is some evidence to suggest that, even whilst at Harrow, Byron may have been unaware of just how automatic his rhetorical facility had become.[72] Against this, however, we must place the fact that

Byron confessed that the only man that he wished to exclude from reading his poetry was his old headmaster.[73] But perhaps the most telling factor in this debate is the freedom with which Byron employs these techniques throughout his tales. He does not reserve them exclusively for rhetorical displays such as the one we have been discussing, but uses them with an intemperance that has more than a hint of fully conscious exhibitionism about it. In his purple passages, he is prepared to use them gracefully; elsewhere they are exploited with a crudity that amounts to brashness. It is as if he wishes to recompense himself for what are fairly obviously, in part, 'poetical' concessions to the public and the reviewers.

One motive behind these poetical displays is Byron's desire to demonstrate to reader and reviewer alike that he is neither a 'balladmonger' nor a parvenu translator, but a poet and a gentleman. However loose Byron's decorum was by eighteenth-century standards, it was sufficient in his own day to convey a sense of his gentility. For different reasons, refinement was a desirable asset to reader and reviewer alike. To critics such as Jeffrey and the readers of the coteries, it was that which kept their literature exclusive, whilst paradoxically, to the middle-class reader, it was a mark which reflected their own social achievement. Scott, whose recognition of this demand we have noticed, probably taught Byron much in this respect. He carefully selected the kind of mode that would at once provide easy reading and persuade the reader that he was involved in a sophisticated pursuit. The simple ballad rhythms and directness of narration that had proved successful for Lewis and for his own *Minstrelsy of the Scottish Border* were retained for *The Lay of the Last Minstrel*, and to these he added a hint of refinement and sophistication to gratify his readership's genteel demands. Thus, in the Preface, the minstrel is introduced as 'the last of the race, who, as he is supposed to have survived the Revolution, might have caught somewhat of the refinement of modern poetry, without losing the simplicity of his original model'.[74] Scott obviously wants it both ways. To the critics, however, the 'refinement of modern poetry' was something that required greater emphasis in Scott's verse, and alongside general approbation there occurred numerous complaints about irregular versification, uncouth rhymes, bathos, and an over-generous use of expletives.[75] The poetry subsequent to *The Lay of the Last Minstrel* never fully satisfied the critics in these respects. It is clear that they welcomed Byron's modifications to the verse tale, its liberation from the quaintness and 'vulgarity' of its antiquarian and foreign connections, and its retention of the 'powerful emotions' associated with these more 'primitive' contexts.[76] Byron thus capitalized on Scott's uneasy relationship with the reviewers, and yet his success depended not so much upon the kind of manoeuvring which Scott attempted as upon a tailor-made opportunity for the kind of rhetorical adroitness in which he was skilled. Byron did not have to exert himself to captivate the reading public and the critics. And whilst the history of Scott's rise to fame suggests that he worked for success with some diligence and astuteness, the tongue-in-cheek replies to the critics' cavils to be found scattered throughout the Introduction in *Marmion* may well have demonstrated to Byron that once a poet found his popularity established he could openly confess authorial diffidence without impairing the reception of his verse:

> Need I to thee, dear Erskine, tell
> I love the licence all too well,
> In sounds now lowly, and now strong,
> To raise the desultory song?

> (Introduction to Canto III)[77]

Scott's awareness of the relaxed critical atmosphere in which he is working is thus made explicit. He does not choose to elevate the larger proportion of his narrative to the level of his interspersed descriptions – the level preferred by his reviewers. Almost certainly Byron learnt something from this, realizing not only that the critics might be easily placated if not satisfied by an adequate provision of 'strong sounds' within the narrative, but also (and perhaps as a consequence of this critical enervation) that the majority of his readers were unlikely to make serious distinctions about the relative qualities of particular passages. The reception of *Childe Harold I & II*, of course, had proved much the same point.

Yet it would be wrong to imply that the poetic displays of Byron's tales were included merely for the reviewers' approval. Undoubtedly Byron enjoyed indulging his rhetoric here as much as he did in *Childe Harold I & II*. Indeed, it is partly the freedom granted by this sense of enjoyment (which in many ways is akin to that confessed by Scott in the passage cited above) that invests the poetry of this period with its characteristic facility. Had Byron not relished his rhetorical performances, and regarded them purely as part of a tactical plan, it is unlikely that he would have been able to move in and out of them with such abandon as he does. These sudden shifts of modulation suited Byron temperamentally, and simultaneously allowed him to lay claim to an image of the poet that was exempt from the kind of professionalism he abhorred. A remark recorded by Medwin exemplifies how Byron was able to marry his temperamental propensities to his social attitudes, under the guise of an aesthetic that belongs to early Regency taste: 'Like Gray . . . Campbell smells too much of the oil: he is never satisfied with what he does; his finest things have been spoiled by over-polish – the sharpness of the outline is worn off. Like paintings, poems may be too highly finished. The great art is effect, no matter how produced.'[78] The most significant part of this, however, is the final sentence, which to some extent summarizes Byron's compositional attitudes during his years of fame. It also testifies to Byron's limited but nonetheless accurate assessment of his public's taste, but our main interest is likely to be absorbed by its ambivalence. I think there is more than a grain of cynicism here, yet necessarily a cynicism that is not directed bluntly against the popular taste, but includes a reference to his own weaknesses. It is therefore a complex attitude, and akin to that which gives the tales their real interest.

'Effect', in the tales, amounts to more than simple rhetorical indulgence. Exoticism, adventure, hints of incest, murders, and swashbuckling yet occasionally gentlemanly heroes all have their part to play in the performance. A measure of concentrated sensationalism also has a role:

> The Mind, that broods o'er guilty woes,
> Is like the Scorpion girt by fire;
> In circle narrowing as it glows,
> The flames around their captive close,
> Till inly search'd by thousand throes,
> And maddening in her ire,
> One sad and sole relief she knows,
> The sting she nourish'd for her foes,
> Whose venom never yet was vain,
> Gives but one pang and cures all pain,
> And darts into her desperate brain
>
> (*The Giaour*, 422–32)

However, because this image is utilized to illustrate an idea somewhat sententiously presented by the poet as a fact, it need not necessarily be seen as a sensational indulgence. This is less true of the passage in *The Corsair* wherein the reader is invited to imagine Conrad's impalement:

> The leech was sent – but not in mercy – there,
> To note how much the life yet left could bear;
> He found enough to load with heaviest chain,
> And promise feeling for the wrench of pain;
> To-morrow – yea – to-morrow's evening sun
> Will sinking see impalement's pangs begun,
> And rising with the wonted blush of morn
> Behold how well or ill those pangs are borne.
> Of torments this the longest and the worst,
> Which adds all other agony to thirst,
> That day by day death still forbears to slake,
> While famish'd vultures flit around the stake.
> 'Oh! water – water!' smiling Hate denies
> The victim's prayer, for if he drinks he dies.

(II, 310–23)

This is too much like the ending of *The Monk* to be regarded as anything other than an attempt to create a sensational effect, and Byron is clearly exploiting the kind of sadistic spice that Lewis had found so successful. A passage from *The Siege of Corinth* may possibly convince us of Byron's weakness for sensationalism:

> And he saw the lean dogs beneath the wall
> Hold o'er the dead their carnival,
> Gorging and growling o'er carcass and limb
> They were too busy to bark at him!
> From a Tartar's skull they had stripp'd the flesh,
> As ye peel the fig when its fruit is fresh;
> And their white tusks crunch'd o'er the whiter skull,
> As it slipp'd through their jaws, when their edge grew dull

(454–61)

Yet this offers more of interest, and requires us to go further than simply concluding that Byron was not averse to using elements of Gothic horror as part of his showmanship. There is something very close to malice in the line 'As ye peel the fig when the fruit is fresh', and it is indicative of Byron's awareness of his readership's desire to be shocked. A little spitefully, Byron pushes the content of his verse beyond all tasteful limits. It is a deliberate violation of decorum, and the impropriety is not merely 'literary', for it insists on involving the reader in a way to which he was unaccustomed, no longer allowing him or her to relish horror in the comfortable aegis provided by the circumstances of drawing-room reading. This discomfiting and provocative intrusion into the reader's world is not an isolated instance of what might be described as Byron's teasing of his readership in the Turkish Tales. The subject of the reader's relation to the poem apparently affords him occasional amusement:

> Ours the wild life in tumult still to range
> From toil to rest, and joy in every change.
> Oh, who can tell? not thou luxurious slave!
> Whose soul would sicken o'er the heaving wave;
> Not thou, vain lord of wantonness and ease!
> Whom slumber soothes not – pleasure cannot please –
> Oh, who can tell, save he whose heart hath tried,
> And danced in triumph o'er the waters wide,
> The exulting sense – the pulse's maddening play,
> That thrills the wanderer of that trackless way?
>
> (*The Corsair*, 7–16)

Obviously this is not intended as a flagrant denial of the worth of the reading experience; it has a local reference within the poem which dulls its edge. Nevertheless, this implication cannot be easily eradicated. Like the line from *Parisina*, 'It was a thing to see, not hear!' (339), this passage seeks to expose something of the artificiality of reading fiction. It may be that it can be regarded as a perceptive comment by Byron on the reading habits of his time, on the genteel substitution of novelty and purely literary excitement for real experience. But most important, it is at once Byron's means of refusing to comply with the rules of the poetry game and an assertion that the proper validation of what he is writing about is only to be found in his own experience. Whilst this implies a basic dissatisfaction with a poetry that attempts to recreate the events and emotions of real-life experience, the verse of the tales proves only too emphatically that a recreation of this kind has not been an aim that Byron has taken at all seriously. Thus although 'It was a thing to see, not hear!' may be masquerading as a cry of artistic frustration, it therefore cannot possibly be read as such. Like the tricks of rhyme and the odd effects of metre, the sensationalism and what appears to be its maliciousness, this is a taunt made with no confidence that it will be received as such. The games of the tales are internal ones, conducted for Byron's own satisfaction, and amusing only to the extent that their drollery consists of his assumption that his readers will either miss them completely or interpret them in the wrong way.

Ostensibly, the tales present us with a poet who amuses himself with his own prolixity, discovering at the same time some of the verbal tricks and possibilities that he was to exploit later in his career. His addiction to this amusement might be seen as a consequence of his boredom, but, given the economic circumstances in which these poems were produced, it seems more likely that Byron was conducting an internal private performance for himself in order to create an illusion of independence. By building a dimension in the verse of which he can be fairly sure his audience will remain ignorant, he is able to dissociate himself from a productive process wherein the poet has become subsumed into the trade of orientalism. He is able, therefore, to delude himself about the real nature of his relationship to his audience. Simultaneously, by amusing himself in this way, the writing of verse is for the most part sustained at a non-serious level. He is thus able to see himself as distinct from his conception of the literary parvenu, but, more important, the fact that he is able to postpone a serious consideration of the nature of his art creates a situation in which he is able vaguely to believe in it as a mechanism which actually allows him to make extravagant claims for his capacity for real experience. The tales implicitly declare that their events are based upon the poet's familiarity with their exotic settings, but, further, the movement of the verse, together with the interspersed reflective passages ('What boots the oft-repeated tale of strife, / The feast of vultures, and the waste of life?' – *Lara*, II, 264–5), suggest something of a capacity for emotional sympathy and worldly wisdom that is based upon experience.

Despite these illusions, the anomalies of the verse tales suggest that at this point in his career Byron recognized himself as a producer, a poet providing a commodity in demand. This recognition simultaneously stimulates a review of his productive processes, a review which goes no further than allowing him to realize the nature of his poetic facility and his habitual evasion of real difficulties. Accordingly, his writing becomes self-consciously flippant as a means of defence against an audience which threatened to confront him with the less acceptable aspect of his poetry, by exerting their control over it as a commodity. The writing of the verse tales may not have resolved the problematic relationship between Byron and his poetry that manifested itself in *Childe Harold I & II*, but their careless assurance suggests that his discovery of his own position vis-à-vis his readers at least allowed him to live more happily with it.

3

Shelley and the new school of poetry: *Childe Harold III* and *The Prisoner of Chillon*

Not in the lucid intervals of life
. . .
Is nature felt, or can be; nor do words,
Which practised talent readily affords,
Prove that her hand has touched responsive chords[1]

(Wordsworth)

In this chapter I wish to concentrate upon certain features of Byron's poetry in 1816 which have either been ignored or inadequately discussed in the past. Most of these features, directly or indirectly, are a consequence of Byron's meeting with Shelley in the same year. In 1821, in answer to Medwin's accusation that he was indebted to Wordsworth in *Childe Harold III*, Byron allegedly replied: 'Very possibly . . . Shelley, when I was in Switzerland, used to dose me with Wordsworth physic even to nausea: and I do remember then reading some things of his with pleasure.'[2]

The embarrassment latent in the facetiousness of this remark is not surprising. It is not to be expected that Byron would readily have conceded the influence of Wordsworth on his writings at any time in his career. Indeed, in the light of his well-known derogatory comments on the older poet, this influence now presents itself as such an improbable possibility that it is largely discounted.[3] The fact remains that not only Byron and his contemporary reviewers, but also Wordsworth, were aware of it.[4] The offhand nature of Byron's confession, however, is not merely a consequence of his embarrassment. It is also entirely consistent with the nature of his use of Wordsworth, which can be aptly introduced by another remark to be found in Medwin: 'The lyrical ballads, jacobinal and puling with affectation of simplicity as they were, had undoubtedly a certain

64

merit: and Wordsworth, though occasionally a writer for the nursery masters and misses . . . now and then expressed ideas worth imitating; but like brother Southey, he had his price.'⁵ 'Wordsworth . . . now and then expressed ideas worth imitating' – this is exactly the kind of comment we might expect from the poet of the Turkish Tales.

This remark does not tell us the whole story, however. It confirms that Byron's use of Wordsworth in 1816 was not the result of a serious reassessment of his own art, and that it did not amount to an acknowledgement of Wordsworth's poetic achievement. But it would be untrue to say that the new elements of Byron's poetry in 1816 were a consequence of his exploitation of a few Wordsworthian motifs that he considered to be marketable. The relationship is far more complex than this: the question that demands to be answered is why Byron should have become interested in Wordsworth at all. This immediately concerns us with the issue of Shelley's part in recommending Wordsworth to Byron.

Of course Shelley was not responsible for introducing Wordsworth to Byron. Byron knew the *Lyrical Ballads*, and reviewed the *Poems in Two Volumes* (1807) for *Monthly Literary Recreations*. By 1815 he had read *The Excursion*, and he was also acquainted with the collected poems published that same year.⁶ In fact, Byron had probably kept a fairly close eye on Wordsworth, and whilst the conventionality of the comments on the older poet scattered through the letters and journals suggests that his reading need not have been particularly attentive, the fact that Wordsworth was an established poet of the age by 1815 cannot have escaped his notice. Shelley may have had a relatively simple task, therefore, in directing Byron's attentions to Wordsworth in 1816. He was dealing with somebody who was reasonably well acquainted with Wordsworth's work, and somebody who was also ready to reconsider him, though probably not for the reasons that Shelley would have wished. Byron would have been curious to know how Wordsworth had become established. Here was a poet whose opposition to him in style and manner was so marked that their mutual acceptance by the same public would seem to be an impossibility. As the most popular poet of the day, and fully conscious of what made him new and fashionable, Byron was unlikely to feel any resistance towards Jeffrey's suggestion that his talents were perfectly suited to his era.⁷ We could say, in fact, that he liked to consider himself as the embodiment of the 'spirit of the age'.⁸ Wordsworth, for a while, could be dismissed as an irrelevant eccentric by the derisive jokes of which Byron was so fond. But by 1816 these jokes were wearing a little thin, and Byron must have been dimly aware that Wordsworth deserved to be considered as an authentic product of his era, an established figure of the age. When Shelley urged him to read Wordsworth, this dim awareness may well have been transformed into a fully conscious recognition, and this recognition, in turn, would have forced Byron to realize that if he really were to be regarded as the embodiment of the spirit of his age, he would have to open his eyes to that part of it that was manifesting itself in Wordsworth. Of course all this is hypothetical, but in keeping, I believe, with what we know of Byron's character and the historical facts.

We are still in the area of hypotheses when we come to consider the way in which Shelley represented Wordsworth to Byron. There is no evidence to help us discover which poems Byron read at Shelley's suggestion, for example, although Wordsworth himself had no doubt as to which of his poems Byron had been reading.[9] Further, although Leavis has called attention to the 'fine critical intelligence' of Shelley's appreciation of Wordsworth in *Peter Bell the Third*,[10] I cannot imagine that this intelligence would have been allowed free play in the early stages of the friendship between the two poets, even supposing that it existed as early as 1816. Certainly the sonnet 'To Wordsworth' which Shelley published in 1816 with *Alastor* (although composed, admittedly, in 1814) offers no evidence of an intelligent understanding of Wordsworth's verse. Despite these obfuscations we can be fairly sure of two things. First, the radical sympathies which Byron and Shelley shared would have resulted in a basic agreement over Wordsworth's political apostasy, and it seems likely that this aspect of Wordsworth's career would have been of sufficient consequence to Shelley, and sufficiently agreeable to Byron's preconceptions and prejudices, to allow both poets to find a wide area of agreement within which it could be mooted by either that Wordsworth was 'improvable'. That is to say, no matter how much more sensitive and fully aware Shelley's reading of Wordsworth may have been than Byron's, his sense of betrayal was such that he was liable to be tolerant of Byron's less sensitive criticisms. 'To Wordsworth' is sufficiently endowed with this sense of betrayal to allow us to suppose that this would have been so. From Shelley's point of view, there would have been considerable consolation in finding sympathy, however broad, in such a potentially powerful ally. From Byron's point of view, however, this point of agreement may have been so reassuring as to encourage him to simplify his conception of where Wordsworth had gone wrong. Secondly, there can be little doubt that when Byron met Shelley, he met the first person (and probably the only person) in his life who was to tell him with conviction that Wordsworth was a great poet. And Shelley's reasons for claiming greatness for Wordsworth were so intimately bound up with his own highly individual sense of poetic vocation that this conviction would have carried with it the weight of Shelley's absolute, almost religious, commitment to his art. It cannot be said that the force of this would have made Shelley's proposals irresistible to Byron: on the contrary, Byron probably felt inwardly resistant to many of Shelley's ideas. But it would have been sufficient to convince him of Shelley's authenticity, and thereby of Wordsworth's too.[11]

The meaning which Shelley attached to Wordsworth's 'greatness' undoubtedly lay at a considerable distance from any concept that Byron had of the word's usage – and there is plentiful evidence to demonstrate how loose and unthinking this concept probably was. We can be almost certain that Shelley thought Wordsworth was a great poet largely on account of his claims for the centrality of the poet's position. The emphasis which Wordsworth places upon the poet's social responsibilities, his 'truth', and his sensitivity to the 'goings-on' of the Universe'[12] were after all to be transformed by Shelley's conviction into one of his most famous statements:

poets . . . are the institutors of laws, and the founders of civil society, and the inventors of the arts of life, and the teachers, who draw into a certain propinquity with the beautiful and the true, that partial apprehension of the agencies of the invisible world which is called religion . . . A poet participates in the eternal, the infinite, and the one.[13]

One cannot imagine Byron coming to terms with this, and there is little evidence to suggest that by 1816 Shelley was able to articulate these ideas with such confidence. Nevertheless, *Alastor*, published in 1816, has its roots in a closely related set of ideas, and suggests that Shelley was liable to place Byron in deep water fairly quickly. In Shelley's own words, the poem 'represents a youth of uncorrupted feelings and adventurous genius led forth by an imagination inflamed and purified through familiarity with all that is excellent and majestic, to the contemplation of the universe'.[14] Its allegory may be designed to express the agonies of the too-sensitive poet, but it also stresses the fact that he is one of the world's 'luminaries'. Thus far *Alastor* is related to Wordsworth by the general (but nevertheless important) claims made for the poet's role in the Preface to the *Lyrical Ballads*. But *Alastor* also demonstrates how Shelley assimilated and transformed aspects of Wordsworth's poetry. In this extract, as the first phrase given suggests, Shelley is working on 'Intimations of Immortality':

> Whither have fled
> The hues of heaven that canopied his bower
> Of yesternight? the sounds that soothed his sleep,
> The mystery and the majesty of Earth,
> The joy, the exaltation? His wan eyes
> Gaze on the empty scene as vacantly
> As ocean's moon looks on the moon in heaven.
> The spirit of sweet human love has sent
> A vision to the sleep of him who spurned
> Her choicest gifts. He eagerly pursues
> Beyond the realms of dream that fleeting shade;
> He overleaps the bounds. Alas! Alas!
> Were limbs, and breath, and being intertwined
> Thus treacherously? Lost, lost, for ever lost,
> In the wide pathless desert of dim sleep,
> That beautiful shape! Does the dark gate of death
> Conduct to thy mysterious paradise,
> O Sleep?

(196–213)[15]

Of course this is nothing like Wordsworth, and perhaps one is most conscious here of how Shelley was able to lose Wordsworth by marrying him so easily to other elements of his reading. In addition, it shows only too clearly Shelley's lack of sympathy with Wordsworth's theories of composition. Further, the allegorical scheme of *Alastor* has no Wordsworthian equivalent. What this demonstrates is that Shelley, in exploiting ideas that he believes are to be found in Wordsworth, totally divorces them from the sense of authentic, deeply contemplated experience upon which they depend in the older poet's work. The poetic experience in Wordsworth primarily consists of the evocation of feelings through which the ideas and circumstances of the poem become significant – 'the feeling therein developed gives importance to the action and situation, and not the action and situation to the feeling'.[16] Shelley is not interested in the poetry of experience: unlike Wordsworth his emphasis is not on the philosophical reflections and generosity of sentiment that the acts of perception are liable to elicit, but on the mystical implications of his Poet's extreme sensitivity. The 'truth' of Wordsworth's poems is experienced through the text; Shelley's 'truth', however, is always esoterically mysterious, an alchemical factor to be discovered. 'The spirit of solitude' in *Alastor* is mingled with the ether of magic.

This particular aspect of Shelley's conception of the poet does not fully manifest itself in Byron's poetry until *Manfred*. Nevertheless, *Alastor* is immediately relevant to Shelley's representation of Wordsworth to Byron. It may not allow us to delineate precisely the manner in which Shelley read Wordsworth, but it demonstrates the relation of Shelley's concept of the poet to the definition of the poet's role and poetry as described in Wordsworth's poetry and prose. Most important, it suggests the location of Shelley's emphasis in defining Wordsworth's greatness to Byron. In addition, we might reasonably suppose that Shelley, as a poet of ideas, gave Byron his own abstract of the 'ideas' of Wordsworth's poetry.

As an intelligent man, Byron may have been confused by Shelley's version of Wordsworth, and struck by how alien it was to his own notions of poetry, but he would not have been totally mystified by it. Convinced by the authenticity of Wordsworth and Shelley, he was left with the task of discovering a method of absorbing their 'ideas' into his own verse. The method he discovered, we shall see, involved reducing them to a manageable and more familiar state.

Childe Harold's Pilgrimage III

The stanzas in *Childe Harold III* which have been identified as bearing the marks of Wordsworth's influence, principally stanzas 72–4, 88–9, and 97,[17] bear little stylistic affinity to Wordsworth. They are delivered in the typical mode of *Childe Harold's Pilgrimage*. What is new is the sentiment to which they lay claim. A detailed examination of the most frequently quoted of these stanzas reveals how Byron is attempting to master new material with his old compositional habits:

> I live not in myself, but I become
> Portion of that around me; and to me
> High mountains are a feeling, but the hum
> Of human cities torture: I can see

> Nothing to loathe in Nature, save to be
> A link reluctant in a fleshy chain,
> Classed among creatures, when the soul can flee,
> And with the sky – the peak – the heaving plain
> Of Ocean, or the stars, mingle – and not in vain.

(III, lxxii)

This marks a point of departure for Byron, and regarding this move in the wider context of his complete works, we can see it as an excursion and nothing more. But even within this stanza, the fact that Byron is on a literary sortie is made abundantly clear, and the tyranny of style over matter signifies the relative unimportance of the actual sentiment of the verse to him. He is only concerned with the effect of its presentation. He knows full well how to begin, and the confidence of his entry into this new field bears all the characteristics of a virtuoso improviser who believes himself equal 'to anything'.[18] But it is surprising how quickly he loses himself after such a grandiloquent entry. By the third line he stumbles into vagueness: the tenor of the delivery promises something more precise than 'a feeling', which in this context is bathetic. At this point Byron may well be trying to understand what has been described as 'the most notorious feature of Shelleyan optics . . . the vagueness bred of his seeking "in what I see the manifestation of something beyond the present & tangible object"'.[19] In doing so he is possibly equating Shelley's vagueness with the deliberate vagueness ('I cannot paint what then I was') of Wordsworth in 'Tintern Abbey':

> Their colours and their forms, were then to me
> An appetite; a feeling and a love

(79–80)

Byron is clearly not at ease in his line, and the fact that he feels compelled to make such an uncomfortable assertion should perhaps be read as an inevitable consequence of an inability to understand poetry as anything other than a form of declamation. The failure to be impressively aphoristic in the third line causes him to seek refuge in something more familiar in his next phrase: an exaggerated emotion to which an unscrupulous exploitation of verbal crudity ('torture') allows him to lay claim. And this is promptly followed by a piece of equally familiar condescension. Byron is finding his feet again, and 'A link reluctant in a fleshy chain' is sufficiently compact and meretricious to re-establish his confidence. Back in the business of creating 'effect', his improvising continues in the old self-propagating manner of the Turkish Tales. The brief list comes easily, and conveniently provides an appropriate rhapsodic effect. But Byron falls into a trap by relapsing into his safe techniques too near the end of the stanza. His usual means of avoiding a demanding climax – a diversion of some kind or a change of subject – cannot possibly be accommodated by the last line, and the result is a particularly awkward alexandrine. Byron later insisted that the finishing line of the Spenserian stanza 'must be good'.[20] The number of uncomfortable stanza endings in *Childe Harold III & IV*, given this awareness, can only testify to his abandonment of the kind of self-consciousness (however lacking in finesse) identifiable in the first two cantos.

If this is Byron's version of Wordsworth – and it is worth reiterating that both he and Wordsworth were prepared to accept it as such – then it is a version that depends heavily on Shelley. 'Classed among creatures, when the soul can flee' probably derives from Shelley's neo-Platonic sympathies. Shelley's summary of Wordsworth, being a rather mystical one, has apparently resulted in Byron's seizing upon the most familiar aspect he can discover in Shelley's thinking to help him rationalize it. In addition, this neo-Platonic reading of Wordsworth, where 'the feeling infinite' (stanza 90) is almost always presented as a sense of the soul's immortality, would have been entirely consistent with a literal reading of 'Intimations of Immortality', a poem which may have proved attractive to Byron precisely because of its vulnerability to a literal approach. Byron is both literalizing Wordsworth and Shelley and simplifying them, by taking a hold on what may have been the one thread of Shelley's thinking with which he was familiar. And it is this tendency to interpolate familiar areas of his reading between himself and Shelley and Wordsworth that results in the rather confused relationship between the poet and nature that *Childe Harold III* proposes.

Rousseau is mentioned more than once in the third canto, but he plays a more significant part in the poetry than simply providing Byron with decorative topographical allusions. Byron's references to scenery as a presence governing his emotions (stanzas 85, 89, 93) strongly recall Saint-Preux's descriptions in *La Nouvelle Héloise*. Similarly, the idea that Byron, expelled from the world of men, finds spiritual rejuvenation in the world of nature (stanzas 73, 85, 98) is a reiteration of the prevalent concern of the *Rêveries d'un Promeneur*

Solitaire.[21] When Byron wrote these later stanzas of *Childe Harold III* he was touring the territory of *La Nouvelle Héloise* with Shelley, who was enthusiastically reading the novel for the first time.[22] It therefore seems quite likely that his own reading of Wordsworth could have been significantly coloured by his recall of Rousseau. This becomes an even stronger possibility when one considers how easily Byron could have identified himself with Rousseau as a social outcast seeking to redefine his position in the world.

At the beginning of the *Rêveries*, Rosseau asks, 'But I, withdrawn from them and from everything, what am I then?'[23] His reference is to the society that has rejected him, and the *Rêveries* answers the question by the claim that it is only through the disengagement of 'social passions and their troublesome attendants'[24] that the individual can rediscover the spiritual calm that nature elicits. This claim, and the position from which it is delivered, is remarkably similar to that which Byron makes in the third canto. The position which Byron finally adopts in relation to the world of men, that of indifference ('I have not loved the world, nor the world me, / But let us part fair foes'), is arrived at through what he has claimed to be the spiritual consolations of his solitude. Simultaneously, this is presented as some kind of victory, an abjuration of the kind of worldly hatred or spite that he has transcended. The ignominy of exile is thus denied, and again this coincides with Rousseau's position in the *Rêveries*:

Do all they can, my repugnance can never reach aversion . . . I had rather shun than hate them. Their aspect strikes my senses, and through them my heart, with impressions which a thousand cruel looks render painful; but the uneasiness leaves me the moment the object which caused it disappears . . . They are indifferent to me no farther than they relate to me . . . The conclusion I am able to draw from all these reflections is, that I never was truly adapted to society where all is constraint, obligation, devoirs; and that my independent disposition always rendered me incapable of a subjection necessary to him who wishes to be something in the world.[25]

Byron's weakness for posturing may have naturally resulted in drawing him away from Wordsworth and towards Rousseau, but it is not merely this single element of Rousseau that he absorbs. Rousseau's belief that the happiness of his reveries proceeded from the invasion of his senses by ecstasies induced by contemplating the objects of nature[26] and the subsequent exclusion of the 'agitation of continual passions' and the distraction of 'terrestrial impressions'[27] finds an easy passage into Byron's poetry:

> Clear, placid Leman! thy contrasted lake,
> With the wild world I dwelt in, is a thing
> Which warns me, in its stillness, to forsake
> Earth's troubled waters for a purer spring.
> This quiet sail is as a noiseless wing
> To waft me from distraction
>
> (III, lxxxv)

It is this aspect of the *Rêveries* which leads Rousseau into a neo-Platonic position: 'in this inactivity of body, my soul remains active, it still produces sentiments, thoughts; and internal and moral life seem to grow out of the death of all terrestrial and temporal interests. My body is nothing now but a trouble, an obstacle, and I disengage myself from it before-hand as much as I can.'[28] This is not where Rousseau places his emphasis. In fact this passage may be regarded as a lapse into an easy and conventional mode of thinking that Rousseau resists for the most part. Significantly, it is a mode which Byron cannot resist:

> And when, at length, the mind shall be all free
> From what it hates in this degraded form,
> Reft of its carnal life, save what shall be
> Existent happier in the fly and worm, –
> When elements to elements conform,
> And dust is as it should be, shall I not
> Feel all I see, less dazzling, but more warm?
> The bodiless thought? the Spirit of each spot?
> Of which, even now, I share at times the immortal lot?
>
> (III, lxxiv)

Byron's model here, and the reasons for his dependence on this mode and idea, is something to which I shall return.

Whilst it seems quite likely that what Byron vaguely claims to be the 'soul' of nature, that which makes natural objects 'felt and feeling' (stanza 96), derives approximately from the 'presence' in 'Tintern Abbey' (line 94), or from Shelley's interpretation of the poem perhaps, it is unclear how he wishes to represent his relation to this 'soul'. Towards the end of the canto, he apparently attempts to resolve the difficulty in a note to stanza 99:

the feeling with which all around Clarens, and the opposite rocks of Meillerie, is invested, is of a still higher and more comprehensive order than the mere sympathy with individual passion; it is a sense of the existence of love in

73

its most extended and sublime capacity, and of our own participation of its good and of its glory: It is the great principle of the universe, which is there more condensed, but not less manifested; and of which, though knowing ourselves a part, we lose our individuality, and mingle in the beauty of the whole.

The use of 'mingle' suggests that what is being described here is an experience similar to that of stanza 72. This note is not merely a paraphrase of stanzas 99–104: its emphasis upon the 'loss of individuality' (which recalls the *Rêveries*) and the 'great principle of the universe' (which sounds rather like the Shelley who was just about to write 'Mont Blanc' and 'Hymn to Intellectual Beauty') suggests that Byron is attempting to marry all the eclectic elements which he has enlisted in his efforts to create a new role for himself as poet. The 'sense of the existence of love in its most extended and sublime capacity', which, as the note confesses, derives from *La Nouvelle Héloise*, is thus that quantity in which Byron chooses to house his vague collection of ideas and motifs which he has gleaned from Wordsworth, Shelley, and Rousseau's other writings.

An ideal and abstract love of this kind is not, strictly speaking, an essential part of Rousseau's thinking in *La Nouvelle Héloise*. Byron is closer to Petrarch here:

> Undying Love's, who here ascends a throne
> To which the steps are mountains; where the god
> Is a pervading life and light, – so shown
> Not on those summits solely, nor alone
> In the still cave and forest; o'er the flower
> His eye is sparkling, and his breath hath blown

(III, 100)

> Ma pur sì aspre vie né sì selvagge
> cercar non so ch'Amor non venga sempre
> ragionado con meco, ed io con lui.

(Petrarch, Sonnet 35)[29]

And it is Saint-Preux, in *La Nouvelle Héloise*, who is constantly reminded of Petrarch when he surveys the landscape around him:

Il semble qu'en s'élevant au-dessus du séjour des hommes, on y laisse tous les sentiments bas et terrestres, et qu'à mesure qu'on approche des régions éthérées, l'âme contracte quelque chose de leur inaltérable pureté . . . Je doute qu'aucune agitation violente, aucune maladie de vapeurs pût tenir contre un pareil séjour prolongé, et je suis surpris que des bains de l'air salutaire et

bienfaisant des montagnes ne soient pas un des grands remèdes de la médi-
cine et de la morale.

> Qui non palazzi, non teatro o loggia;
> Ma'n lor vece un' abete, un faggio, un pino,
> Tra l'erba verde e'l bel monte vicino
> Levan di terra al ciel nostr' intelletto.[30]

It may well be that Saint-Preux and Petrarch have permitted Byron
to feel that he has understood and assimilated these lines from
'Tintern Abbey':

> well pleased to recognise
> In nature and the language of the sense
> The anchor of my purest thoughts, the nurse,
> The guide, the guardian of my heart, and soul
> Of all my moral being.

(107–11)

But the kind of spiritual sanctity to which Byron lays claim is far
closer to Saint-Preux's Petrarchan pretensions than to Wordsworth:

> He who hath loved not, here would learn that lore,
> And make his heart a spirit; he who knows
> That tender mystery, will love the more;
> For this is Love's recess, where vain men's woes,
> And the world's waste, have driven him far from those,
> For 'tis his nature to advance or die;
> He stands not still, but or decays, or grows
> Into a boundless blessing, which may vie
> With the immortal lights, in its eternity!

(III, ciii)

And the omnipresence of Love upon which Byron places so much
emphasis (stanzas 100–1) almost certainly derives from
Saint-Preux's Petrarchan habit of transposing the landscape into a
visual representation of his love:

Si tu goûtes ce plaisir tous les soirs, je le goûte cent fois le jour: je vis plus
solitaire, je suis environée de tes vestiges, et je ne saurais fixer les yeux sur les
objects qui m'entourent sans te voir tout autour de moi.

> Qui canto dolcemente, e qui s'assise;
> Qui si rivolse, e qui ritenne il passo;
> Qui co' begli occhi mi trafise il core;
> Qui disse una parola, e qui sorrise.[31]

1 Francis Wheatley, *St Preux and Julia*, 1785

Byron thus finally attempts to resolve the vagueness of his use of landscape in *Childe Harold III* by resorting to Saint-Preux and Petrarch, and in doing so he calls our attention to an interesting aspect of the culture of the late eighteenth and the early nineteenth centuries: the acceptance of Petrarch as an atemporal poet. It was almost certainly the popularity of the scenic descriptions of *La Nouvelle Héloise* that attracted Byron,[32] but his use of Petrarch depends upon the alacrity with which Petrarch comes to hand in Saint-Preux's descriptions. Byron's Petrarchan stanzas can be seen as a consequence of a highly sentimental reading of Rousseau's novel, for they are also a direct consequence of the kind of tourism in which he and Shelley were indulging. Although Byron wrote manfully to Murray, 'I have traversed all Rousseau's ground – with the Heloise before me – & am struck to a degree with the force & accuracy of his descriptions',[33] a letter from Shelley to Peacock may give a more truthful picture of their tour:

We proceeded with a contrary wind to Clarens against a heavy swell. I never felt more strongly than on landing at Clarens, that the spirit of old times had deserted its once cherished habitation. A thousand times, thought I, have Julia and Saint-Preux walked on this terraced road looking towards these mountains which I now behold; nay, treading on the ground where I now tread. From the window of our lodging our landlady pointed out 'le bosquet de Julie.' At least the inhabitants of this village are impressed with an idea that the persons of that romance had actual existence. In the evening we walked thither. It is indeed Julia's wood . . .

On the following day we went to see the castle of Clarens . . . We gathered roses on the terrace, in the feeling that they might be the posterity of some planted by Julie's hand. We sent their dead and withered leaves to the absent.[34]

The fact that Byron chooses to close his descriptive and 'metaphysical' pieces in *Childe Harold III* with the third-hand sentiments which this kind of indulgence elicited can only be seen as indicative of the amount of serious thought which lay behind his adoption of this new poetical role.

One more aspect of Byron's new departures in *Childe Harold III* remains to be discussed, and this relates back to his coming to terms with Wordsworth through a literal interpretation of 'Intimations of Immortality' and through the neo-Platonism of Shelley and the coincidental parts of Rousseau's *Rêveries*. The nature of Byron's established style, and his stanza, clearly preclude an emulation of these writers' respective modes. The mode which comes to his mind is distinctly eighteenth-century:

And when, at length, the mind shall be all free
From what it hates in this degraded form,

Reft of its carnal life, save what shall be
Existent happier in the fly and worm, –
When elements to elements conform,
And dust is as it should be, shall I not
Feel all I see, less dazzling, but more warm?
The bodiless thought? the Spirit of each spot?
Of which, even now, I share at times the immortal lot?

(III, lxxiv)

The impression received here is that Byron is not trying to emulate Wordsworth, but to improve upon him by extracting what he believes to be Wordsworth's central philosophical premises and expressing them in a more dramatically impressive manner. In doing so he recalls and uses Rousseau's belief in the 'reverie' as a means of suspending the pains of quotidian sensory experience, and marries this to a quasi-religious mode of poetic expression that almost certainly derives from Young. Byron's ugly phrase 'Reft of its carnal life' has its roots in Young's rhetoric and preoccupations:

Death is victory;
It binds in chains the raging ills of life;
Lust and ambition, wrath and avarice

(*Night Thoughts*, III, 498–500)[35]

But the likeness to Young is broader than this. Byron apparently cannot grasp what he considered to be the essential part of Wordsworth's thinking without relating it to the kind of crudely logical reasoning that lends itself to Young's equally crude rhetoric. Thus stanza 73 derives its mode directly from the style of Young's questioning self-examinations:

Who looks on that, and sees not in himself
An awful stranger, a terrestrial god?
A glorious partner with the Deity
In that high attribute, immortal life?
If a God bleeds, he bleeds not for a worm:
I gaze, and as I gaze, my mounting soul
Catches strange fire, Eternity! at thee;
And drops the world – or rather, more enjoys:
How chang'd the face of nature! how improv'd!

(*Night Thoughts*, IV, 495–503)

Byron comes to equivalent conclusions through the same kind of rhetorical process:

Are not the mountains, waves, and skies, a part
Of me and of my soul, as I of them?

> Is not the love of these deep in my heart
> With a pure passion? should I not contemn
> All objects, if compared with these? and stem
> A tide of suffering, rather than forego
> Such feelings for the hard and wordly phlegm
> Of thou whose eyes are only turn'd below,
> Gazing upon the ground, with thoughts that dare not glow?
>
> (III, lxxv)

Young's attraction for Byron, and hence the reason why his mode was likely to come to hand so readily, probably lay not merely in the extempore yet logical nature of his rhetorical questionings, but also in his aphoristic and consciously impressive manner:

> When mount we? when these shackles cast? When quit
> This cell of the creation? this small nest,
> Stuck in a corner of the universe,
> Wrap'd up in fleecy cloud, and fine spun air?
>
> (*Night Thoughts*, VI, 137–40)

It is this kind of impressiveness that could have induced Byron to regard Young as a successful 'philosophical' poet.

It is significant that in trying to absorb Shelley's version of Wordsworth into his own verse, Byron is reminded of Rousseau's *Rêveries*, Saint-Preux's Petrarch, and the style of Young. This alone tells us something about the nature of Byron's thinking, and how this thinking seriously affected the shape of his poetry. Also it warns us against taking Byron's new role in *Childe Harold III* as an aspect of his verse that can be explained in terms of his philosophical development or his 'vision'.[36] More important, it suggests that Byron's attempt to stake a claim for himself in an area of poetry which he had ignored previously was founded upon a trust in his own peculiar artistry – an artistry which depended not only upon verbal dexterity, but, as we have seen, also upon the extrapolation and exploitation of what he believed to be the essential ideas from whatever areas of his reading presented themselves as relevant. The 'few ideas worthy of imitation' in Wordsworth thus become transformed through the nature of Byron's précis of them.

We are left to wonder what Byron thought he had done with Wordsworth when he had finished *Childe Harold III*. At least three reviewers were in no doubt that Wordsworth had been improved upon:

the finer passages of Wordsworth and Southey have in them wherewithal to give an impulse to the utmost ambition of rival genius; and their diction and manner of writing is frequently both striking and original. But we must say, that it would afford us still greater pleasure to find these tuneful gentlemen returning the compliment which Lord Byron has here paid to their talents, and forming themselves on the model rather of his imitations, than of their own originals.[37]

The descriptive power displayed in the next specimen we shall transcribe, is of the very highest order of excellence. Wordsworth, whose strength lies in enduing materiality with intelligence, has nothing finer of the kind.[38]

In the third canto of *Childe Harold*, accordingly, he has delivered up his soul to the impulses of Nature, and we have seen how that high communion has elevated and sublimed it. He instantly penetrated into her heart, as he had before into the heart of Man . . . He leapt at once into the first rank of descriptive poets. He came into competition with Wordsworth upon his own ground, and with his own weapons; and in the first encounter he vanquished and overthrew him. His description of the stormy night among the Alps – of the blending, – the mingling, – the fusion of his own soul, with the raging elements around him, – is alone worth all the dull metaphysics of *The Excursion*, and shews that he might enlarge the limits of human consciousness regarding the operations of matter upon mind, as widely as he has enlarged them regarding the operations of mind upon itself.[39]

This may lead us to suppose that Byron also may have believed that he had improved upon Wordsworth. This belief, as I have suggested, could have been accommodated and even encouraged by Shelley in the circumstances of his and Byron's early friendship. But given the nature of Byron's compositional habits, and the implications of his summary of Wordsworth, it seems unlikely that he seriously considered himself to be involved in such a process. It was probably no part of Byron's aim to improve upon Wordsworth's actual poetry in *Childe Harold III*. Acquiescing in the public's notion of him as the representative poet of the age, and therefore encouraged to absorb those aspects of it which he had previously avoided, Byron was probably less concerned with Wordsworth's verse than with its inherent claims to draw directly upon experience. Wishing to believe so much in the advantages of having lived in 'three or four worlds', and conceiving of Wordsworth as living in only one,[40] he felt that whatever Wordsworth had discovered he could discover somewhere in his own wider range of experience. Looking into himself to make this discovery, however, he is led into reiterating motifs and ideas that depend heavily upon other areas of his reading. His primary concern, nevertheless, was with himself as a better subject than Wordsworth, and the relative merits of the poetry itself were thus of secondary importance.

Byron would thus have been pleased by the critical response with which *Childe Harold III* was greeted, but amused, perhaps, by the fortuitousness and ease by which this approval had been won. For in one sense Shelley and his volumes of Wordsworth arrived in Byron's life at a particular appropriate time. Having offered himself as the subject of his poetry at the beginning of the third canto, Byron was uneasy with the prospect of proceeding beyond making a few appropriate gestures:

> Yet must I think less wildly: – I *have* thought
> Too long and darkly, till my brain became,
> In its own eddy boiling and o'erwrought,
> A whirling gulf of phantasy and flame:
> And thus, untaught in youth my heart to tame,
> My springs of life were poison'd. 'Tis too late!
> Yet am I changed; though still enough the same
> In strength to bear what time cannot abate,
> And feed on bitter fruits without accusing Fate.
>
> (III, vii)

This is one of those moments at which we may recognize a certain inherent truth in the poetry that is communicated in spite of its extreme mannerism. Here is a man who is frustrated by his own limitations, whose only recourse is to transfigure them into a 'romantic' gesture ('My springs of life were poison'd'). This recourse, it seems to me, must be regarded as a means of postponing the problems of self-knowledge. The theatrical extravagance of Byron's gestures offered an apparently limitless number of useful diversions:

> Something too much of this
>
> (III, viii)

> Stop! – for thy tread is on an Empire's dust!
>
> (III, xvii)

> Away with these!
>
> (III, xlvi)

But these diversions must also be seen as the manifestations of a restlessness disturbing in its implications. They are closely related, in fact, to those of *Don Juan*. Yet whilst *Don Juan* explores the implications of such gestures, *Childe Harold III* offers them in the hope that they will prove sufficiently absorbing in themselves to detract from the uneasiness of Byron's dilemma: the dilemma of a poet who does not wish to know too much about himself, but nevertheless intends to present himself as the subject of his poem. From Byron's point of view the canto is saved from the impending bankruptcy towards which its aimless postponements are proceeding by his realization that he could marry his predilection for self-dramatization to Shelley's description of the role of the poet as represented by Wordsworth. What Byron understood to be Wordsworth's 'theme' provided him with a necessary focus, but, more important, Wordsworth's and Shelley's claims for the poet allowed him to offer his own experience as that of a 'more comprehensive soul' than that which is 'supposed to be common among mankind'.[41]

The Prisoner of Chillon

The Prisoner of Chillon, contemporaneous with *Childe Harold III*, is a poem in which Byron continued his attempts to expand his poetic accomplishments. Just as he involved himself with Wordsworth in the third canto of *Childe Harold*, so in this dramatic monologue, because of the approximations of critical thought to which he was accustomed, he involved himself with 'Lakism'.[42] There are two major reasons why Byron may have assumed the subject of imprisonment to be a suitable one for this exercise.

First, he probably felt that the 'more comprehensive soul' to which he had, with Shelley's help, laid claim in *Childe Harold III* demanded exemplification. The suffering prisoner presented itself as a likely subject by which he could demonstrate his 'disposition to be affected more than other men by absent things as if they were present' and his 'ability of conjuring up in himself passions which are indeed far from being the same as those produced by real events, yet . . . do more nearly resemble the passions produced by real events, than anything which . . . other men are accustomed to feel in themselves'.[43] *The Prisoner of Chillon*, then, was conceived as a poem about the kind of feelings and sympathies which Byron believed to be the subjects of Lakist writings, and in this respect it differs sharply from his earlier narratives. Secondly, regarding the Lakists from a distance, and perhaps thinking of Southey as being only peripheral, Byron could easily have persuaded himself that imprisonment, as a subject and a metaphor, was somehow central to Lakist thinking. Even if he did not know 'This Lime Tree Bower My Prison' or 'Frost at Midnight' – and on account of the history of the publication of these poems the chances are perhaps not very great – he would have been acquainted with the reiteration of the theme of spiritual imprisonment within the city and the means of liberation in 'Tintern Abbey', one of Wordsworth's most popular poems.[44] Further, attracted possibly to 'Intimations of Immortality' because of its vulnerability to paraphrase, he would have had a ready recall of 'Shades of the prison-house begin to close / Upon the growing boy' (lines 67–8) on account of the central metaphorical significance of these lines in such an interpretation. Looking more generally at Wordsworth's *Poems in Two Volumes* he would have seen twenty-six sonnets 'Dedicated to Liberty' including 'To Toussaint l'Ouverture' and 'There is a bondage which is worse to bear', and moving from there back to the *Lyrical Ballads*, he would have encountered three poems dealing specifically with imprisonment: Wordsworth's 'The Convict' and Coleridge's 'Foster Mother's Tale' and 'The Dungeon'. In addition, he may also have recalled the use of the image of imprisonment in 'The Rime of the Ancient Mariner' (line 179).

Byron would have been particularly well acquainted with one of these poems. As well as being published in the editions of the *Lyrical Ballads* published in 1798 and 1800, 'The Dungeon', taken originally from the earlier drama of *Osorio*, was included in Coleridge's revised version of the play *Remorse*. Byron was largely responsible for the production of *Remorse* at Drury Lane in 1813, and the poem therefore would have been doubly familiar to him.

The Prisoner of Chillon shows signs of this familiarity. After an account of the inhumanity of his prisoner's confinement, and the 'unmoulding' of the 'essence' of 'his very soul', Coleridge's poem praises the restorative powers of Nature:

> With other ministrations thou, O Nature!
> Healest thy wandering and distemper'd child:
> Thou pourest on him thy soft influences,
> Thy sunny hues, fair forms, and breathing sweets,
> Thy melodies of woods, and winds and waters,
> Till he relent, and can no more endure

To be a jarring and a dissonant thing,
Amid this general dance and minstrelsy;
But, bursting into tears, wins back his way,
His angry spirit heal'd and harmoniz'd
By the benignant touch of Love and Beauty.

(20–30)[45]

Byron, with no investments in pantisocratic schemes, has no wish to make a socio-political issue out of his poem. There is no question of Bonnivard being a social delinquent who may be restored to virtue by the 'ministrations' of nature. But *The Prisoner of Chillon* employs the same focal point as 'The Dungeon': the comparison between the dehumanizing effects of imprisonment and the restorative powers latent in the 'benignant' felicity of the natural world. The destruction of the prisoner's soul in Coleridge's poem, and the 'stagnation' of his energies (8–9) is comparable to the state of limbo and 'stagnant idleness' into which Bonnivard is thrown in section IX of *The Prisoner of Chillon*, and the emphasis upon the 'harmonizing' effect of Nature in 'The Dungeon' has a direct equivalent in lines 337–55 of Byron's poem. And whilst Byron may have stood at a considerable distance from pantisocracy, he recognized enough of Godwin in 'The Dungeon' and 'The Convict', and no doubt in Shelley too, to persuade himself into a belief that Godwin also was an essential prop in this new school of poetry, and subsequently to conclude his poem with what amounts to a Godwinian motto:

My very chains and I grew friends,
So much a long communion tends
To make us what we are

(389–91)

Although 'The Dungeon' can be regarded as a source for the ideas of *The Prisoner of Chillon*, it exerts no influence upon the poem's style. The diction is markedly more simple than that of Byron's previous works, and it is apparent that here he is attempting to discover an alternative to his habitual mode. A prominent and rather surprising feature of the poem is its consistent recourse to trite detail and enumeration; both motifs that can be readily associated with the Wordsworth who exposed himself to ridicule with the publication of 'The Thorn' and 'We Are Seven':

We were seven – who now are one
Six in youth, and one in age

(17–18)

> And in each pillar there is a ring,
> And in each ring there is a chain
>
> (36–7)

> They chain'd us each to a column stone,
> And we were three – yet, each alone;
> We could not move a single pace,
> We could not see each other's face
>
> (48–51)

> And it was liberty to stride
> Along my cell from side to side,
> And up and down, and then athwart,
> And tread it over every part;
> And round the pillars one by one,
> Returning where my walk begun
>
> (306–11)

This cannot be seen as anything other than a deliberate attempt to emulate a poetic mode that Byron would have associated with Wordsworth and Southey.[46] And when reading the following lines, one could easily be persuaded that Byron has taken 'the *innocence* of Ambrose Philips', which Jeffrey identified as a prominent ingredient of Lakist writing, as his model:[47]

> And then there was a little isle,
> Which in my very face did smile,
> The only one in view;
> A small green isle, it seem'd no more,
> Scarce broader than my dungeon floor,
> But in it there were three tall trees,
> And o'er it blew the mountain breeze,
> And by it there were waters flowing,
> And on it there were young flowers growing,
> Of gentle breath and hue.
>
> (341–50)

The generous use of conjunctions in the poem (see also for example lines 306–10 and 355–65) is perhaps more reminiscent of Ambrose Philips than of Wordsworth or Southey.

There are lines in *The Prisoner of Chillon* that smack unmistakeably of Wordsworth and Coleridge, and could perhaps be happily lodged in their poetry:

Which neither was of life nor death;
A sea of stagnant idleness

(248–9)

to bend
Once more, upon the mountains high,
The quiet of a loving eye.

(329–31)[48]

But for the most part Byron's attempt to come to terms with what he believes to be a Lakist mode results in the production of a dangerously parodic kind of poetry. Indeed, the conspicuous shorter couplets which recall Southey's irregular versification ('Nor grew it white / In a single night' (2–3) and 'I know not why / I could not die' (227–8)) are not dissimilar in their effect to the parody of Southey in *Rejected Addresses*. Like the parodist, Byron has identified and exploited what he believes to be the essential features of the poetry he is imitating, and, as a not particularly studious reader of this poetry, he has adhered fairly closely in this process of identification to the commonplace preconceptions about the style of the Lakist school. Conscious of the innovatory nature of this style, he has made an attempt to avoid the kind of excitement that his use of the verse form in his previous tales was designed to generate. But largely unaware of the actual constitution of these innovations, he falls back upon what little he knows about the new school of poetry, and that slight acquaintance has been significantly if not wholly consciously influenced by the familiar criticisms of lukewarm reviews. His writing in a manner reminiscent of Ambrose Philips is therefore not inexplicable. We have no reason to believe that Byron had any more respect for the style he was adopting in *The Prisoner of Chillon* than that which he had accorded to the style of the Turkish Tales. The possibility that he is again consciously practising the 'art of sinking' therefore cannot be dismissed.

Looking backwards at the *Lyrical Ballads* and *English Eclogues*, it is quite likely that Byron would have defined a Lakist poem as a poem about a non-event. The new mode of *The Prisoner of Chillon* suggests that he believes himself to be discovering how the Lakers could write about a non-event. Since his previous modes had been so eventful – in terms of emotional production if not of actual incidents – we might initially suppose that this presented him with a challenge. But it is unlikely that this was the case. Perhaps the most significant conclusion to be drawn from Byron's rather easy and unceremonious adoption of a new mode in *The Prisoner of Chillon* is that this confirms his readiness to conceive of his art as a commodity produced by a standardized process. Indeed, the style of *The Prisoner of Chillon* does not allow us to suppose that the deductions made by Byron after his survey of the Lakist writers were significantly different from those made by Jeffrey with reference to 'Mr Wordsworth and his friends': 'They are, to the full, as much mannerists, too, as the poetasters who ring changes on the commonplaces of magazine versification; and all the difference between them is, that they borrow their phrases from a different and a scantier *gradus ad Parnassum*.'[49] Byron thinks he has a sufficiently accurate assessment of the contents of this imaginary gradus to write a poem based upon its structures. The result is a curiously aimless kind of poetry, and very bad it is too:

> His spirit withered with their clank,
> I saw it silently decline –
> And so perchance in sooth did mine:
> But yet I forced it on to cheer
> Those relics of a home so dear.
> He was a hunter of the hills,
> Had followed there the deer and wolf;
> To him his dungeon was a gulf,
> And fetter'd feet the worst of ills.

> (97–105)

The recourse to expletives and clichés betrays the fact that Byron does not really know where he is going. It seems as though his concept of Lakist poetry is based upon the assumption that its significances are not elicited from the contemplated experience, but are implicit in a chosen mode of presentation. He consequently believes that by emulating this mode he may discover its significance during the process of composition. But it is only too clear that he discovers very little:

> And I have felt the winter's spray
> Wash through the bars when winds were high
> And wanton in the happy sky;
> And then the very rock hath rock'd
> And I have felt it shake unshock'd

> (119–23)

Byron's established repertoire of improvisations may be said to have admitted the advantage of distracting his readers' attention away from considering the possibility that he has very little to say. Similarly, this repertoire can also be regarded as an antidote to his own boredom. When, as here, it has been replaced by a new set of gambits precluding the kind of diversions which he so badly needed, the primary structure of his compositional method is exposed, and his boredom, if not identifiable in the text itself, is more easily diagnosed. The adoption of a new mode has not coerced Byron into a reassessment of the nature of his poetry. The old habits are merely rechannelled, and their new course only serves to reveal the fundamentally arbitrary nature of his creative process. When he was a bored man writing for a bored audience, he knew how to arouse what passed for attention and excitement. In writing *Childe Harold III*, he was seduced by the fantasy of a new relation to his audience (stimulated by the meeting with Shelley); and this, coupled with the sense that he was no longer a member of the 'bores and the bored', clearly deprived him of his most familiar resources and left him floundering.

Byron is not completely lost, however. The subject of imprisonment had a sufficient number of literary precedents to allow him to find his way through his poem by accepting some of the guidelines they offered. The Romantic imprisonment metaphor (as exemplified in 'This Lime Tree Bower My Prison' and 'Tintern Abbey' for instance) would have been read by Byron as a development of the kind of commonplace to be found in Lovelace's 'To Althea, from Prison': that is, in its most simple form, that the body's confinement need not inhibit the mind. The verbal echo of Lovelace pointed out by E. H. Coleridge in lines 377–8 indicates that his poem may well have been in Byron's mind. No doubt 'To Althea, from Prison' presented itself as a sufficiently elegant extract to Byron's era for him to be well acquainted with the poem, and he may also have known 'Loyalty Confined', a ballad reiterating Lovelace's theme included in Percy's *Reliques*. Ultimately, we may feel that the phrase from Lovelace probably offered itself to Byron as a rather clever thing to say about imprisonment in precisely the same way as did that from Dryden at lines 322–3 (again identified by E. H. Coleridge). However, lines 332–55 of *The Prisoner of Chillon* suggest that Byron may have been attempting to transform this commonplace into what he probably believed to be a Lakist idea. That is, by re-establishing his sense of harmony with the felicity of the natural world (by bending 'once more upon the mountains high / The quiet of a loving eye') Bonnivard might be recognized as achieving the equivalent of the Ancient Mariner's salvation, or the 'sensations sweet' and 'tranquil restoration' that sustain Wordsworth's 'hours of weariness' in 'Tintern Abbey' (27–30). One critic has persuaded himself that *The Prisoner of Chillon* lends itself to this kind of interpretation, and he thereby implies that it qualifies for a respectable place in the Romantic canon.[50] But whilst Byron does show a tendency to move in this direction, it is most important to notice the sudden diversion at line 356, which represents his inability to use Bonnivard's imprisonment as a Romantic metaphor. This metaphor is of course finally precluded by Byron's decision to rely on Godwin to help him expand his poetic territory into that normally occupied by the Lakists. Godwin, after all, was accessible in a way that 'Tintern Abbey' and 'The Ancient Mariner' were not.

Byron may have the ambition to transform his subject, but the poem's change of direction at line 356 confirms that he lacks the means by which he may do so. Instead of Bonnivard's contemplation of the scenery outside his prison becoming a vision that induces his spiritual restoration, as the celebratory nature of the poetry might lead us to expect, it becomes instead a means of emphasizing the pathos of his confinement. The quality of this pathos, so badly served by Byron's unsympathetic use of his mode, depends entirely therefore on the contrast between the simple pleasures of freedom and the deprivations of confinement. In fact, Byron is treating a popular subject in a popular way.

In Sterne's *A Sentimental Journey*, Yorick, frightened by the possible consequences of not having a passport, imagines what it must be like to be imprisoned:

– I took a single captive, and having first shut him up in his dungeon, I then looked through the twilight of his grated door to take his picture.

I beheld his body half wasted away with long expectation and confinement, and felt what kind of sickness of the heart it was which arises from hope deferred. Upon looking nearer I saw him pale and feverish: in thirty years the western breeze had not once fanned his blood – he had seen no sun, no moon in all that time – nor had the voice of friend or kinsman breathed through his lattice – his children –

– But here my heart began to bleed – and I was forced to go on with another part of the portrait.

He was sitting upon the ground upon a little straw, in the furthest corner

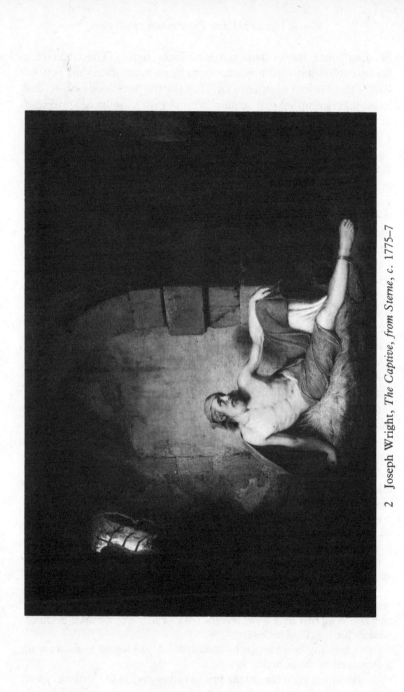

2 Joseph Wright, *The Captive, from Sterne*, c. 1775–7

of his dungeon, which was alternately his chair and bed: a little calendar of small sticks were laid at the head notched all over with the dismal days and nights he had passed there – he had one of these little sticks in his hand, and with a rusty nail he was etching another day of misery to add to the heap. As I darkened the little light he had, he lifted up a hopeless eye towards the door, then cast it down, shook his head, and went on with his work of affliction. I heard his chains upon his legs, as he turned his body to lay his little stick upon the bundle – He gave a deep sigh – I saw the iron enter into his soul – I burst into tears – I could not sustain the picture of confinement which my fancy had drawn – I started up from my chair.[51]

The number of images of Sterne's captive produced in the late eighteenth century (the best of these being an etching by John Hamilton Mortimer and two paintings by Joseph Wright) suggest that this passage became a *locus classicus* for the theme of imprisonment (see fig. 2). A closer look at Wordsworth's 'The Convict' confirms this. 'I pause; and at length, through the glimmering grate / That outcast of pity behold' (11–12) is very close to Sterne's 'I then looked through the twilight of his grated door to take his picture.' Like Sterne's prisoner, Wordsworth's gives a deep sigh (line 13). And what was perhaps supposed to be the most poignant moment of Sterne's portrait, and the moment upon which Wright's second painting concentrates – the prisoner raising his 'hopeless eye towards the door' – finds its way into Wordsworth's poem and receives further sentimental embroidery:

> But now he half-raises his deep-sunken eye,
> And the motion unsettles a tear;
> The silence of sorrow it seems to supply,
> And asks of me why I am here.

(41–4)

The significance of the passage from *A Sentimental Journey* to *The Prisoner of Chillon* does not consist so much in specific echoes of this kind as in its overall structure (although 'I had no hope my eyes to raise' (368) does sound like another variation of the eye-raising motif). Like Sterne, Byron relies for his pathos on the painful act of the prisoner looking outward, and, like Sterne also, he has prepared the way for this by emphasizing his captive's exclusion from the objects of the natural world. But perhaps most important, Byron follows Sterne in his use of the symbol of the bird as a means of presenting his prisoner as a victim.

Sterne's passage, published in 1768, is a distinctive product of its

3   Henry Fuseli, *Ugolino*, 1806

era in its treatment of its prisoner as a matyr.[52] No doubt after 1789 it
was easier for people to conceive of prisoners in this way, whether
their sympathies lay with those who stormed the Bastille or those

who were suffering under the Terror. But Sterne's aim to 'teach us to love the world and our fellow creatures better than we do'[53] had nothing to do with current affairs, and accordingly he needs to overcome his readers' prejudicial assumptions that confinement is society's means of protection and punishment, that all prisoners are dangerous or wicked criminals. The means that he employs is the image of the caged bird, by which he implies that imprisonment is an offence against nature. Byron has reversed the process. Sterne carefully guides his reader into the prison by initially concentrating on the caged bird: Byron points his reader towards the natural pleasures from which Bonnivard is excluded by having a bird perch on top of his prison. The bird, further, has perhaps escaped from its cage:

> I know not if it late were free,
> Or broke its cage to perch on mine

> (279–80)

In this detail Byron is following the post-revolutionary emblematic tradition of popular art (interestingly anticipated by Sterne's coat of arms)[54] wherein a bird perched upon a cage commemorates political emancipation.[55] Despite the reversal, and the use of this more recent motif, it is clear that Byron is depending heavily on Sterne's basic formula. And in doing so, he may have persuaded himself that he was remaining within the precincts of Lakist writing. In addition to the precedent of 'The Convict' (excluded from all editions of the *Lyrical Ballads* after 1798), Byron may not have felt that there was any real distinction to be made between the Lakist poet's 'disposition to be affected more than other men by absent things as if they were present' and the sensitivity of a Yorick who declares himself to be a man of feeling by the details and emotional sympathies of his imaginary exercise.

In addition to the passage from *A Sentimental Journey*, Byron enlists the aid of the other classic image of imprisonment in his time, the Ugolino episode from Dante's *Inferno* (XXXIII). This episode, as it has been shown, was almost certainly the most famous piece of Dante's poetry in England in the eighteenth century.[56] Before the first complete translation of the *Inferno* appeared in 1785, there were six translations of the Ugolino episode already in existence, and it remained a popular fragment for translation until the second decade of the nineteenth century.[57] In 1773, Reynolds exhibited his painting of Ugolino and his sons at the Royal Academy, and the impact of the work was such that a critic writing for the *Quarterly Review* in 1823 claimed that 'Dante was brought into fashion in England by Sir Joshua Reynolds.'[58] In 1806, Fuseli exhibited his version of Ugolino at the Royal Academy, and this precipitated a controversy over the relative merits of the two paintings.[59] The kind of currency enjoyed by the Ugolino passage in the late eighteenth and early nineteenth centuries meant that it presented itself to Byron as an obvious and a useful point of reference for the treatment of the theme of imprisonment. Unsure of the areas in which he should be concentrating in a poem about feelings rather than incidents, Byron attempts to describe the sufferings of confinement by attributing some brothers to Bonnivard so that they may drop dead around him.[60] No historical account of Bonnivard mentions the fact that his brothers were imprisoned with him, and by introducing them Byron is able to represent his hero as the strongest of a group of figures who suffers his fate nobly. Somewhere behind *The Prisoner of Chillon*, therefore, there exists a tableau that closely resembles the *Laocoön*. (It is perhaps significant that Byron begins by giving Bonnivard seven brothers, but places only two in confinement with him.) Indirectly, Byron is capitalizing on the *Laocoön's* fame and prestige, and more precisely, yet still perhaps as an indirect inheritance, he has taken Winckelmann's identification of the exemplary nature of its spiritual qualities as the foundation for the kind of feelings he feels he ought to be describing.[61] Byron's imagination, therefore, is largely (but not completely) governed by the tyrannies of Winckelmann's philhellenism.

The prestige of the *Laocoön* in this period is almost certainly an additional reason for the appeal of the Ugolino episode to its artists. Fuseli certainly makes the most of Dante's line 'Io non piangea, sí dentro impetrai' (which as the epigraph to his painting he translated 'Bereft of tears I inward turned to stone')[62] to transpose the Laocoön-like qualities as defined by Winckelmann into a new statuesque context by which the suppression of emotional excess, or perhaps its annihilation by the extremity of the situation, becomes even more forceful. Significantly, it is this line from Dante that we find echoed in *The Prisoner of Chillon*:

> I had no thought, no feeling – none –
> Among the stones I stood a stone.

(235–6)

Shelley later suggested that 'Byron had deeply studied this death of

Ugolino, and perhaps but for it would never have written *The Prisoner of Chillon*',[63] and his remark confirms the dominant role played by the Ugolino extract in Byron's composition of the poem.

Whether or not Byron finally seriously believed that he was writing a Lakist poem in *The Prisoner of Chillon* is not the point. What is significant is that the attempt to write a Lakist poem leads him – with a disturbing lack of resistance on his part – into a position where he finds himself recognizing common denominators in such divergent authors as Sterne and Dante. Such a recognition might be interpreted as symptomatic of an impoverished imagination, but we might more profitably regard it as the disorientation produced by the meeting with Shelley. This disorientation has resulted in Byron allowing his imagination to be almost completely tyrannized by his eye for 'effect'. In one respect, Byron's eye for effect can be regarded as an extension of the gradus-habit: his search for and use of examples derives finally from the same cultural inheritance that produced Bysshe's 'Collection of the Most Natural, Agreeable, and Noble Thoughts' in *The Art of English Poetry*. In another respect, it is analogous to Fuseli's eye for attitude. But what we notice in Fuseli – the exploration of the ironies of employing old poses in new contexts[64] – we find lacking in Byron's poetry of this period. The restriction of the analogy therefore allows us to discern a gap in Byron's poetry, and it is perhaps Byron's recognition of this gap that brings him into a position wherefrom he is able to write *Don Juan*.

The kind of processes in which we find Byron involved in 1816 are a direct consequence of this unique historical situation. In an era when in one quarter literary dilettantism suddenly finds itself deeply involved with a reading public that is expanding at an unprecedented rate, thereby producing poets liable to be recognized as 'great' on account of their massive sales, whilst in another quarter there are claims being made for the poet's greatness which are formulated on the centrality of his position and his responsibilities towards a spiritually deprived populace, it is perhaps inevitable that there should arise a poet who finds himself attempting to reconcile the antipathetic elements of this impossible, but nonetheless unavoidable, dialectic. To define Byron's role in this conflict more precisely, we must recapitulate his position prior to 1816. Until this date and the meeting with Shelley, he was able to ignore Wordsworth's claims for the poet's position. As an amateur with distinctive talents in verbal dexterity and aspirations for a fashionable reputation, he 'awoke one morning' to find himself entertaining an audience that was disproportionately huge for an amateur performance. But their applause rendered modifications to this performance unnecessary, and helped Byron to define a relationship to his audience that allowed him to slip comfortably into easy habits of writing. The most significant consequence of the meeting with Shelley in 1816 is that Shelley's modifications to Wordsworth, in stressing the centrality of the poet's position but in ignoring the problems of the creative act, eroded this stable and well-defined relationship. Byron is thus made aware that if he is to expand his poetic concerns to include the area occupied by the writing of this new school, he must depend less upon the sense of there being a clearly defined audience for whom he is writing, and more upon the issues of subject and mode. But he has no real means of recognizing that the significance of making new concerns the subject of poetry and the significance, too, of employing new modes were dependent upon a completely new concept of compositional method. It is this which throws Byron hopelessly off balance, and causes him to move towards areas which offer him obvious support. Thus, his poetry becomes subject to the kind of bizarre conflations identifiable in *Childe Harold III* and *The Prisoner of Chillon*.

4

Tourist rhetoric: *Childe Harold IV*

In the fourth canto of *Childe Harold*, we can see Byron attempting to recover the equilibrium lost in *Childe Harold III* and *The Prisoner of Chillon*. Here he finds himself committed to his poetry in a way that was alien to him before 1816, but rather than trying to complement this new seriousness by emulating the mode or embracing the subjects of Lakist writings, he attempts to compose great poetry by relying almost entirely on his own rhetorical resources. It is true that as an afterthought, towards the end of the canto, he goes through the Wordsworthian motions once again, but the tiredness of the verse is so patently obvious that we cannot help but recognize in it a confession of failure:

> There is a pleasure in the pathless woods,
> There is a rapture on the lonely shore,
> There is society, where none intrudes,
> By the deep Sea, and Music in its roar:
> I love not man the less, but Nature more,
> From these our interviews, in which I steal
> From all I may be, or have been before,
> To mingle with the Universe, and feel
> What I can ne'er express – yet cannot all conceal.
>
> (IV, clxxviii)

Yet the kind of commitment we find in *Childe Harold IV* is not of such a nature that it encourages us to regard it as the consequence of Byron's acceptance of Shelley's artistic seriousness. It is far more desperate than that. It is, more important, a result of Byron writing as his public and reviewers expected him to write. An extract from Jeffrey's review of *Childe Harold III* may give some idea of what Byron had to live up to:

If the finest poetry be that which leaves the deepest impression on the minds of its readers – and this is not the worst test of its excellence – Lord Byron, we think, must be allowed to take precedence of all his distinguished contemporaries . . . in force of diction, and inextinguishable energy of sentiment, he clearly surpasses them all. 'Words that breathe, and thoughts that burn' are not merely the ornaments, but the common staple of his poetry . . . To produce great effects, he felt that it was necessary to deal only with the greater passions – with the exaltations of a daring fancy, and the errors of a lofty intellect – with the pride, the terrors, and the agonies of strong emotion – the fire and air alone of our human elements.[1]

This commentary has something in common with earlier reviews of Byron's poetry, but its general tenor is pitched at a far higher level. The separation controversy, and Byron's new style in the third canto, encouraged Jeffrey to couch his review in an even more histrionic idiom than that to which he was accustomed. 'Beautiful as this poetry is, it is a relief at last to close the volume. We cannot maintain our accustomed tone of levity, or even speak like calm literary judges in the midst of these agonizing traces of a wounded and distempered spirit.'[2] A less complimentary, but nevertheless equally significant, facet of the reception of the poetry written in 1816 is represented by another critic's accusation that Byron had 'out-Fuselied Fuseli'.[3] The figure of the poet that Byron found had been created for him in England therefore did not allow him to produce anything so tame as the first two cantos or a mere swashbuckling verse tale. 'The fire and air alone of our human elements' were what was expected, and these indeed were what Byron attempted to provide. The fundamental failure of *Childe Harold IV* is that its subjects were incapable of producing such effects (although *Manfred* stands as an example of the different kind of failure achieved by successfully producing them). Consequently the gestures, distractions, and postures are far more exaggerated and extreme than those found anywhere else in *Childe Harold*, as Byron forces himself to declaim upon everything from the horses of St Mark to the ocean in a wild and desperate attempt to convert the experience of being a tourist into the experience of being a poet. We can clearly see where this leads him in such passages as the following:

> The roar of waters! from the headlong height
> Velino cleaves the wave-worn precipice;
> The fall of waters! rapid as the light
> The flashing mass foams shaking the abyss;

The Hell of Waters! where they howl and hiss,
And boil in endless torture; while the sweat
Of their great agony, wrung out from this
Their Phlegethon, curls round the rocks of jet
That gird the gulf around, in pitiless horror set

            and how the Giant Element
From rock to rock leaps with delirious bound,
Crushing the cliffs, which downward worn and rent
With his fierce footsteps, yield in chasms a fearful vent

To the broad column which rolls on, and shows
More like the fountain of an infant sea
Torn from the womb of mountains

Horribly beautiful! but on the verge,
From side to side, beneath the glittering morn,
An Iris sits, amidst the infernal surge,
Like Hope upon a death-bed, and, unworn
Its steady dyes, while all around is torn
By the distracted waters, bears serene
Its brilliant hues with all their beams unshorn:
Resembling, 'mid the torture of the scene,
Love watching Madness with unalterable mien.

                          (IV, lxix–lxxii)

It may be that 'Mont Blanc' and its claim to be an 'undisciplined overflowing of the soul' written under 'the immediate impression of the deep and powerful feelings excited by the objects which it attempts to describe'[4] is of some significance here, but it is the attempt to make '"Words that breathe, and thoughts that burn" . . . the common staple of his poetry', rather than Shelley's theories of composition, that leads Byron into such a poetic disaster. It is the critics' vague admiration for power, proceeding perhaps from half a century of confused discussion of 'the sublime', that results in the frenzied attempt to produce a sensational effect. And perhaps what is most conspicuous in this passage is Byron's unhappy response to the compulsion to feel and express his feelings. This induces him to seize upon words and gestures and weld them into conglomerates that by their very combination divorce themselves utterly from the contexts in which their references gave them meaning. 'More like the fountain of an infant sea / Torn from the womb of mountains' may be taken as an example. This fails not merely because its meaning cannot be extrapolated by a literalizing interpretation (how can a fountain be torn?) but also because the gulf between the meta-phorical use of the phraseology and any of the semantic connota-tions, however vague, that it excites is so huge and choked by other denotional comings and goings that only the most indistinct impres-sion of emotional or sensory experience is finally conveyed. The ex-perience of writing poetry like this, no doubt, was instrumental in convincing Byron that he knew exactly what he was talking about in his famous criticism of Keats.[5]

The struggle to meet the demands of contemporary critical opin-ion manifests itself clearly in the pressure which Byron places upon his words, and the resultant descriptive extravagance is comple-mented by a supply of meditative passages of equivalent potency:

> We wither from our youth, we gasp away –
> Sick – sick; unfound the boon – unslaked the thirst,
> Though to the last, in verge of our decay,
> Some phantom lures, such as we sought at first –
>
> (IV, cxxxiv)

Byron's claim that he has grown 'weary of drawing a line which every one seemed determined not to perceive'[6] has of course made no real difference to the poem. But it marks his awareness of the redundancy of a surrogate hero such as that formerly proposed, and his sense, possibly, of the advantages of the poem's narrator, rather than the hero, laying claim to the weight of experience that allows him to promulgate his own feelings and opinions. This, after all, is the case of *Don Juan*. Whilst Byron may have been attracted by this idea, the style of delivery which his mode demands only induces frustration. His desperation is registered everywhere, from the very beginning where he enlists the aid of Mrs Radcliffe's eloquence – and in the attempt to link it to his own gesture still manages to make an absurd slip that even Rogers noticed ('a Palace and a prison on each hand') – through the point where he finds himself confronted by the Apollo Belvedere, and turns to Winckelmann (who by this time had been in currency for fifty years) to inform his response,[7] to the very end of the canto where he falls back upon Wordsworth amidst a string of uncomfortable attempts to make his exit (clxiv, clxvi, clxxix, clxxxv). The inability to end his poem convincingly may be accepted as the evidence by which we can detect Byron's dissatisfac-tion with what he has written, his awareness that his poem could not be described as 'the fire and air alone of our human elements'. And indeed, apart from the many good reasons that were probably beyond Byron's comprehension why such a description could not be applied to any poetry, there was one less substantial reason, of which he must have been conscious, why it could not be applied to his own. That reason was his own indolence and lack of commitment, which did not allow him to look much further than the likes of Mrs Radcliffe and Winckelmann for assistance. 'What is writ, is writ, – / Would it were worthier!' (clxxxv), and we detect in this a moment of sincerity which evaporates when the sentiment is transformed, predictably, into a tragic gesture:

> but I am not now
> That which I have been – and my visions flit
> Less palpably before me –
>
> (IV, clxxxv)

No doubt it is true, but the truth is obscured by its presentation, and Byron's dissatisfaction with the mode and circumstances by which his sentiments are damaged is expressed in the very last stanza, where he reminds us, and perhaps himself, of the less than serious innocent spirit in which *Childe Harold's Pilgrimage* was begun:

> if in your memories dwell
> A thought which once was his – if on ye swell
> A single recollection – not in vain
> He wore his sandal-shoon, and scallop-shell
>
> (IV, clxxxvi)

Although Byron's desperation and dissatisfaction may be recognized in the fourth canto, the very attempt to be successful within the terms prescribed for him by the reviewers testifies to his uncritical acceptance of the idiom in which they wrote. The vocabulary of Jeffrey's review of *Childe Harold III* places it firmly at the beginning of the nineteenth century. It looks backward to that plethora of ostentatious adjectives that Gray's odes drew from certain literary circles in the late eighteenth century,[8] and sideways to the kind of extravagant rhetoric that John Wilson was employing in his review of *Manfred* (a rhetoric that needed only the slightest of modifications to make Wilson an acceptable Victorian editor). Gray occupies a crucial position historically. The adverse criticism of Johnson's 'Life of Gray' (1781), in itself a reproach to the enthusiasm of Mason's *Memoirs* (1775) and Langhorne's review in which it was claimed that

Gray's effects 'could be felt, could be tasted only by the few',[9] was responded to by Gray's faithful admirers in terms echoing Langhorne's esoteric claims. Gilbert Wakefield, in his edition of *The Poems of Mr. Gray* (1786), accused Johnson of an 'inelegance of taste, a frigid churlishness of temper, unsubdued and unqualified by that melting sensibility, that divine enthusiasm of soul, which are essential to a hearty relish of poetical composition',[10] and Robert Potter, in *An Inquiry Into Some Passages in Dr Johnson's Lives of the Poets* (1783), disqualifies Johnson from criticizing Gray on the grounds that he has none of 'that etherial flame which animates the poet' and, therefore, he is 'as little qualified to judge of these works of imagination, as the shivering inhabitant of the caverns of the North to form an idea of the glowing sun that flames over the plains of Chili'.[11] These sentiments find a chilling echo in Arnold's peremptory treatment of Johnson: 'But Johnson was not by nature fitted to do justice to Gray and his poetry; this by itself is a sufficient explanation of the deficiencies of his criticism of Gray.'[12] In the process which sees a discerning critic like Mattthew Arnold inheriting the critical legacy of Gray's admirers, the close relationship between Byron's poetry and its reviews occupies a central position. Reading Jeffrey one is struck by the fact that the critical climate that he was brought up in was one upon which the Gray controversy must have had a considerable influence. Whilst Jeffrey does not explicitly reiterate Langhorne's exclusive claims, he draws heavily upon the idiom which such claims licensed, an idiom which drew its vocabulary from the poetry itself. And Arnold, responding positively to the aspects of Byron's verse that impressed Jeffrey, albeit for different reasons, necessarily assimilated some of the vague critical terminology and assumptions upon which the critics of Byron's time depended so heavily. The way in which Arnold's adoption of Wordsworth's theories was interfered with by this kind of criticism and the poetry it condoned is exemplified in his description of poetry as 'a thing which has been plunged in the poet's soul until it comes forth naturally and necessarily'.[13] To see the extent to which this 'poetic' criticism proceeded in Byron's era, one has only to turn to John Wilson's review of *Manfred*,[14] and Byron's comment on this review – 'it had all the air of being a poet's, and was a very good one'[15] – emphasizes his unqualified acceptance of the critical idiom which played such an important role in shaping his poetry.

Childe Harold IV may be taken as representing a critical phase in

the history of English poetry. Its search for effect, more obvious
here than anywhere else in Byron's verse because he has to struggle so
hard, is not only the consequence of the victory of the critical heritage of Gray's admirers over Johnson; it is also that which gave
Byron's poetry its Victorian lustre:

> And, Byron! let us dare admire
> If not thy fierce and turbid song,
> Yet that, in anguish, doubt, desire
> Thy fiery courage still was strong.[16]

But without the 'fierce and turbid song' the 'fiery courage' would
have had no currency. And in justice to Byron and Arnold, Byron's
positive response to the critical idiom of his time is also that which
distinguishes him from Rogers, Campbell, and Moore. I cannot
agree with Robson's observation that 'the staple language of Byron's
poetry is afflicted everywhere with the effeteness of a verse idiom in
decline'.[17] Byron could never be found writing like this:

> With thee beneath my windows, pleasant Sea,
> I long not to o'erlook earth's fairest glades
> And green savannahs – Earth has not a plain
> So boundless or so beautiful as thine;
> The eagle's vision cannot take it in:
> The lightning's wing, too weak to sweep its space,
> Sinks half-way o'er it like a wearied bird:
> . . .
> The Spirit of the Universe in thee
> Is visible; thou hast in thee the life –
> The eternal, graceful, and majestic life
> Of nature, and the natural human heart
> Is therefore bound to thee with holy love.[18]
>
> My mule refreshed – and, let the truth be told,
> He was nor dull nor contradictory,
> But patient, diligent, and sure of foot,
> Shunning the loose stone on the precipice,
> Snorting suspicion while with sight, smell, touch,
> Trying, detecting, where the surface smiled[19]

This may be described as 'effete'; it certainly represents the limitations and feebleness of the Regency poet attempting to respond to a
'modern' influence (Wordsworth) without any real reassessment of
his well-practised rhetorical routine. Even though we can recognize

in Byron the same reluctance to submit the material of his poetry to close inspection, he does not share the complacency of Campbell and Rogers. Arnold's admiration for Byron depended on his recognition of an uneasy spirit behind the courage and his valuation of Byron's self-assertion in spite of this uneasiness. His moral standpoint perhaps encouraged him to conceive of Byron's rhetoric as that element by which the less acceptable side of his character was kept under control: the more forceful the rhetoric, therefore, the greater the value Arnold was liable to place upon it. But appreciating Byron in this way also entailed the investment of a considerable amount of emotional sympathy; the identification of the troubled man with the pageant of the bleeding heart. Unlike Arnold, the present-day reader cannot allow this myth to stand between him and the uneasiness within the verse:

> Have I not –
> Hear me, my mother Earth! behold it, Heaven! –
> Have I not had to wrestle with my lot?
> Have I not suffered things to be forgiven?
> Have I not had my brain seared, my heart riven,
> Hopes sapped, name blighted, Life's life lied away?
> And only not to desperation driven,
> Because not altogether of such clay
> As rots into the souls of those whom I survey.
>
> (IV, cxxxv)

Whatever is expressed through this, it does not coincide with the paraphrasable meaning of the stanza. What is conveyed here, and throughout *Childe Harold IV*, in the extent to which so many lines are highly overcharged, is Byron's dissatisfaction with his means, the sense that, whatever the obscure and possibly confused reasons for writing, they are not satisfied by what is written. Hazlitt, apparently baffled but still astute, had this to say about the canto: 'There is in every line an effort at brilliancy, and a successful effort; and yet, in the next, as if nothing had been done, the same thing is attempted to be expressed again with the same labour as before, the same success, and with as little appearance of repose or satisfaction of mind.'[20] We may quibble over the word 'brilliancy' and question the 'success' of Byron's 'efforts', but as a general comment on the impressions received from reading *Childe Harold IV*, this observation penetrates to the very heart of the poem. Its gestures may not succeed in conveying the weight of emotional experience to which they lay claim, but the

monotonous forcefulness with which they are repeatedly performed 'with little appearance of repose or satisfaction of mind'
registers the poet's dissatisfaction with his mode. In *Childe Harold
IV* we see Byron exhausting the possibilities of the style he had been
encouraged to adopt. He has fallen into the rut of creating effect
only. The bankruptcy that is postponed by spinning the poem out to
its inordinate length, however, is not to be interpreted merely as an
index to Byron's personality, any more than we can interpret this
canto in terms of Byron's 'mood' – as does Rutherford.[21] It is, more
important, a consequence of his belonging to a culture that inherited
a relaxed yet ostentatious vocabulary for the criticism of its poetry. It
is no coincidence that a shrewd critic like Hazlitt comments on this
canto in a manner that recalls Johnson on Gray, and no coincidence
either that some of Johnson's criticisms of Gray can be applied to
Childe Harold IV with equal force: 'These odes are marked by glittering accumulations of ungraceful ornaments; they strike, rather than
please; the images are magnified by affectation; the language is
laboured into harshness. The mind of the writer seems to work
with unnatural violence . . . His art and his struggle are too visible,
and there is too little appearance of ease and nature.'[22]

Unlike *Childe Harold I & II* and the Turkish Tales, this canto is
devoid of that interesting dimension provided by Byron's toying with
his art or his audience, and, unlike *Childe Harold III* and *The Prisoner of Chillon*, here he is not stimulated by the challenge of his
poetic interests. If Paul West were right in suggesting that the act of
composition for Byron entailed a compulsion to keep writing in the
expectation that something would 'turn up',[23] then *Childe Harold IV*
could be simply described as that work in which nothing does turn
up. But as a general theory this is not accurate enough. It cannot be
happily applied to the Turkish Tales, for instance. Nevertheless, it
may prepare the way for a more satisfying hypothesis. The phrase
from which Paul West begins – 'what composition meant to Byron' – is one which raises too many unresolvable problems. A
descriptive rather than a prescriptive approach is required, and what
we can recognize in Byron's poetry is that as the act of composition
moves between being easy and being difficult, so he is allowed a
directly proportional degree of detachment. Thus in the Turkish
Tales, where it is excessively easy, Byron is able to stand back from
his poetry, and in the leisure of relaxed contemplation he is able to
recognize and exploit the interesting possibilities of his method and

circumstances. In the latter parts of *Childe Harold III* and in *The Prisoner of Chillon*, however, where the act of composition is less easy, Byron's efforts to write a different kind of poetry preclude a simultaneous review of his productive processes. At the same time, the steady supply of useful references which feed his attempts to tread new ground create the illusion of inspiration, and therefore the act of composition, although not easy, is not sufficiently difficult to place the poetry under any real stress. Byron is watching himself perform in a new role, and this is as far as his detachment proceeds. In *Childe Harold IV*, however, the effort which Byron has to invest in the act of writing does not allow him to watch himself at all. It is this complete lack of detachment which renders him critically impotent. The result is a poetry wherein he is caught in an interminable circuit of rhetorical declamations, a poetry which attempts to surpass itself at every turn. Even though we may be momentarily distracted by the odd turn of phrase, the pitch at which the declamations resume and are repeatedly delivered betrays Byron's frustration with monotonous forcefulness.

5

Modernizing the Gothic drama:
Manfred

Manfred has proved irritating to at least one critic:

This new spiritual superman, in fact, has an emotional and intellectual
immaturity of a kind usually associated with adolescence, and while this
would not have mattered so much in a verse-tale entertainment, it is fatally
disabling in a moral-metaphysical play like *Manfred*. The more seriously we
are asked to take the hero, the more serious must be our criticism of his
defects.[1]

Rutherford seems confident of what constitutes a good 'moral-
metaphysical play', yet whatever he has in mind, we can be sure it is
not the kind of success which Robert F. Gleckner claims for *Manfred*.
He apparently interprets that which exacerbates Rutherford as the
classic embodiment of the Romantic *Weltanschauung*:

In *Manfred* the character himself is the human condition, aware of his own
nature and his world, and creating out of despair a meaningful framework
within which to die . . . But we also know that his death is the final surrender
to his own mortality: he is Prometheus dead upon the Caucasus, Christ
eternally crucified, the creative artist's imaged life dying as it is born.
'Darkness . . . was the universe.'[2]

Manfred, admittedly, is an extravagant and peculiar piece of poetry.
But its sensational and emotional generosity need not commit us to
an equally excessive critical response. We do not have to lose the play
behind Robert Gleckner's rhetoric any more than we have perfuncto-
rily to dismiss it in the manner prescribed by Rutherford. We might
profit more by a perusal which concerns itself less with hazardous
guesses at what we think Byron is – or ought to be – saying through
his drama and more with the tones of his delivery. We shall not find
ourselves in company with either Gleckner or Rutherford if we begin
by stating plainly that *Manfred* is a very bad drama, and then pro-

ceed to show that it is a bad drama of a peculiar kind: it bears everywhere the stamp of its period, and yet it could not have been written by anyone but Byron. To suggest that 'more than any other English poem *Manfred* is typical of the Romantic period; it is an expression of the mood of Romanticism, an epitome of the time'[3] is to miss precisely this point. *Manfred* belongs so unmistakeably to Byron's *oeuvre* fundamentally because it is so eclectic and unstable. It offers us the opportunity to investigate the position in which Byron stood to the theatre of his time and to the other possibilities in drama that his contemporaries discerned outside it. The nature of *Manfred*'s instability not only permits such an approach, but demands it.

Shelley's role in *Manfred*'s inception is important and complex. We may begin its description by making the simple observation that Manfred takes his approximate outline from Alastor: he is the insatiate hero of extraordinary talent destroyed, apparently, by a self-consuming passion. But this is as far as the likeness proceeds. Whilst Manfred is given moments in which to display his 'sensitivity' (this must be what we are supposed to recognize in the inadequate and tedious Childe Harold-like effusions; see for instance III, iv, 1–45), he is neither a poet nor an uncorrupted youth, and we are not asked to regard his death as the world's loss. Manfred is no 'luminary', although his being a magician probably derives in part from the mysticism of *Alastor*. But the most obvious difference between *Manfred* and *Alastor* lies in their implicit proposals of the heroic, and, by studying the props which Byron enlists for the purposes of creating his heroic ideal, we may see the kind of processes identifiable behind the poetry of *Childe Harold III* repeated. Again Byron takes a basic formula for being 'modern' from Shelley, but the transformations which this formula undergoes in his poetry only serve to emphasize his limitations and dependence upon more familiar areas of his reading for guidance. It has been suggested that we can trace a philosophical argument between Shelley and Byron by comparing *Manfred* and *Alastor* (amongst other pairs of poems).[4] This demands that we accept both poets as serious philosophers, and in the case of Byron this is especially hard. Apparently it also entails the acceptance of *Manfred* as Byron's 'estimate of the human condition',[5] which leads to even more intractable problems. And indeed the nebulousness and uncritical crudity of the discussion which this approach has produced only emphasize its wrong-headedness.[6] If anything, *Manfred* confirms how uncomfortable Byron was in the area of philosophical

108

poetry. For if we are willing to recognize the influence of Shelley in the drama's beginnings, when we come to trace the extent of this influence we must inevitably recognize how unsolicitous Byron's care of it was. *Manfred* shows Byron taking a cue from Shelley once again but being more seriously diverted than before, and almost certainly the lack of resistance on his part is due to his realization that by readily accepting the material which the outline of his poetic drama called to mind he could make its composition a relatively easy exercise. This being so, he would be allowed the kind of detachment which he had exploited for the purposes of self-amusement in the Turkish Tales. The games played in *Manfred* are not of the same kind, and neither are they indulged in with any confidence. But they exist nevertheless, and it is this aspect of the drama which allows us to understand it as belonging to the same period of Byron's development as *Beppo*, a period which is also characterized by his exhaustion of the possibilities of *Childe Harold*.

Perhaps the most noticeable feature of *Manfred* is the stagecraft behind the presentation of the hero. Although it is one of the most unstageable of his dramas, *Manfred* nevertheless draws on Byron's experience of the theatre more extensively than any other play he wrote. During his years in London Byron was an enthusiastic patron of the theatre. In 1814 he assured Moore that he was 'acquainted with no *im*material sensuality so delightful as good acting',[7] and his admiration for Kean above all other actors is well known. He was so jealous of the attention Miss O'Neil drew from his favourite that he refused to watch her act, and at Kean's benefit in *Macbeth* in 1814, despite being part of Lady Jersey's party, Byron preferred his own box, which he shared with Moore only, to savour an uninterrupted performance, whilst 'every other in the house was crowded almost to suffocation'.[8] Despite ample evidence of this kind of enthusiasm, Byron can still be found claiming that he has only 'the greatest contempt for the stage'.[9] The remark suggests that Byron recognized his taste for the theatre as a weakness, and what makes *Manfred* such an interesting part of Byron's *oeuvre* is the way in which it continuously indulges this weakness, while qualifying this indulgence by suggesting the existence of the will to caricature it, a will which lacks both the means and the conviction needed for its successful implementation.

Excusing himself to Murray for writing *Manfred*, Byron confessed himself to be 'a devil of a mannerist' and expressed his intention to 'leave off'.[10] However sincere or otherwise this intention may have been, there is no 'leaving off' in the drama itself. Its major structural determinant is the amount of space provided for great moments, moments wherein the kind of skills in which Edmund Kean excelled could be indulged to their fullest extent. Indeed, the acting tradition which runs through Garrick, Kemble, and Kean, a tradition which emphasized the uniqueness of the individual's experience, and one which depended heavily on physical expression in the attempt to convey the particularities of emotional and psychological conditions, is a vital element of *Manfred*'s constitution. Because the drama does not propose a situation capable of supporting a psychological or emotional dimension worthy of serious interest, it becomes a string of empty stage mannerisms which belong to Byron's time, hopelessly divorced from the contexts which gave them meaning.

Perhaps the greatest moments of the Regency theatre were to be found in the most popular plays of the period: *Richard III* and *Macbeth*. Richard faced by the spectres in his tent, Macbeth by Banquo's ghost, the dagger, or the witches, gave the actor of talent the opportunity to invest these moments with the kind of energy that might suggest something of the complex issues which hung upon them in the wake of eighteenth-century criticism. These were points of moral crisis, where the actor's horror could elicit a sympathetic response from an audience whose first inclination was towards unsympathetic moral condemnation, and also points at which the audience could be persuaded to see the hero as a man fighting against the uncontrollable and mysterious workings of his own mind.[11] Although these moments undoubtedly retained the potential to promote a consideration of their critical significance in the Regency theatre, the impression received from Byron's enthusiasm is that they were more frequently regarded as the marks by which an actor's prowess was evaluated as an achievement in itself. Byron's gladiatorial interest in Kean appears to be more like the behaviour of one who regarded himself as a connoisseur of style than as a literary critic.

It is the connoisseur of style that allows himself free rein in *Manfred*. Whereas the popular tragedies offered only a limited number of great moments, Byron's drama is almost wholly a succession of such: an indefatigable stream of apparitions followed by the responses of the hero. If the play were to have been acted in Byron's time, the actor would have had not merely one or two opportunities to eclipse the performances of his rivals, but many, each more terrible and magnificent than the last. In such a role Kean could have exerted his grotesque postures and impassioned gestures to the full:

> Oh God! if it be thus, and *thou*
> Art not a madness and a mockery,
> I yet might be happy. I will clasp thee,
> And we again will be – (*the figure vanishes*)
> My heart is crush'd!
> (*Manfred falls senseless*)
>
> (I, i, 188–91)

> I do defy ye, – though I feel my soul
> Is ebbing from me, yet I do defy ye;
> Nor will I hence, while I have earthly breath
> To breathe my scorn upon ye – earthly strength
> To wrestle, though with spirits; what ye take
> Shall be ta'en limb from limb.
>
> (III, iv, 99–104)

Manfred in performance would have provided more than ample scope for the kind of 'physical' acting Byron admired in Kemble and Kean.[12] Its hero is involved in very little movement prompted by dramatic circumstances that are normally evolved by the presence of other characters on the stage. His actions are minimal, and the only people with whom he converses normally are the hunter and the abbot. Unless Manfred is to stand passive, his movements upon the stage must take the form of emotional gestures. The style of acting which lies behind *Manfred* and Byron's later dramas is a style which received its approval and encouragement from an audience whose culture had developed a taste for attitude and rhetorical gesture, a taste that by Byron's time was not merely well established, but almost passé.

In tracing the influence of the contemporary stage on *Manfred*, the topic of scenery deserves some consideration. Apologizing to Moore for the drama before its publication, Byron claimed, 'I wrote a sort of mad Drama, for the sake of introducing the Alpine scenery in description',[13] and some years after publication, protesting against charges of plagiarism, he wrote that 'it was the *Staubach* and the *Jungfrau*, and something else, much more than Faustus, that made me write *Manfred*'.[14] These comments imply that Byron conceived of *Manfred* as continuing the attempts to show an interest in landscape begun in *Childe Harold III*, but when one turns to the drama, very few descriptive passages are to be found. Manfred's speech upon the

Jungfrau (I, ii), the few lines that preface the entry of the Witch of the Alps (II, ii), the address to the sun (III, ii), and the lines which open Act III, Scene iv make up the total, and to call these lines 'descriptive' is to use the term extremely freely. Whilst there is little actual description in the text of the play, the response which it elicited from its contemporary reader inevitably must have entailed the imaginary construction of a stage set, or rather a theatrically conceived landscape, in which the action could take place. And this imaginary exercise would have been both prompted and well served by a familiarity with the scenic extravagance of the post-de Loutherbourgian theatre. Scenic descriptions such as those offered as directions before Act I, Scene ii (*The mountain of the Jungfrau. – Time, Morning. – Manfred alone upon the cliffs*), Act II, Scene ii (*A lower valley in the Alps. – A Cataract*), and Act III, Scene iii (*The summit of the Jungfrau Mountain*) may be minimal, but in the context of the lavish parade of effects displayed in the large-scale Regency theatres, they were doubtless sufficiently suggestive to arouse a whole chain of associations capable of exerting a considerable effect upon the way in which the drama was read. Similarly Manfred's speech to the sun at sunset was probably composed and read with an awareness of the spectacular effects of stage-lighting, as too were such lines as 'yon red cloud, which rests / On Eiger's pinnacle' (III, iii, 36–7) and 'the Sunbow's rays still arch / The torrent with the many hues of heaven' (II, ii, 1–2).

The anomaly that exists between Byron's claims for *Manfred*'s relation to landscape and the text confirms that its composition was heavily supplemented by his familiarity with the theatre; so much so, indeed, that he assumed the quality of scenic effect to be one of its most obvious features, even whilst there is little material in the text to support such an assumption. Further, and more important, this anomaly betrays his natural tendency to move away from a landscape tradition that centred on Wordsworth and towards one that centred on de Loutherbourg. As a glance at the last two cantos of *Childe Harold* confirms, Byron's attempts to emulate a Wordsworthian response to landscape were consistently subjected to his weakness for effect (amongst other things). The description of Terni in Canto IV and the storm scene in Canto III, for example, suggest that Byron found it difficult to liberate himself from his preconception that spectacle was the most desirable end of description. Such an assumption is the consequence of his living in an era which some years previously had thrilled to the effects of de Loutherbourg's Eidophusikon, and had prefaced some of its dramatic productions with a theatre of nature in order to allow the audience a full and uninterrupted appreciation of the innovatory sophistications of the scenic machinery. Bearing in mind Wordsworth's diagnosis of one of his society's diseases as a 'craving for extraordinary incident', the reproduction of elemental phenomena within the theatre can perhaps be seen as more spectacular, more stimulating, and altogether less demanding on what Wordsworth regarded as the faculty of creative perception than the real thing. And thus *Manfred* provides a depressingly telling statement upon Byron's ultimate reaction to Shelley's recommendation of Wordsworth: after various unhappy attempts to write a poetry that impressed his readership with his response to nature, Byron finds the alternative of implicitly referring his reader to the machinists of Drury Lane more attractive.[15]

The Gothic extravagance of *Manfred*, another aspect of its constitution drawn from the contemporary stage, is hard to avoid, and raises interesting yet awkward problems. The air of mystery surrounding the hero's past life, his sense of sin and remorse, the strong supernatural element, and the settings (such as 'a Gothic gallery' and 'a hall in the Castle of Manfred') – all these motifs announced the play as Gothic, and thereby encouraged the reader to dedicate to *Manfred* the kind of attention and expectations that might accompany his experience of a drama such as *The Castle Spectre* or his reading of a novel like *The Mysteries of Udolpho*. Manfred's Gothic allegiances, however, arouse suspicion. Why does Byron, a fully established member of the literary canon of his age, employ a series of motifs that were more commonly associated with writers outside of this canon, or writers in search of their first success? The answer, I believe, again lies with Shelley. It is not that Shelley (whose attraction to Gothic writing is well known) simply encouraged Byron to write a Gothic play, but that, because of the way in which Shelley's mind worked, his attempt to interest Byron in writing philosophical poetry may well have involved the use of Gothic examples. In 1816, Shelley's admiration for Coleridge was at its zenith, and there is therefore every reason to suppose that the latter was implicated in the discussions of the significance of the new poetic school with Byron.[16] For Coleridge was a writer who apparently bridged the gulf between Gothic writing and the philosophical interests of the new school. The connection is not immediately clear, but Peacock demonstrates how it may be made:

No one could call up a *rawhead and bloody bones* with so many adjuncts and circumstances of ghastliness. Mystery was his mental element. He lived in the midst of that visionary world in which nothing is but what is not. He dreamed with his eyes open, and saw ghosts dancing round him at noontide. He had been in his youth an enthusiast for liberty, and had hailed the dawn of the French Revolution as the promise of a day that was to banish war and slavery, and every form of vice and misery, from the face of the earth. Because all this was not done, he deduced that nothing was done; that the overthrow of the feudal forces of tyranny and superstition was the greatest calamity that had ever befallen mankind; and that their only hope now was to rake the rubbish together, and rebuild it without any of those loopholes by which the light had originally crept in. To qualify himself for a coadjutor in this laudable task, he plunged into the central opacity of Kantian metaphysics, and lay *perdu* several years in transcendental darkness, till the common daylight of common sense became intolerable to his eyes.[17]

This is our introduction to Mr Flosky (Coleridge) in *Nightmare Abbey*. Subsequently, Flosky complains, 'the great evil is, that there is too much commonplace light in our moral and political literature; and light is a great enemy to mystery, and mystery is a great friend to enthusiasm'.[18] This is far from a satiric *tour de force*. Peacock's relation of Coleridge's interests presents him as a child of Romanticism reacting against the Enlightenment, whose post-revolutionary disillusion drives him from individualism to egotism. Coleridge's 'ghosts', Peacock suggests (served up to the reading public with 'goblins and skeletons', but now abandoned on account of their popularization),[19] originally presented him with a useful means of reawakening certain aspects of individual experience that had been repressed by the Enlightenment, but subsequently assume a modified place in his thinking on account of their supporting a philosophy that extended Berkeley's denial of external physicality to include a denial of external utilitarian ethics and emotions. 'It is the mind that maketh well or ill', Flosky quotes happily, and later he asserts, 'I can safely say I have seen too many ghosts myself to believe in their external existence.'[20] On the appearance of a ghost, Flosky is the first of the company to disappear in fright, and thus Peacock emphasizes Coleridge's discomfort with himself, the dilemma that the writer of *Christabel*, the student of Kant, and the author of *The Friend* inevitably confronted.

I have concentrated on Peacock here to demonstrate how much could be perceived by a shrewd and intelligent observer of the period. Turning to Shelley and Byron, the emphasis is on how little, relatively speaking, they perceive. Shelley, searching for ghosts in his youth, warming to *Caleb Williams* on the one hand and *Frankenstein* on the other, was likely to be less aware of the complexity of the historical context of Coleridge's Gothic sympathies than Peacock. It seems plausible that he would have read Flosky as a joke made against obscurantism, a joke, therefore, in which he was included. Shelley's fascination with the Gothic had little to do with the interest in the supernatural proposed by the authors of the *Lyrical Ballads*, and nothing to do with Kant and Berkeley. If we are to accept Peacock's critique of him in *Nightmare Abbey*, where Scythrop is to be found 'taking his evening seat, on a fallen fragment of mossy stone, with his back resting against the ruined wall, – a thick canopy of ivy, with an owl in it, over his head',[21] Shelley's Gothic sympathies are the result of an early taste for romance that he never fully transcended as a result of the role played by this taste and the imaginative extravagance that it licensed in supporting his fantasies. Shelley's response to Coleridge's philosophical interests, Peacock suggests, is not informed by a fully conscious awareness of their historical significance, but is subjected to his alchemical preoccupation with the mysterious, a preoccupation which protects itself and develops into soi-distant theorizing by way of Shelley's absolute trust in his own mind:

He began to devour romances and German tragedies, and, by the recommendation of Mr Flosky, to pore over ponderous tomes of transcendental philosophy, which reconciled him to the labour of studying them in their mystical jargon and necromantic imagery. In the congenial solitude of Nightmare Abbey, the distempered ideas of metaphysical romance and romantic metaphysics had ample time and space to germinate into a fertile crop of chimeras, which rapidly shot up into vigorous and abundant vegetation.[22]

It is this 'congenial solitude', Shelley's satisfaction with his own ideas and fantasies, of which Peacock is implicitly critical, and it is this, too, which places Shelley in a position where he is unlikely to appreciate or fully understand Coleridge.

If Shelley stood at some distance from Coleridge, then how much more of a gulf was there between Coleridge and Byron, and how alien too were Shelley's Gothic interests, so intimately connected with his theorizing, to any responses which Byron may have had to the Gothic novel or drama! But Coleridge was nevertheless available to Shelley in a way that might have allowed him to claim spiritual kinship.

What seems to have happened in *Manfred* is that Byron found himself writing a 'metaphysical' drama (his own description)[23] in which, as a consequence of Shelley's confused sympathies and probable representation of Coleridge, he also found himself exploiting Gothic machinery. And his unhappiness with the philosophical dimension of his drama (an unhappiness that manifests itself for instance in the borrowing of one of *Manfred*'s most pithy 'philosophical' aphorisms from Young)[24] leads him into a heavier dependence on the Gothic motifs by way of compensation. Again Byron responds to Shelley by taking refuge in more manageable material, but in this instance the consequences are different from those that ensued from his falling back upon Rousseau or Dante. For his prop here is the Gothic drama, something that was not only far closer to home, but something also, in all probability, for which he had very little respect.

The stage traditions that seduce Byron away from Shelley, and which Byron exploits in an unashamedly exaggerated manner, cause *Manfred* to become a very stagey, yet ultimately unstageable, drama. The abundance of great moments, suggestions of lavish scenery, and atmosphere of Gothic mystery combine to create a drama that was too extravagant even for Drury Lane. Nevertheless, this is where *Manfred* belongs: the moment the hero is taken from this context and placed in the arena of critical speculation (such as that wherein Robert Gleckner places him) he becomes not merely implausible, but ridiculous. Only the theatre of the mind, the theatre imaginatively constructed out of the most sensational aspects of contemporary production, could have found room for *Manfred*, and indeed, to the typical theatre-goer of the time, such imaginative speculation, however frivolous, was probably most enjoyable. In Byron's exorbitant arrangement of his props and crescendos we detect his own enjoyment too, and in addition the drama offered him another fantastic attraction. For by banning its performance, the acting implicit in the text is preserved as his own. To the reader accustomed to identifying the heroes of Byron's poetry with Byron himself, *Manfred*, by proposing a wholly new and fundamentally dramatic relationship between author and reader, transforms the poet into the actor: the drama presents Byron as Kean, fully responsible for the representation of the leading role. Hazlitt perhaps sensed something of this when he wrote that Byron's dramas 'abound in speeches . . . such as he himself might make when lolling on his couch of a morning'.[25]

Could it be, however, that the inordinate indulgence of *Manfred* is not a mark of naive conceit, as Hazlitt apparently supposed, but a symptom of Byron's enjoyment of the excesses of overacting and his concomitant emerging awareness of the potentialities of self-caricature? If the answer to this question is affirmative, *Manfred* assumes some significance as a preconditioning exercise for *Don Juan*, and such an answer would also allow us to make sense out of the juxtaposition of Byron's proclaimed contempt for the stage alongside his exploitation of its sensationalism. We have a strong precedent, too, for expecting an affirmative answer in the shape of the Turkish Tales, for, as with these lays, the composition of *Manfred*, partly because of Byron's familiarity with the theatre, has cost him little effort. But how can such an answer be sanctioned? If we were to identify elements of self-caricature in *Manfred* on the basis of its exorbitance alone, then we might be forced to identify the same elements in other Gothic dramas of the period, even though *Manfred* might generally be recognized as the most spectacular of them all.[26] Its exaggerations need to be complemented and supported by some other factor before they can be taken as symptomatic of anything other than a predilection for the crude excitement of sensationalism. That factor can be found in the drama's deliberate trifling with decorum, which gives it a ubiquitous quasi-burlesque tone.

It is at this point that we must turn again to Shelley and his relation to the texts that influenced *Manfred*. When Byron's drama was reviewed, two literary resemblances were spotted immediately: Goethe's *Faust* and the *Prometheus Vinctus* of Aeschylus.[27] Both dramas had been brought to Byron's attention in 1816. Lewis gave Byron and Shelley an oral translation of parts of *Faust* whilst visiting Geneva, and Shelley, as well as reading *Prometheus* in Greek that year (according to Mrs Shelley), allegedly translated the whole of the drama orally to Byron. If anything is to be made of these commonly acknowledged relationships, we must endeavour to imagine how Byron might have responded to these translations.

We might begin by subjecting Shelley's oral translations of the *Prometheus Vinctus* to more scrutiny than Timothy Webb sees fit. His accounts runs as follows:

For Lord Byron he sometimes translated orally – occasionally portions of *Faust*, 'to . . . impregnate Byron's brain', and in 1816 the whole of Aeschylus's *Prometheus Bound*. This had such an effect that Byron composed his poem 'Prometheus' shortly after and later declared that *Prometheus* was at the back of almost everything that he had written. Shelley also translated *Prometheus* for his cousin in 1821–2. Medwin described him . . . '. . . reading it as fluently as if written in French or Italian; and if there be any merit in my own version . . . it is much due to the recollection of his words, which often flowed on line after line in blank verse, into which very harmonious prose resolves itself naturally.'[28]

By making a case for Shelley's extraordinary talents as a translator, Webb here avoids two rather awkward questions. First, Medwin's claim looks suspiciously like a ploy by which he hoped to attract attention to his own translation. Is it true, therefore? Webb immediately follows this account with another of Medwin's anecdotes which he demonstrates to be extremely suspect.[29] But even if we accept that Shelley translated *Prometheus* with fluency to Byron in 1816, we must place this translation, and for that matter *Prometheus Unbound* and *Manfred*, in the historical context of the late-eighteenth-century revival of Aeschylus. The two works largely responsible for taking Aeschylus out of Parson Adams's study and the public school syllabus and into English literary culture were Robert Potter's translation of the tragedies (1777) and Flaxman's *Compositions from the Tragedies of Aeschylus* (1795).[30] Considering Flaxman's European impact, and considering too how influential Retzsch's *Outlines* were in awakening Shelley's interest in *Faust*,[31] the possibility that Flaxman's *Compositions* were instrumental in creating his taste for Aeschylus must be strong. But Potter (from whom Flaxman took his captions) is of more immediate relevance. For if indeed Shelley did give Byron a fluent oral translation of *Prometheus* in 1816, it was a translation that almost certainly would have been informed and strongly coloured by Potter's.[32]

The Aeschylus revival, itself part of the growing regard for 'primitive' writers, was not a simple matter of rediscovery. For Aeschylus's tragic style contained many elements that were antipathetic to the late eighteenth century. His dramas were non-realistic and frequently plotless. In the case of *The Persae* and *The Eumenides* there was no real hero. In an era when the stage was highly influential in the interpretation of dramatic texts, Aeschylus's 'stage' must have been difficult to visualize: in a drama like *Prometheus*, for instance, spatio-temporal relationships are extremely ambiguous, and the definition of a location and a sequential pattern of events is not helped by the apparently arbitrary entrances and exits. Here also, Aeschylus dramatizes not events, but emotions; the purpose of each 'scene', therefore, is not to be interpreted in terms of its causal relationships, but is rather to be understood as the means by which the dramatized emotion is intensified. In the late eighteenth century there was no code of decorum which could happily accommodate a dialogue amongst supernatural agents or between these agents and men. Finally, there was the difficulty presented by the high proportion of choral pieces in rhythms that reminded the eighteenth-century gentleman that in Aeschylus's time tragedy admitted music and dance within its precincts. Flaxman and Potter cannot be said to have solved these problems, but by emphasizing, and in effect reinterpreting, other aspects of Aeschylus's texts, they successfully diverted attention away from them.

By 'dramatizing' scenes which in the text form no part of the dramatic action, but lie somewhere beyond it, Flaxman made the tragedies look more eventful than they actually were.[33] His 'primitive' forms and deliberate abandonment of illusionistic perspective complement the 'severity' of Aeschylus (simultaneously resolving the problem of spatial ambiguity), and the precise contours of his outlines, together with an occasional quality of two-dimensional elegance that derives from his era's taste for Greek vase-paintings, also imbued his compositions with a correctness that in the mind of the beholder might easily be associated with the original text.[34]

Potter begins by attempting to guide his reader into Aeschylus by suggesting how he may be visualized in terms defined by contemporary aesthetic interests. *Prometheus*, he suggests in his Preface, has 'sublimity of conception, a strength, a fire, a certain savage dignity'; its 'scenery is the greatest that the human imagination ever formed' and its scenes 'would require the utmost effort of Salvator Rosa's genius to represent them'.[35] The 'sober spirit' of *The Supplicants*, however, together with its characters and scenery, forms 'a picture that would have well employed the united pencils of Poussin and Claude Lorraine'.[36] Thus, by the associations these names readily evoked, the former drama is sublime, and the latter beautiful.[37] But the most important point about Potter's translation is that he represents Aeschylus in a style that was used and approved by the circles in which he moved:

> Fav'ring seasons grace the year,
> Crown with rich fruits your cultured plains;
> The joyful flock, the sportive steer,
> Bound wanton o'er your wide domains.

Each immortal showering treasures,
Wake the soft melodious measures;
Let the chastely-warbled lay
The Muses' rapture-breathing shell obey.
Firm may the honours of your laws remain,
And prudence in your counsels reign:
Just to yourselves, and to the stranger kind,
May peace to sleep consign the bloodless sword;
Each honour to your country's gods assigned;
Each laurelled shrine with hallowed rites adored;
The parent's hoary head with reverence crowned;
View this, ye righteous gods, and stretch protection round![38]

Potter's regard for Gray and Collins is his means of reconciling Aeschylus to the tastes of the late eighteenth century: what he sees in the original text is transformed by his awareness of how easily he might transpose it into this 'sophisticated' diction and movement. He also eradicates the problems raised by the chorus partly by modifying the original text into a more rigid strophe–antistrophe–epode formation, and partly by employing rhythms more reminiscent of the 'correct' chanting of Gray's *The Bard* than of barbaric song and dance.[39] Potter also partly solved the problem of decorum raised by the supernatural element by employing an appropriately dignified medium in the shape of his strongly Miltonic narrative.[40]

To answer the question of how much Potter there is in Shelley would take more space than can be allowed here. But if nothing else, Potter almost certainly demonstrated to Shelley how the subjects of Aeschylus lent themselves to a poetic rendering, for whilst Potter cannot be said to have made anything of Aeschylus as a dramatist, he represented him as a poet of tragic dignity. A sympathy for Potter may also have been awakened in Shelley by the ease with which Potter's Prometheus could have been associated with Gray's Bard on account of the similarity of Gray's style to Potter's. There are also direct verbal echoes in *Prometheus Chained* that suggest the presence of Gray's poem in Potter's translation, such as his generous use of the word 'ruin' in Prometheus's predictions of Jove's fall.[41] Interestingly, Shelley uses the word in the same context at the beginning of *Prometheus Unbound*:

> Disdain! Ah no! I pity thee. What ruin
> Will hunt thee undefended through wide Heaven!

(I, 54–5)

The problems of decorum and dramatic narrative raised by Aeschylus's art were thus submerged by Flaxman and Potter. The fact remains, however, that anyone familiar with the original text could still be aware of these problems if he chose to be. Shelley, we might hypothesize, attracted to the Prometheus myth and Potter's style, his self-confessed purpose as a poet being 'simply to familiarize the highly refined imagination of the more select classes of poetical readers with beautiful idealisms of moral excellence',[42] was altogether unlikely to apprehend Aeschylus as a problematic poet. But Byron, with no interest in 'beautiful idealisms of moral excellence', and being well practised in the dramatization of emotions rather than events, might have found much to ponder over. However, the main reason for his seeing things in Aeschylus that Shelley was willing to ignore, I would suggest, is to be found in his familiarity with *Macbeth* upon the stage, a familiarity that interfered with his reading and conception of the Greek dramatist to a far greater extent than whatever interferences may have been caused by an acquaintance with Potter and Flaxman. In addition, his response to Aeschylus probably would have been significantly affected by Lewis's readings of *Faust*.

I will deal with each of these connections separately. It may seem a little odd to connect Aeschylus with *Macbeth*, but if indeed Byron made this link, he was not the only significant figure of his age to do so. Hazlitt, discussing the effects of *Macbeth* upon the stage, wrote, 'The Witches of Macbeth indeed are ridiculous upon the modern stage, and we doubt if the Furies of Aeschylus would be more respected.'[43] Hazlitt's comment (as well as being an announcement of the advantages of closet criticism) alerts us to the kind of problems posed by *Macbeth* in the early nineteenth century. *Macbeth*'s particular difficulty, of course, might be located in the quasi-comical tones in which the witches converse, particularly in the Hecate episode. But Hazlitt's mention of Aeschylus demonstrates that it was not this particular element of *Macbeth* that was troubling him. His emphasis is on 'the modern stage'. It seems likely, therefore, that he is thinking of its insistence upon spectacular effect. But there is an additional reason why *Macbeth* may be regarded as a work around which a controversy was quietly building up in Byron's time.

In 1802, Philipsthal exhibited a magic lantern which he christened the 'Phantasmagoria' at the Lyceum. By means of a transparent screen and a system of lenses and reflectors, Philipsthal was able to conjure up apparitions and spectres which were seen to move towards and away from the audience. Whether or not the Phantasmagoria had any immediate effect upon the productions of *Macbeth* in the theatre, Philipsthal's exhibition must have brought about a serious reorientation of the way in which people visualized imaginary phenomena that had no empirical ratification, a reorientation that was directly relevant to their conception of plays like *Macbeth*, *Manfred*, and even the dramas of Aeschylus. For the Phantasmagoria brought mechanics into the world of fantasy: no longer was the romantic thrill of imagining an apparition such a private experience. Philipsthal demonstrated, in a most spectacular way, that such excitements could be standardized. And this demonstration must have had an indirect but nevertheless consequential impact upon the audience watching *Macbeth* in the theatre, who of necessity subsequently must have been struck not merely by the visual concreteness of the actor's body playing Banquo or the armed head, but also by the intrusion of make-up, costume, and direction upon the ghost's representation. That is to say, in the theatre, however sophisticated the lighting and cosmetics, the audience was always likely to be aware of the mechanics behind the spectre, whereas the excitement of Philipsthal's Phantasmagoria, no doubt heightened by its technical crudity and lack of focus, had allowed them, albeit momentarily, to forget that these images too were the result of conscious and workmanlike contrivance.[44] The mystery of the mechanism no doubt contributed to the mystery of the effect. Further, Philipsthal's exhibition offered Gothic thrills as a commodity, and, by presenting spectre-raising as a novel entertainment worth paying for in itself, the Phantasmagoria made the exhilaration of the fantastic a mechanical wonder, and finally a fashionable indulgence. And in doing so, it threw *Macbeth* into a particularly dangerous position. Nowhere is this better realized than in Gillray's *A Phantasmagoria; – Scene – Conjuring-up an Armed Skeleton* (1803), a political satire that makes its point by a conflation of Philipsthal's spectacle and Act IV, Scene i of *Macbeth* (see fig. 4). And Gillray's implicit and mischievous reference to Fuseli's *Macbeth and the Armed Head* announces how the Phantasmagoria, as well as stirring up problems in the representation of *Macbeth* upon the stage, also placed Fuseli's serious challenge to the restrictions of academic art (as conceived by Reynolds) into a new context. Fuseli had perhaps hoped to endow his licence with academic respectability by concentrating upon 'academic' subjects

4　James Gillray, *A Phantasmagoria; – Scene – Conjuring-up an Armed Skeleton*, 1803

5   Henry Fuseli, *Macbeth and the Armed Head,* c. 1774

such as those offered by *Macbeth*. He cannot therefore have been pleased to find that licence sanctioned – however accidentally – by Philipsthal's particular brand of illusionism (see fig. 5). Gillray's freedom in using *Macbeth* as the means by which he makes Philipsthal Fuseli's ally emphasizes the central position Shakespeare's play was liable to assume in controversies over illusionistic licence.

Philipsthal's Phantasmagoria had perhaps only quickened and heightened the effects of an inevitable convergence: the identification of the cheap thrills of Gothic horror, never to be taken seriously, with the ghost scenes of Shakespeare, and *Macbeth* in particular. Looking at Aeschylus in 1816, Byron was more likely to see the dramas in the phantasmagorical light shed by the modern stage and its association than in the dim light of Shelley's mystical philosophizing, or that of Flaxman and Potter. In short, the nature of *Macbeth*'s standing in Byron's culture could easily have distorted his reading of Aeschylus. And the problems thus perceived in Aeschylus, no doubt, would have been heightened by his awareness that underneath the *Prometheus* of Potter and Flaxman there was a drama composed of little more than a series of supernatural visitations, with no real plot or narrative of connected events.

A slightly ambivalent regard for *Macbeth* and Aeschylus must have been strengthened by the kind of acquaintance which Byron had with *Faust* in 1816. Whilst Lewis may have restricted his translated extracts to those scenes which he found most impressive – and certainly the pieces of *Manfred* that are most obviously taken from *Faust* suggest a strong Gothic influence at work[45] – he can hardly have avoided conveying an impression of the jocularity of Mephistopheles's dialogue. And Byron would have had a ready-made means of accommodating this apparent violation of tragic decorum by recognizing in it a quasi-parodic response to the problem of raising spectres upon the contemporary stage. The case for this being so can be reinforced by reference to his other source for *Faust* (a source too frequently neglected or underestimated) – Madame de Staël's *De l'Allemagne*. Published in England in 1813, in French and in translation, the book was a great success. Byron read it upon its publication, 'liked it prodigiously',[46] and in *Don Juan* made it clear that *De l'Allemagne* was the obvious source for the average littérateur's knowledge of Goethe.[47] The book devotes forty-five pages to *Faust*, consisting largely of translated extracts and paraphrases. This chapter, and the extracts from the drama that appeared later with

Retzsch's *Outlines*,[48] were probably the most accessible accounts of *Faust* available to the non-German-speaking public before the first complete English translation was published in 1835.

Madame de Staël emphasized the amusement provided by the 'audacious gaiety' of Mephistopheles and the drama's peculiar blend of tragedy and levity.[49] Her determination to represent *Faust* as a work of genius leads her into a rather confused response to its ambiguous tenor: 'But to derive pleasure from this sort of comedy, reason must be set aside, and the pleasures of the imagination must be considered as a licensed game without any object . . . nothing but the excess, the very extravagance, of genius can confer any merit on these productions.'[50] *Faust* is represented as a work with 'intentional defects', for which Madame de Staël apologizes by claiming that 'when such a genius as that of Goethe sets itself free from all restrictions, the crowd of thoughts is so great, that on every side they break through and trample down the barriers of art'. Her attempt to reconcile German extravagance to the seriousness of French tragic theatre is no happier: 'The belief in evil spirits is to be met with in many pieces of German poetry; the nature of the north agrees very well with this description of terror; it is therefore much less ridiculous in Germany, than it would be in France, to make use of the Devil in works of fiction.'[51] What she might have added was that 'making use of devils' in England, when Philipsthal's show, a plethora of German ballads, and other Gothic entertainments had popularized them to the extent that they had become a common motif in contemporary political caricature and satire, was fraught with even greater problems.[52]

Perhaps the most directly relevant part of Madame de Staël's account of *Faust* occurs in her description of the Witch's Kitchen. This, she suggests, 'may, in some respects, be considered as a parody of that of the Witches in *Macbeth*'.[53] There is every reason to suppose that Byron recalled this description when he was writing *Manfred*:

FIRST DES.	Welcome! – Where's Nemesis?
SECOND DES.	At some great work;
	But what I know not, my hands were full.
THIRD DES.	Behold she cometh.
	ENTER NEMESIS
FIRST DES.	Say, where hast thou been?
	My sisters and thyself are slow to-night.

NEMESIS.   I was detain'd . . .

(II, iii, 58–62)

The echo of *Macbeth* is strong:

FIRST WITCH.   Where hast thou been, sister?
SECOND WITCH.   Killing swine.
THIRD WITCH.   Sister, where thou?
FIRST WITCH.   A sailor's wife had chestnuts in her lap,
                And mounched, and mounched, and mounched.

(*Macbeth*, I, iii, 1–5)

Again, Nemesis's exit in *Manfred* recalls that of Hecate in *Macbeth*:

Away!
We have outstay'd the hour – mount we our clouds!

(*Manfred*, II, iii, 71–2)

Hark! I am called; my little spirit, see,
Sits in a foggy cloud and stays for me.

(*Macbeth*, III, v, 34–5)

Clearly this is a pastiche of some kind. Whilst Byron does not actually parody *Macbeth*, the absurd gesture of Nemesis's exit suggests that he may have been toying with the ambiguous tones of the Hecate episode. Is it then to be assumed that Byron took Madame de Staël's description of the Witch's Kitchen as a Shakespearean parody as a precedent for a similar kind of licence in *Manfred*? Whilst he obviously had no real understanding of the mode of *Faust*, Byron may have persuaded himself, with the help of *De l'Allemagne*, that his emulation of it in *Manfred* provided him with the right kind of context for a 'parody' of this nature.

Although Madame de Staël may have helped Byron to guess at the manner in which the supernatural element was handled in *Faust*, this guess was heavily informed by the handling of the supernatural in English popular literature and art. Thus, Byron's attempt to follow *Faust*'s allegedly parodic response to *Macbeth* is subject to his familiarity with the manner in which artists such as Gillray used the supernatural as a satiric device. The Nemesis episode provides two obvious examples. This song, for instance, clearly refers to Napoleon:

The Captive Usurper,
Hurled down from the throne,
Lay buried in torpor,

127

Forgotten and lone;
I broke through his slumbers,
I shivered his chain,
I leagued him with numbers –
He's Tyrant again!
With the blood of a million he'll answer my care,
With a nation's destruction – his flight and despair!

(II, iii, 16–25)

The idea of presenting an evil supernatural personage as the satirical target's guardian was a common one in Regency caricature. Gillray's *The Tables Turn'd*, for instance, shows two pictures, 'Billy in the Devil's claws', wherein the devil gloats over an Englishman's horror at the news of the French landing in Wales, and 'Billy sending the Devil packing', in which the devil is frightened off by the news of the Spanish fleet's defeat.[54] The second song in the Nemesis episode, which Coleridge suggests refers to Thomas Lord Cochrane,[55] also belongs to this satiric tradition:

The Ship sailed on, the ship sailed fast,
But I left not a sail, and I left not a mast;
There is not a plank of the hull or the deck,
And there is not a wretch to lament o'er his wreck;
Save one, whom I held, as he swam, by the hair,
And he was a subject well worthy my care;
A traitor on land, and a pirate at sea –
But I saved him to wreak further havoc for me!

(II, iii, 26–33)

If in one light we are prepared to see *Manfred* as Byron's guess at the kind of drama Goethe had written, then we can recognize how Madame de Staël's description of the Witch's Kitchen has led him into taking the more familiar use of Gothic parodies in popular art as his immediate model. The consequence is this peculiar interlude of mild political satire. In the attempt to write a supernatural drama, Byron is thus drawn away from the spirits of Aeschylus, Goethe, Shelley, and *Macbeth*, and towards the phantasmagorical apparitions utilized in Gillray's caricatures.

Yet although we may take this odd diversion as evidence of Byron being out of his depth, fleeing from the confusion of metaphysics to the relative security of a familiar form of satire, we can also recognize the ease with which he is sidetracked as indicative of a high level of indifference. Were Byron really interested in maintaining the tragic tenor which so much of the drama's rhetoric lays claim to, then elements such as this would be rigidly excluded. Their inclusion alerts us to a certain aimless quality in the drama, resulting perhaps from Byron's boredom as much as from his awareness that he really has nothing to say or achieve apart from the monotonous dramatization of the defiance motif. What we also detect here is that Byron's discomfort with the pretensions of his poetry, for the first time since the early verses of *Childe Harold I* and the Turkish Tales, is manifesting itself in the verse itself: his nonchalance about the risk that his poverty might be discovered is remarkable. The Nemesis episode amounts to a deliberate violation of tragic decorum, and the effect is intensified to the point of self-caricature in Nemesis's speech:

> I was detained repairing shattered thrones –
> Marrying fools, restoring dynasties –
> Avenging men upon their enemies,
> And making them repent their own revenge;
> Goading the wise to madness; from the dull
> Shaping out oracles to rule the world
> Afresh – for they were waxing out of date,
> And mortals dared to ponder for themselves,
> To weigh kings in the balance – and to speak
> Of Freedom, the forbidden fruit.

> (II, iii, 62–71)

Nemesis here becomes a vehicle for the promulgation of the political views that Byron was expected to hold. Nemesis is a political cynic and a republican with a sceptical attitude towards marriage. In addition her speech is couched in an exaggerated version of the world-weary tones of *Childe Harold*. She thus adopts one of Byron's most famous poses, and this glib and mischievous substitution, emphasized by the speech's flippant delivery, causes us to question how seriously Byron is taking himself and his spirits.

Byron may not have expected his public to recognize the implicit farce of the poet presenting himself as Nemesis, but he might have anticipated the kind of reaction to the breach of decorum that we find in Jeffrey's review:

This we think is out of place at least, if we must not say out of character; and though the author may tell us that human calamities are naturally subjects of derision to the Ministers of Vengeance, yet we cannot be persuaded that satirical and political allusions are at all compatible with the feelings and impressions which it was here his business to maintain.[56]

Jeffrey would have been far more shocked had he read this song, included in the first draft of *Manfred*:

> A prodigal son, and a maid undone,
> And a widow re-wedded within the year;
> And a worldly monk, and a pregnant nun,
> Are things which every day appear.[57]

Had this remained, the 'feelings and impressions' which Jeffrey insisted were Byron's 'business to maintain' would not merely have been impaired, but wrecked. What seems to be happening in *Manfred* is that Byron's attempt to write a metaphysical non-realistic drama on the basis of models in which songs are a prominent feature presents him with problems of decorum that occasionally he cannot be bothered to avoid. In this rather extreme instance, he was clearly tempted to abandon whatever compunction he may have had about interrupting and modifying the attention paid to his drama. And the fact that the waggish worldly scepticism of these lines is reminiscent of *The Beggar's Opera* again suggests that whilst writing *Manfred* Byron was moving away from Shelley and towards something more familiar. *The Beggar's Opera* was also evoked for a critic reviewing *Manfred* for the *Gentleman's Magazine* in July 1817, who wrote that the measure of 'Mont Blanc is the monarch of mountains' (I, i, 60–75) 'unluckily reminds us of "How happy could I be with either" ',[58] and certainly not only the metre but also the particularly frivolous limerick-like extra rhyme in the seventh line of this song was more likely to remind the contemporary reader of the songs of Gay than those of Aeschylus:

> Mont Blanc is the monarch of mountains;
> They crown'd him long ago
> On a throne of rocks, in a robe of clouds,
> With a diadem of snow.
> Around his waists are forests braced,
> The Avalanche in his hand;
> But ere it fall, that thundering ball
> Must pause for my command.

(I, i, 60–7)

Shelley's Mont Blanc has been remarkably transformed, and the form in which the echoes are found suggests that behind *Manfred* there is a strong inclination towards a parodic critique of Shelley's poetry of 1816, and the tacit condonation it received in *Childe Harold III*.[59]

Although many of the songs in *Manfred* share the peculiar blend of the qualities of lyric and dirge that characterize the songs in *Prometheus Unbound* and Potter, the existence of these occasional pieces of apparent flippancy and the use of metres more readily associated with light verse raise interesting questions. In the Witch's Kitchen scene in *Faust*, one of the songs sung by the apes contains the following:

> Wir reden und sehn,
> Wir hören und reimen.
> . . .
> Und wenn es uns glückt,
> Und wenn es sich schickt,
> So sind es Gedanken!

Mephistopheles responds with 'Nun, wenigstens musz man bekennen, / Dasz es aufrichtige Poeten sind.'[60] We cannot tell if Byron knew of these lines. If he did, then we might say with conviction that their articulation of a sentiment that had occasionally been drawn into the conscious art of writing, but for the most part had lain dormant (though not without influence) behind so much of his own verse, had an immediate impact upon the songs in *Manfred*. That is to say, the summary of these lines and Mephistopheles's response (if something fits in rhyme then it has the look of a thought and its composer may be regarded as a poet) were so close to home that Byron may have invested the songs of *Manfred* with their flippant experimentalism to see indeed if they would pass for poetry, simultaneously recognizing them as paradigms of his usual productive processes. But even if Byron did not know these particular lines, we could still propose that listening to the songs of *Faust* in translation would have had a similar effect. Reading *Manfred*, one is only too aware that Byron is finding the task of filling the page easy:

> By thy cold breast and serpent smile,
> By thy unfathom'd gulfs of guile,
> By that most seeming virtuous eye,
> By thy shut soul's hypocrisy:
> By thy perfection of thine art
> Which passed for human thine own heart;
> By thy delight in other's pain,
> And by thy brotherhood of Cain,
> I call upon thee!
>
> (I, i, 242–50)

This is a typical example of the drama's heavy dependence upon Byron's competence in lightweight rhetoric. Behind such a shamelessly exaggerated use of anaphora there is the announcement that the poet is holding the poetry cheap. He knows this, but he does not expect his reader to. By going one stage further, however, and incorporating the same productive processes in a metre of light verse which implicitly proclaims a meaningless if self-consciously 'clever' arrangement, he makes his recognition of the nature of these processes more blatant, and increases the risk of his audience discovering that they are being abused. At the same time, he makes room within the verse for what looks suspiciously like more deliberate 'sinking':

> Where the slumbering earthquake
> Lies pillow'd on fire,
> And the lakes of bitumen
> Rise boilingly higher:
> Where the roots of the Andes
> Strike deep in the earth,
> As their summits to heaven
> Shoot soaringly forth
> . . .
>
> I am the Rider of the wind,
> The Stirrer of the storm;
> The hurricane I left behind
> Is yet with lightning warm;
> To speed with thee, o'er shore and sea
> I swept upon the blast:
> The fleet I met sail'd well, and yet
> 'Twill sink ere night be past.

(I, i, 88–107)

Although in retrospect it may seem predictable, we might still be initially surprised by the fact that the lyrical qualities of *Manfred* are far closer to those of the *Irish Melodies* than to those of *Prometheus Unbound*. The casual facility of this extract consists in the poet's surrender to rhyme and rhythm. As in the Turkish Tales and the 'versicles' of the letters, it is this which carries him along:

> Here goes for a swim on the stream of old Time
> On those buoyant supporters, the bladders of rhyme.[61]

Whereas *Childe Harold III* and *The Prisoner of Chillon* can be regarded as attempts to be modern which are controlled by a relatively conventional idea of what great poetry might be, *Manfred* cannot. Its instability stems from the fact that Byron's conception of himself as the embodiment of the spirit of the age lacked the support of inner conviction: the fantasy could only be sustained by postponing the question of how seriously to take his art and the figure of the poet projected to his public. Further, whilst the poetry of the Lakers presented itself as material that could be processed, whatever Shelley had suggested to Byron about the possibilities of 'non-realistic' closet drama was not so malleable. Evidently the only way in which Byron can handle this problem is by falling back upon his acquaintance with the stage, and this perhaps signifies a confused attempt to define Shelley's suggestions antithetically which cannot resist the temptation to include the agents of definition in the final product. Whether or not this was the case, *Manfred* represents an aggressive but nonchalantly cheerful response to Byron's dilemma, one which assuages his frustration by its inordinate exaggeration of stage mannerisms, and one which indulges it by its perverse inclination to explore the problems of writing a drama from which dramatic event has been excluded rather than to find a way around them. The carelessly quarrelsome nature of this reaction results in an uninhibited indulgence in his habitual methods of evading compositional difficulties and the transformation of Shelley's magus into a phantasmagorial spectre-raiser on the one hand, and a mechanism for the perpetuation of infantile fantasies of omnipotence on the other: the hero, by exorcizing Satan with none of the usual aids, virtually controls the fiction.

In a society where such divergent artists as Shelley, Philipsthal, Coleridge, Gillray, Maturin, Fuseli, Lewis, and Peacock are to be found exploiting a common range of motifs whilst expecting different kinds of attention, it is perhaps inevitable that Byron's employment of these motifs should result in confusion. His desire to be received as the most prominent poet of his age could only be sustained by a suppression of his discriminatory faculties, and *Manfred*, as a response to this desire, is accordingly absurdly eclectic. At the same time its nonchalance is symptomatic of the absence of anxiety over this. The writing of the drama, rather like the writing of the Turkish Tales, has been sufficiently easy to allow him a generous measure of detachment. Accordingly, he is more conscious of the implications of his compositional processes, more conscious (although never fully conscious) of how the essentially frivolous conception of *Manfred* is able to absorb the same kind of artistic ambivalence as that evident in *Childe Harold I and II*. Like this earlier piece, *Manfred* seems to be moving close to a point at which Byron could caricature the self he loved to indulge. The mode of *Manfred*, of course, prevents him from reaching this position. But the very act of writing the drama, perhaps, made the recognition of this tendency more likely. Looking at *Manfred* from this point of view, its proximity to *Don Juan* is no mystery.

6

Heroic tableaux: the three historical tragedies

Reviewing *The Corsair* and *The Bride of Abydos* in 1814, Jeffrey felt himself sufficiently moved to pay Byron a great compliment:

We hope he is not in earnest in meditating even a temporary divorce from his Muse – and would humbly suggest to him to do away the reproach of the age, by producing a tragic drama of the old English school of poetry and pathos. He has all the air, we think, of being the knight for whom the accomplishment of that great adventure is reserved.[1]

But when Byron wrote his three historical tragedies in 1820 and 1821, it cannot be said that he did so with all the confidence that such a tribute might have inspired. On the contrary, when placed in their context as works contemporary with *Don Juan*, and as rather unlikely sequels to the peculiar dramatic experimentalism of *Manfred*, I believe we must approach these dramas as pieces in which, as in *Childe Harold IV*, Byron attempted to discover whether indeed he owned the talent that his society had been ready to credit him with. Unlike *Childe Harold IV*, however, they are not desperate reruns of an ailing mode. They are efforts to formulate a new programme, and as such they must be considered as the only fully serious works that Byron wrote that involved him in a reassessment of his poetic abilities and ambitions in which Shelley played no part. Here Byron is not writing for Shelley, nor for his bookseller, nor for the fashionable coteries, but for the version of himself that he wished to pass on to posterity. Accepting his limited abilities and deploying them in *Don Juan*, however successfully, seems to have left him dissatisfied, and the venture into the new realm of tragedy was an attempt to regain the status of a major author.

The major author, Byron apparently believed, needed a great European tradition behind him:

6 Benjamin West, *Cleombrotus ordered in Banishment by Leonidas II, King of Sparta*, 1770

I am however persuaded that this is not to be done by following the old dramatists – who are full of gross faults – pardoned only for the beauty of their language – but by writing naturally and *regularly* – & producing *regular* tragedies like the *Greeks* – but not in *imitation* – merely the outline of their conduct adapted to our own times and circumstances – and of course *no* chorus. – . . . If you want to have a notion of what I am trying – take up a *translation* of any of the *Greek* tragedians. If I said the original – it would be an impudent presumption of mine – but the translations are so inferior to the originals that I think I may risk it. – Then Judge of the 'simplicity of plot – &c.' – and do not judge me by your mad old dramatists – which is like drinking Usquebaugh – & then proving a fountain – yet after all I suppose that you do not mean that Spirits is a nobler element than a clear spring bubbling in the Sun – & this I take to be the difference between the Greeks & those turbid mountebanks – always excepting B. Jonson – who was a Scholar and a Classic. – – Or take up a translation of Alfieri – & try the interest &c. of these my new attempts in the old line – by *him* in *English*. – And then tell me fairly your opinion. – But don't measure me by YOUR OWN *old or new* tailor's yards. – Nothing so easy as intricate confusion of plot – and rant.[2]

However empty the terms seem that Byron employs for promoting his classicism, and however improbable his choice of allies (Jonson, Potter, and Alfieri) appears, the critique of the contemporary stage implicit in the dramas and the remarks that accompany them are apparently sincerely felt. What remains to be discovered is whether he was able to find the resources to make this critique anything more than an expression of dissatisfaction.

First it must be noted that Byron made his classical claims at a time when the label of classicism was used freely and without precision. It is unnecessary again to emphasize how relaxed the critical mode of Byron's day was, but is perhaps worth mentioning here that Coleridge's *Remorse* could be dismissed as 'incorrect' and spectacular in some quarters,[3] and greeted as gracefully classical in others: 'The style is, throughout, poetical and classical, and far above the common level.'[4] 'Genius he certainly possesses; the graces of diction, and brilliant passages in this tragedy distinguish it among the efforts of modern times; and once more correct language and classical graces adorn the stage.'[5] Byron may have persuaded himself that he had a more legitimate access to the term 'classical' than such reviewers as these, and his dependence upon the weight carried by such phrases as 'studiously Greek', 'regular', and 'severe', being bereft of precise application and discussion, looks suspiciously like trading on a vocabulary that was unlikely to be challenged on account of its currency among the littérateurs. And Byron does not help his case by suggesting that his dramas should be compared with Potter's translations (probably the most readily available editions in Byron's time), for such an exercise only emphasizes how distant his concept of Greekness was from Potter's.[6]

Byron believed he had established the neo-classicism of these dramas by a rigorous control of his form; by a 'severer approach to the rules' and by including 'nothing *melo*-dramatic – no surprises – no starts, nor trap-doors, nor opportunities "for tossing their heads and kicking their heels" '.[7] The subject that falls into this simple and regular mould is a common one in neo-classical art. It is the *exemplum virtutis*, the example of a man whose actions are the result of his uncommonly heroic devotion to his principles: the abused Doge sacrificing all for the principles of justice or republican freedom (*Marino Faliero* and *The Two Foscari*), or the philosophical and poetic king who rediscovers the traditional virtues and responsibilities of kingship but not at the expense of his pacifistic beliefs (*Sardanapalus*). The latter half of the eighteenth century had seen many such examples in its paintings: the Horatii, Germanicus, Brutus and his sons, Virginia, Socrates – to name but a few (see fig. 6). And it is the ethos of these paintings, rather than that of any particular literary texts, that we find reflected in Byron's three tragic dramas. The reasons for this are not to be found in a theory that proposes a direct relationship between these dramas and the paintings of David or Benjamin West, but in the subtle and pervasive process by which the kind of gestures that characterized the neo-classic rendering of the *exemplum virtutis* in the visual arts were disseminated through Byron's culture as representative of the spirit of antiquity.

In the late eighteenth century, the Greco-Roman world received a new kind of attention from artists whose anti-Rococo seriousness combined with a tendency to political idealism that was a consequence of living in a revolutionary era. The result was a flood of paintings that concentrated on the most celebrated examples of high-minded virtuous behaviour from antiquity, here used for the purposes of moral propaganda: At their best, these paintings are characterized by a rigorous concentration upon the central gesture through which the ethic is displayed. This is the principle by which they are arranged: extraneous material is excluded, and the contents of the paintings are arranged to emphasize their central motifs.[8] The use of antiquity in this way, however, necessarily resulted in a strong coloration of the popular concept of Greco-Roman culture. Thus the gestures of the new politics and an antihedonistic style became concomitantly the characteristic gestures of the antique world. Byron's attempt in his dramas to recreate the experience of what he believes to be Greek tragic action feeds largely off this reading of Greco-Roman culture rather than one that attempted to extrapolate the ethos of ancient tragedy from a scholarly examination of its literary texts.

The 'severity' and 'regularity' which Byron claims for his dramas, therefore, cannot be readily interpreted in purely literary terms. Although these descriptions have some reference to a rigorous adherence to the unities, the superfluous amount of poeticizing in all three of the plays (apparently there to remind the reader that these were dramas written by the major poet of the day) precludes a reference to the verse itself. His insistence upon formal regularity, however, may be seen as broadly analogous to the disciplined arrangement of figures and environment that is characteristic of late-eighteenth-century neo-classical painting. And the analogy goes further than this. The *exemplum virtutis*, as a dramatic subject, demands a rendering that concentrates its audience's attention upon situations in which the central ethic can be conveyed in the glow of emotional excitement, rather than upon situations in which the primary interests are psychological or metaphysical. It is perhaps not surprising, therefore, that we discover in Byron's dramas a tendency to think in terms of tableaux that recall the ethos of neo-classical painting and relief sculpture. These plays are structured around situations in which the reader is expected to feel the weight of the moral by recognizing its embodiment in particular gestures which frequently arrange themselves into tableaux:

DOGE.   My unhappy children!
MAR.   What!
          You feel it then at last – *you*! – Where is now
          The stoic of the state?
DOGE   (*throwing himself down by the body*). *Here*!
                              (*The Two Foscari*, IV, i, 212–14)

Angiolina refusing in her faintness to sit before her husband at his trial (*Marino Faliero*, V, i), the Doge's farewell (V, ii), Sardanapalus before his funeral pyre or watching the death of Salemenes (V, i) – all these are examples of moments in the dramas in which Byron may have persuaded himself that he was imagining and conveying the essence of Greek tragic action by arranging tableaux in a neo-classical manner.

A propensity to conceive of tragic action in terms of tableaux and rhetorical gestures would have been augmented by the acting styles of Byron's time. In this respect, Kemble appears to stand in a relation to these three tragedies approximately equivalent to Kean's relation to *Manfred*. Kemble's style was noted for its 'studied grace of action' and its finish.[9] A note Byron provided to the Preface of *Marino Faliero* suggests how the distinctive grace of Kemble (and Mrs Siddons) could be readily identified with the spirit of antiquity:

The long complaints of the actual state of the drama arise, however, from no fault of the performers. I can conceive nothing better than Kemble, Cooke, and Kean in their very different manners, or than Elliston in *gentleman's* comedy, and in some parts of tragedy . . . Siddons and Kemble were the ideal of tragic action; I never saw anything at all resembling them even in *person*: for this reason, we shall never see again Coriolanus or Macbeth. When Kean is blamed for want of dignity, we should remember that it is a grace, and not an art, and not to be attained by study. In all, *not* SUPER-natural parts, he is perfect; even his very defects belong, or seem to belong, to the parts themselves, and appear truer to nature. But of Kemble we may say, with reference to his acting, what the Cardinal de Retz said of the Marquis of Montrose, 'that he was the only man he ever saw who reminded him of the heroes of Plutarch.'[10]

The tradition of acting to which Kemble's style belonged, that of Garrick and the French tragic style of the mid-eighteenth century, was closely associated with the revival of a genuine antique acting style.[11] Voltaire considered that his *Mérope* was a recreation of 'pure Greek tragedy',[12] and his success was due to the innovatory mode of three celebrated actresses, Mlle Dumesnil, Mlle Clairon, and Mlle Lekain, whose acting was characterized by an 'expressive panto-mimic style . . . presenting isolated situations in striking, picturesque tableaux'.[13] In the Preface to *Les Scythes*, praising the new acting style, Voltaire includes an interesting reference to Garrick: 'It is in this great art, that of being able to speak to the eye, that England's greatest actor, M. Garrick, has his strength and it is with this that he has shaken and moved us, even those of us who did not understand his language.'[14] Byron, almost certainly, would have known little or nothing about the representation of Voltaire's dramas on the French stage, but it seems likely that what he knew of Garrick, combined

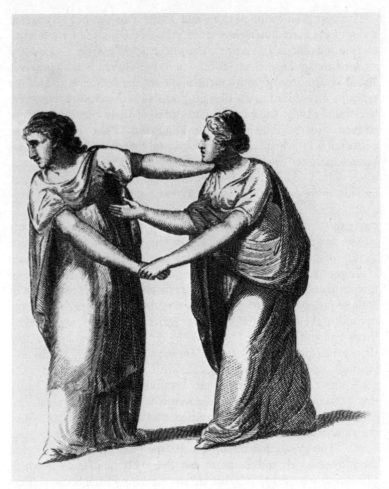

7 'Persuasion repulsed', from Henry Siddons, *Practical Illustrations of Rhetorical Gesture and Action*, 1822

with his admiration for Kemble and Mrs Siddons, would have encouraged him to recognize the grace of rhetorical gesture as his access to the essence of antique tragic action.

The appreciation of posture and attitude in the popular acting styles of the early nineteenth century may be adjudged by reference to Henry Siddons's *Practical Illustrations of Rhetorical Gesture and Action* (first published in 1807), where the illustrations themselves also make the relationship of the stage and its costumes to antique art quite clear (see fig. 7). Elegant postures and antiquity, however, were more closely linked in the 'attitudes' of Lady Hamilton, whose celebrity was at its height in the 1780s and 1790s, when she was performing at private gatherings.[15] Byron therefore would not have been acquainted with these performances at first hand, but public interest in Lady Hamilton's personal life made her a sufficiently famous figure in the Regency for us to assume that the attitudes were a subject of common knowledge. In addition, they stand as testimony to the kind of exclusive entertainment that a man of Byron's station might have been expected to enjoy. Whilst the distinctive quality of the attitudes evidently lay in the skill with which Lady Hamilton made her transitions from one to another, the manner of their attraction for those whose interests centred on the recreation of antique poses can be recognized by a perusal of Rehberg's attempts to capture their static qualities in his series of drawings, engraved by Piroli and published in 1794.[16] Although it has been claimed that there is no evidence for a direct connection between Lady Hamilton's attitudes and the theatre, the ease with which a man of Byron's generation could have related Lady Hamilton's embodiment of antiquity to the acting style of Mrs Siddons is perhaps best demonstrated by comparing Rehberg's illustration of Lady Hamilton as Niobe with a watercolour by Mary Hamilton of Mrs Siddons as Lady Macbeth.[17] The close correlation between the poses, and perhaps even more significantly the costumes, together with the manner in which the shawls are used to supplement the elegance of the body, reflects the common context of tastes and fashions in which Lady Hamilton and Mrs Siddons performed.

Reading Byron's tragedies, one becomes only too aware of the room within them for the arrangement of tableaux and rhetorical gestures, and it is in their incorporation of these 'classical' arrangements and poses, I suspect, that his claims for Greek severity are based. It thus follows that their composition entailed the constant visualization of scenes and episodes, a task made easy for Byron, since the sediments of his culture were thick with popular images of antiquity from the paintings of Benjamin West to the attitudes of

Lady Hamilton. The fact that Byron had little first-hand acquaintance with the subjects so far discussed is important. He probably never saw a work by or after David, and although he would have known something of Poussin's history paintings and the work of West, it seems unlikely that they ever had much effect upon him. Although he saw Kemble and Mrs Siddons, both were well past their prime by Byron's time, and Lady Hamilton he could not have seen. All, in fact, belong more properly to earlier eras, yet all had a rather *passé* currency in Byron's youth, and this, I would suggest, was sufficiently influential to dictate the style of his tragedies and to delude him into thinking that he had succeeded in imagining tragic action and, more specifically, Greek tragic action.

An entry in Byron's diary of 1821 suggests that *Sardanapalus* and *The Two Foscari*, if not *Marino Faliero*, were subject to a more recent influence – his reading of Seneca:

Turned over Seneca's tragedies. Wrote the opening lines of the intended tragedy of Sardanapalus. Rode out some miles into the forest. Misty and rainy. Returned – dined – wrote some more of my tragedy.

Read Diodorus Siculus – turned over Seneca, and some other books. Wrote some more of the tragedy. Took a glass of grog.[18]

It may well be that 'turning over Seneca' was an act no less desultory than 'taking a glass of grog', and the unity of tone suggests in fact that it was. But that Byron read Seneca at all is significant, and that he read him together with his source for the history of *Sardanapalus* is even more so. Interest in Seneca's tragedies in the late eighteenth and early nineteenth centuries was probably even less than it is today. Indeed, between 1701 and 1904 there were no English translations, and the most recent English edition in Latin available to Byron was published in 1659. Byron's reading of Seneca is thus somewhat surprising. He may have been sufficiently acquainted with the Roman theatre to know that Seneca's texts amounted to a renunciation of its spectacular effects. If this were so then he may have turned to Seneca out of authorial sympathy, recognizing a strong parallel between the popular theatre of his own day and that of Seneca's.[19] In addition, as the father of Roman stoicism, an adherent to the unities, and the popularizer of the five-act structure, Seneca offered himself as a suitable model for an author who was attempting to find a classical mode for the dramatic rendering of the *exemplum virtutis*.

Despite the fact that many of the motifs in Byron's dramas that one is tempted to trace to Seneca probably find their way to the early nineteenth century via Elizabethan and Jacobean drama and Otway, there is some evidence to suggest that Byron's reading of Seneca played an important part in the composition of his tragedies. *The Two Foscari*, for instance, like *Marino Faliero*, makes much of offstage suffering:

LOR.　He cried out twice.
BAR.　　　　　　　　　A saint had done so,
　　　Even with the crown of Glory in his eye,
　　　At such inhuman artifice of pain
　　　As was forced on him; but he did not cry
　　　For pity; not a word nor groan escaped him,
　　　And those two shrieks were not in supplication,
　　　But wrung from pangs, and followed by no prayers.

　　　　　　　　　　　　　　　　(I, i, 334–40)

Similarly, the battle in *Sardanapalus* – the most important action of the play – takes place offstage and is narrated by characters onstage. Sardanapalus's character as a hero therefore depends less on the audience's interpretations of his actions than on the rhetoric of the other dramatis personae. The technique is more Senecan than Elizabethan. The death of Astyanax in *The Trojan Women*, for instance, is narrated in a like style:

　　　　There in the grip of hostile hands, the boy
　　　　Stood, as defiant as a lion's cub
　　　　Which, yet unarmed with formidable teeth,
　　　　Small and defenceless though it be, shows fight,
　　　　Snapping with rage and ineffectual jaws.
　　　　The crowd was touched with pity; even the leaders,
　　　　Even Ulysses. Tears were in the eyes
　　　　Of all[20]

In Seneca, 'character' (if it can be called such) is almost totally dependent on conduct, and since a high proportion of significant action takes place offstage, then character is ultimately conveyed by rhetorical narration. It is the technique of a dramatist who will not trust his audience to interpret, and therefore interprets for them, and it is here that Byron and Seneca stand on common ground. Their distrust of audience responses not only results in the setting up of closet drama, but also in the establishment of an imaginary stage that does not present action but a manufactured response to action. The rhetoric of messengers is all-important, the complexity of a plot that is seen to develop onstage is avoided, and the characters are represented devoid of a human context, as starkly pictorial two-dimensional figures:

> He fights now bare-headed, and by far
> Too much exposed. The soldiers knew his face,
> And the foe too; and in the moon's broad light,
> His silk tiara and his flowing hair
> Makes him a mark too royal. Every arrow
> Is pointed at the fair hair and fair features,
> And the broad fillet which crowns both.
>
> (*Sardanapalus*, III, i, 202–8)

Similarly, soliloquy is not the presentation of the character's psychology, but the complete representation of the ideal upon which the notion of character is utterly dependent. In both Byron and Seneca this is usually the noble bearing of suffering:

> But I have other, greater pain to bear;
> No rest at night, no balm of sleep relieves
> My troubled soul. It thrives and grows – my pain
> Burns in me like the burning heart of Etna.
> My loom stands still, the wool drops from my hands;
> I have no heart to make my offerings
> At the god's temples, or to take my place
> Among the dances of the Attic women
> Torch bearing in dark rites around their altars.
>
> (*Phaedra*)[21]

> I had borne all – it hurt me, but I bore it –
> Till this last running over of the cup
> Of bitterness – until this last loud insult,
> Not only unredressed, but sanctioned; then,
> And thus, I cast all further feelings from me –
> The feelings which they crushed for me, long, long
> Before, even in their oath of false allegiance!
>
> (*Marino Faliero*, III, ii, 367–73)

In both Byron and Seneca, the constant reinforcement and emphasis of particular attitudes and gestures make for monotonous drama and a reduction of characterization to the form of bold, uncomplicated outline. T. S. Eliot's description of Seneca – 'though . . . long-winded, he is not diffuse; he is capable of great concision; there is even a monotony of forcefulness'[22] – also provides us with an accurate summary of Byron's achievement in his tragedies.

The most damaging aspect of Byron's tragedies from a historical point of view is that their presentation of the neo-classic Stoic is in want of a political reference. The same cannot be said of the paintings of David or even the dramas of Alfieri. This factor alone may not make Byron's dramas bad any more than it makes Alfieri's good, but to take account of it is to begin to identify the want of conviction that can be detected in the continuous retreats into rhetoric and tableaux. The absence of a political situation in England in 1820 that could promote real excitement from the dramatic presentation of high-minded sacrificial conduct means that the gestures of Byron's tragedies must be regarded as fundamentally aesthetic rather than political. That is to say, they were offered purely as a demonstration against the condition of the contemporary stage. As such they are insufficiently felt to create around them an artistic context through which they could succeed. A comparison with David's paintings helps to identify their deficiency. David's success depends not merely on the anti-Rococo aesthetic principles that are partly responsible for a new pictorial environment, but also upon the strength of ethical conviction that imbues this environment with its life and vigour. The success of *The Oath of the Horatii* has been described as 'the perfect coincidence of style and moralizing intention', the wedding of 'pictorial genius to ethical passion'.[23] And it is this ethical passion, engendered in a turbulent political situation, which gives David's art its disciplined aesthetic strengths. Byron's drama is bereft of an equivalent discipline because it is bereft of its cause. The fact that the old easy and slightly frivolous writing habits are allowed to creep in here and there confirms this.[24] The creative impulses behind these dramas – a will to be recognized as a great artist and a dissatisfaction with contemporary dramatic tastes – are simply not sufficiently felt to discipline or enliven the resultant texts.

In the context of the early-nineteenth-century stage, *Marino Faliero*, *Sardanapalus*, and *The Two Foscari* can be seen as an overstated plea for formality, but as works contemporaneous with *Don Juan* they have considerable significance to any concept of Byron's *oeuvre*. For whilst it is tempting to regard *Don Juan* as definitive of Byron's final position vis-à-vis the cant of his society and its poetry, notice of these dramas should, if nothing else, prevent us from regarding it in this over-simplified manner. Bearing in mind the way in which these tragedies announce their pledges to abstract moral idealism, what Byron said about cant is worth repeating here:

> The truth is, that in these days the grand '*primum mobile*' of England is *cant*; cant political, cant poetical, cant religious, cant moral; but always *cant*, multiplied through all the varieties of life. It is the fashion, and while it lasts will be too powerful for those who can only exist by taking the tone of the time. I say *cant*, because it is only a thing of words, without the smallest influence upon human actions; the English being no wiser, no better, and much poorer, and more divided among themselves, as well as far less moral, than they were before the prevalence of this verbal decorum.[25]

The vigour of this possibly stems from the frustration of a man who knew how to criticize his society but found himself unable to renounce or resign the gestures it would have him rehearse. The rhetorical gestures and tableaux that lie behind the texts of these tragedies were perhaps just old-fashioned enough to deceive Byron into thinking that he had made a demonstration against the cant and tastes of his society by presenting the tragic magnificence of a forgotten ethical system, but at the same time he must have been somehow aware of the hopeless gulf between the world of his dramas and that in which his readers lived. T. S. Eliot described the 'ethic of Seneca's plays' as 'that of an age which supplied the lack of moral habits by a system of moral attitudes and poses'.[26] Such a description might also appear to have an application to the ethic of Byron's tragedies: Eliot's description of Seneca's period is remarkably similar to that quoted above which Byron gives of his society. But the distance between Seneca's Rome and the sense of a real heroic past or future was probably not so great as that which faced Byron's society. The potency of Byron's criticism of his society's cant lies in the fact that it is nothing more than a hopeless harangue, delivered with no illusions about the world's transformation. The dramas, on the other hand, are the last of his exercises in complete self-deception, allowing him to persuade himself of the relevance of their abstract idealism, and creating a context of formally rehearsed attitudes and ethics which facilitated his belief in his talents as a tragic dramatist.

7

Cain, the reviewers, and Byron's new form of old-fashioned mischief

Like *Manfred*, *Cain* has attracted the wrong kind of interest:

Cain . . . represents a distinct shift in Byron's interests, from politics to theology, from society to the cosmos . . . the play is far more than the naive exercise in Satanism that it was sometimes taken to be; at its centre is the temptation of Cain by Lucifer which is a Goethean and metaphysical dialogue, the encounter of good and evil, a second Temptation and Fall in which the mysterious implications of the first are further explored.[1]

Joseph's request that *Cain* be given serious consideration as a philosophical poem only serves to bring into play the kind of attention that rapidly confirms its naivety. It is as well to begin by admitting that Cain is as potent an affirmation of Byron's bankruptcy as a philosophical poet as we are likely to find. Further, it is bad poetry and worse drama. But the poem need not simply be dismissed as a piece of incompetence. It can be regarded alternatively as a provocative work which is concerned less with its artistry than with an assault upon decorum which occasionally borders on literary vandalism. *Cain*'s rebellion may ultimately be evaluated as somewhat childish on account of its limited resources, but it must also be seen as evidence of Byron's new attitude towards his critics: a mischievous exploitation of the space they had given him, and possibly even an attempt to place an unreasonable strain on an unwritten contract that he had grown tired of. *Cain* was also a personal success for Byron in his relationship with Shelley. Shelley was no doubt able to take some credit for what he considered to be *Cain*'s greatness, but he could not have seen that Byron was simultaneously using the poem for his own mischievous and rather trivial purposes. And Shelley's warm approval of the poem can only have convinced Byron that, once discovered, the art of deceiving Shelley into a belief in the greatness of his poetry was as easily contrived, and as full of other possibilities, as the masquerade of genius that he had presented to his readers earlier in his career.

In order to place *Cain* in its proper context, it is necessary to summarize briefly the nature of Byron's relationship with the reviewers. Until 1818, the year of *Don Juan*, the critics had represented Byron as a poetic rebel, and yet it is clear that they regarded him as a rebel of a conventional kind. Byron played the game of poetic revolt strictly according to the rules. He had never really threatened to work outside the mainstream of polite literature. If he became a little too misanthropic or bitter, Jeffrey gently reprimanded him whilst sadly shaking his head over the inevitable maladies of great genius. If he tended to neglect his moral responsibilities, Gifford wagged a paternal finger and suggested that if he remembered them in the future he would be by far the greatest poet of his age. Byron added spice to popular literature, and as he never really threatened its boundaries or its tenets, he was patronized and encouraged. Most important, he never gave the critics anything they could not handle, anything which threatened to subvert the equipment and vocabulary that had been devised for the interpretation of literature. He was therefore 'safe' in a way that Wordsworth, particularly in his early years, was not, and undoubtedly Byron enjoyed being 'safe', for a while at least. He became the safety-valve of literary conservatism; the means by which the critics could preserve their old methods and values whilst creating the illusion that they were moving with the times.

Don Juan disturbed this comfortable relationship, but nevertheless enabled the deeply rooted critical habits to persist. Reading the second canto, Gifford could still remark that 'a little care, and wish to do right would have made this a superlative thing'.[2] In addition, the way in which the poem's mode could be assimilated to that of the popular squib, and the ease with which its poet could be regarded as a man of the world, gave it a familiar and conventional façade. Whilst *Cain* is a far lesser achievement than *Don Juan* in its manipulative possibilities, its crudity succeeded where *Don Juan*'s subtlety failed: it completed the movement begun by *Manfred* away from the conventional conception of the relationship between the poet and his audience. 'It is in my gay metaphysical style, and in the *Manfred* line',[3] Byron wrote, by which he meant that it was wilfully perverse in its refusal to admit of any common ground between the reader and the poet. The poet of *Cain* appeared to his public as inspired, prophetic, and revolutionary; no longer the Byron who wrote with one eye turned towards his audience. But in this poem, as in *Don Juan*, Byron set out to break all the rules whilst remaining ostensibly innocent.

The guise of the inspired poet was one way of preserving this innocence on the printed page. In society, however, another kind of innocence had to be protested: 'Of all my writings, *Cain* has stirred up the most annoyance in England and within my family. I wrote it when I was drunk. When I reread it later I was astonished.'[4] The image of the visionary poet had to be played down in the company of fashionable men. The company Byron was to keep after the writing of *Cain* in 1821, however, was to nurture this image. In 1821, Mary Shelley wrote of Byron:

My Lord is now living very sociably, giving dinners to his male acquaintance and writing divinely; perhaps by this time you have seen *Cain* and will agree with us in thinking it his finest production – To me it sounds like a revelation – of some works one says – one has thought of such things though one could not have expressed it so well – It is not this with *Cain* – one has perhaps stood on the extreme verge of such ideas and from the midst of the darkness which has surrounded us the voice of the Poet now is heard telling a wondrous tale.[5]

To Shelley himself, Byron's achievement in *Cain* had made him a 'spirit of an angel in the mortal paradise of a decaying body'. Cain was 'apocalyptic . . . a revelation not before communicated to man'.[6] Even Moore, whose feelings about the poem were ambivalent, recognized a similar quality in the drama: 'But *Cain* is wonderful – terrible – never to be forgotten. If I am not mistaken, it will sink deep into the world's heart; and while many will shudder at its blasphemy, all must fall prostrate before its grandeur. Talk of Aeschylus and his Prometheus! – here is the true spirit both of the Poet – and the Devil.'[7] It seems improbable to us today that such a decidedly third-rate production as *Cain* could excite such a glorified interest in its poet. Yet Byron's new poetic stance seemed to be invested with 'the true spirit of the Poet', and whilst Shelley could crudely enthuse over it, and Moore was able to embrace it, the arbiters of the public taste were not so tolerant:

We therefore think that poets ought fairly to be confined to the established creed and morality of their country, or to the *actual* passions and sentiments of mankind; and that poetical dreamers and sophists who pretend to *theorise* according to their feverish fancies, without a warrant from authority or reason, ought to be banished the commonwealth of letters. In the courts of morality, poets are unexceptionable witnesses; they may give in the evidence, and depose to facts whether good or ill; but we demur to their arbitrary and self-pleasing summing up; they are suspected *judges*, and not very often safe advocates, where great questions are concerned, and universal principles brought to issue. But we shall not press this point farther at present.[8]

Under the guise of the poet's 'feverish fancy' Byron was able to disregard the poetical code of conduct that was generally observed by the Regency writer. Byron's society had thrilled to the tones of the rebellious free spirit of the poet; *Cain*, obligingly, lays its rude bardic fingers on that society's consecrated taboos.

Jeffrey's criticism of *Cain* objected not merely to the blasphemy of the poem, but to the style of poetry which allowed Byron to articulate unconventional moral opinions:

It is a poor and pedantic sort of poetry that seeks to embody nothing but metaphysical subtleties and abstract deductions of reason – and a very suspicious philosophy that aims at establishing its doctrines by appeals to the passions and the fancy . . . it is the mischief of all poetical paradoxes, that, from the very limits and end of poetry, which deals only in obvious and glancing views, they are never brought to the fair test of argument.[9]

This is important, for it shows just how unreasonable and tyrannical the demands of critics such as Jeffrey were, and to what extremes they were prepared to venture to confine the poet to the habits of thinking of his society. Byron had apparently retreated into his poetry, and chosen to ignore the dimensions of public debate or unpoetical reason which might temper the 'wondrous tale' of the poet. But, Jeffrey insisted, this dimension was of fundamental importance, for poetry had its place *in* society – 'poets ought fairly to be confined to the established creed and morality of their country' – 'poetical dreamers' were not only dangerous, but decidedly bad-mannered in their 'self-pleasing' presumption. Byron had declined to use the stance and mode of expression of the conventional poet in *Cain*, and in addition had been somewhat ungentlemanly in his assumption of a role that admitted of no common ground between himself and his audience. He was breaking his contract with the reviewers by no longer writing for the public, but above them. At least, that was the gesture implicit in the style. Jeffrey did not like it, but perhaps a more typical and less pompous response was that of Edgerton Brydges:

There is another extraordinary poem of which I have not spoken hitherto; because, I will confess, that I know not how to speak of it properly, yet something must be said of it. – *Cain* is a poem much too striking to be passed in silence. But its impiety is so frightful that it is impossible to praise it, while its genius and beauty of composition would demand all the notice which mere literary merit can claim.[10]

From such a prolix man such a confession is of no small consequence.

Cain called the bluff of the reviewers who had made so much of Byron's 'originality' since the success of *Childe Harold*. It presented the reading public with an audacious piece of originality which they could not condone. Sir Edgerton Brydges was perplexed, Jeffrey was indignantly resentful, and Heber (in the *Quarterly*) confessed that 'to apply the severe rules of criticism to a composition of this kind would be little better than lost labour'.[11] *Don Juan* threatened and disturbed Byron's long-standing unwritten agreement with the reviewers, but it was *Cain* that finally forced the more obtuse amongst them to recognize that it had been broken. Even then, some of the old habitual terminology and attitudes devised for the earlier poetry were to be found scattered here and there in the reviews he received for the rest of his career and beyond.

The essentially provocative nature of *Cain* is implicit in the tone of its poetry, a tone at once comic and juvenile, so much so, indeed, that at times Byron seems to be defying his readers to challenge the freedom allowed to his infantilism:

LUCIFER.   Ask the destroyer.
CAIN.   Who?
LUCIFER.   The Maker. – Call him
     Which name thou wilt: he makes but to destroy.

(I, i, 263–4)

Lucifer's audacious crudity of logic is one of *Cain*'s most conspicuous features, and although it is never subtle or witty, its ubiquity transforms the drama's dialogue into something more akin to persiflage. It is this which inspired E. H. Coleridge to suggest that Byron's Lucifer was not related to Milton's Satan but to Goethe's Mephistopheles, and to this I shall return.[12] It must be said of course that like Byron's other dramas *Cain* leans heavily upon a store of rhetoric derived from Shakespearean drama and (particularly in the case of *Cain*) from Milton:

      And yon immense
      Serpent, which rears his dripping mane and vasty

> Head, ten times higher than the haughtiest cedar,
> Forth from the abyss, looking as he could coil
> Himself around the orbs we lately looked on –
> Is he not of the kind which basked beneath
> The tree in Eden?

(II, i, 190–6)

But it also offers something strikingly different in so much of its dialogue, which veers sharply away from such measured, sombre tones:

ADAM.   Son Cain! my first born – wherefore art thou silent?
CAIN.   Why should I speak?
ADAM.   To pray.
CAIN.   Have ye not prayed?
ADAM.   We have, most fervently.
CAIN.   And loudly: I
  Have heard you.
ADAM.   So will God, I trust.
ABEL.   Amen!
ADAM.   But thou my eldest born? art silent still?
CAIN.   'Tis better I should be so.
ADAM.   Wherefore so?
CAIN.   I have nought to ask.
ADAM.   Nor aught to thank for?
CAIN.   No.
ADAM.   Dost thou not *live*?
CAIN.
               Must I not die?

(I, i, 22–9)

The questioning tones of Cain (there are forty-two questions in the first 150 lines) are the evidence of its essentially quarrelsome nature, but, far from being dialectic, the intellectualism is indulged for its own sake. It is perversely dull and unimaginative, yet perhaps to be regarded as the manifestation of Byron's infatuation with his own impertinence. The real threat of the drama is not to conventional theological thinking, or even to the conventions of theological debate, but to literary decorum. Byron plays upon Cain's naivety to bring 'intellectual' debate down to bathetic level. He is playing the vandal, and his wanton damage is inflicted through a perverse indulgence in infantile reasoning:

CAIN.   Did ye not tell me that
  Ye are both eternal?

LUCIFER.	Yea!

CAIN.   And what I have seen –
Yon blue immensity, is boundless?

LUCIFER.   Aye!

CAIN.   And cannot ye both reign, then? – is there not
Enough? – why should ye differ?

LUCIFER.   We both reign.

CAIN.   But one of you makes evil.

LUCIFER.   Which?

CAIN.   Thou! for
If thou canst do man good, why dost thou not?

LUCIFER.   And why not he who made? *I* made ye not;
Ye are his creatures, and not mine.

(II, ii, 388–96)

Lucifer's droll responses to Cain's frantic questionings invest him
with the equanimity of a rather small-minded and self-satisfied Regency gentleman. As the *Quarterly* dryly commented, 'Lucifer,
though his first appearance is well conceived, is as sententious and
sarcastic as a Scotch metaphysician.'[13] Lucifer's tactics of employing
Socratic irony against naivety, and his subsequent amusement at
Cain's expense, transforms the occasionally structured rhetorical
dialogue into facetious bantering. Indeed, Cain's ingenuousness expands to absurd proportions:

. . . To which particular things must melt like snows.

CAIN.   Snows! what are they?

(II, ii, 315–16)

CAIN.

Thoughts unspeakable
Crowd in my breast to burning, when I hear
Of this almighty Death, who is, it seems,
Inevitable. Could I wrestle with him?
I wrestled with the lion, when a boy, .
In play, till he ran roaring from my gripe.

(I, i, 256–61)

The indulgence of this cannot be ignored. Byron is obviously amused
at the concept of Cain's naivety alongside Lucifer's omnipotence. He
thus exaggerates both to the extent that he is prepared to substantiate the exaggeration by the provision of an anecdote befitting Cain's
mythical status ('I wrestled with the lion', etc.). Lucifer frequently
employs not the rhetoric of the heroic tempter, but the modulations

and structures of everyday speech. He is thus given a dramatic character, albeit a limited one, depending for its definition upon his superior and presumptuous familiarity:

```
CAIN.                    would I ne'er had been
               Aught else but dust!
LUCIFER.       That is a grovelling wish,
               Less than thy father's – for he wishes to know!
```
(II, i, 292–3)

```
CAIN.          Thou art not the Lord my father worships?
LUCIFER.                      No.
CAIN.          His equal?
LUCIFER.           No; – I have nought in common with him!
```
(I, i, 304–5)

There is something of the 'Devil's Drive' mentality about *Cain*. The kind of jokes found in this early poem and in *The Vision of Judgement* are to be found in *Cain* too. It is only a short step from

> With us acts are exempt from time, and we
> Can crowd eternity into an hour,
> Or stretch an hour into eternity

(*Cain*, I, i, 535–7)

to

> True testimonies are enough: we lose
> Our time, nay, our eternity, between
> The accusation and defence

(*The Vision of Judgement*, 63)

This kind of poetry has nothing behind it other than a rather frivolous impulse to be offensive. This can be confirmed by referring to *Cain*'s beginnings, which lie not in 'a distinct shift in Byron's interests, from politics to theology', but more probably in the *Quarterly*'s review of Milman's *The Fall of Jerusalem*, published in May 1820, which included a flattering but qualified reference to Byron:

But he must not stop even here. He has yet something to unlearn; he has yet much to add to his own reputation and that of his country. Remarkably as Britain is now distinguished by its living poetical talent, our time has room for him; and has need of him. For sacred poetry, (a walk which Milton alone has hitherto successfully trodden,) his taste, his peculiar talents, his education, and his profession appear alike to designate him; and, while, by a strange predilection for the worser half of manicheism, one of the mightiest spirits of the age has, apparently, devoted himself and his genius to the adornment and extension of evil, we may be well exhilarated by the accession of a new and potent ally to the cause of human virtue and happiness, whose example may furnish an additional evidence that purity and weakness are not synonymous, and that the torch of genius never burns so bright as when duly kindled at the Altar.[14]

Byron was both irritated and amused by this accusation:

I should be glad to know why your Quarter*ing* Reviewers, at the close of *The Fall of Jerusalem*, accuse me of Manicheism? a compliment to which the sweetener of 'one of the mightiest Spirits' by no means reconciles me. The poem they review is very noble; but could they not do justice to the writer without converting him to my religious Antidote? I am not a Manichean, nor an *Any*-chean. I should like to know what harm my 'poeshies' have done: I can't tell what your people mean by making me a hobgoblin.[15]

He made another reference to this accusation in his first letter on Bowles's *Pope*, and also, significantly, in the first draft of the Preface to *Cain*: 'I am prepared to be accused of Manicheism, or some other hard name ending in *ism*, which makes a formidable figure and awful sound in the eyes and ears of those who would be as much puzzled to explain the terms so bandied about, as the liberal and pious indulgers in such epithets.'[16] Byron probably decided against publishing this part of his Preface for Murray's sake, since it could have been construed as a public confession of a heresy. Yet the common usage of 'Manicheism' was probably not so precise, and, according to Byron's letter to Murray on Bowles, amounted to devil-worship.[17] *Cain* is vulnerable to accusations of Manicheism based on either interpretation, for both its heroic portrayal of Lucifer and the 'two Principles' passage which Matthew Arnold has made famous were liable to upset the pious reader.

We may speculate that without the *Quarterly*'s attack on Byron, *Cain* might never have been written. Such speculation, however, cannot take us very far. What is important is to recognize that *Cain* is a provocative piece, and that its provocations are far from haphazard. In fact, they are carefully contrived and attuned to the public's conception of Byron the poet: he was not 'a Manichean, nor an *Any*-chean', but he was prepared to play at Manicheism for the benefit of a public who wished to be scandalized. In addition, he was ready to sacrifice the quality of the poetry for this end. Matthew Arnold is very hard on

> and *thou* wouldst go on aspiring
> To the great double Mysteries! the *two Principles!*

But there can be little doubt that this was composed with the *Quarterly* reviewers in mind, and therefore it is endowed with an element of mischief, which Arnold, for any number of reasons, could not possibly have seen.

For Byron, *Cain*'s indecorum may have had a precedent in the form of Goethe's *Faust*. Although the similarities between *Cain* and *Faust* (depending largely on the parallel to be drawn between Lucifer and Mephistopheles) have been occasionally acknowledged,[18] their implications have remained unexplored. Since Byron did not read *Faust* until 1822, the year after *Cain*'s publication, the nature of this seemingly improbable relationship can only be discovered by investigating the circumstances in which Byron's ideas about Goethe had been formed.

The reception of Goethe's works in England before Carlyle was slow and uneasy, and the reasons for this, perhaps, are not all that complex. First, the German language was not widely known; it was certainly not part of the required equipment of a gentleman, nor even a scholar. The first translations of Goethe's works were not infrequently taken from French versions (such as *Werther* (1779) and *Dichtung und Wahrheit* (1824)). Secondly, German culture was widely regarded by the English as inferior to their own, as retarded and immature. A typical attitude is exemplified in Jeffrey's patronizing opening to his first article on *Dichtung und Wahrheit* in 1816:

The German muse has, of late years, been by far the most prolific of the sisterhood, and has certainly cause enough to be proud of some of her offspring; although, in her time, she has been delivered of a more numerous litter of moon-calves or sooterkins than any of her kindred; and malicious people pretend, that, in the countenances even of her handsomest children, there may be traced a strong likeness to their misshapen brethren. For our own parts, however, we give no credit to that ill-natured surmise; and, considering the German literati as in a great measure the pupils of the English, we cannot help viewing them with parental fondness for their well-meant endeavours, – although, as yet, they have not been able to equal us in the manufacture either of Manchester goods or of Shakespeares.

The astonishing rapidity of the development of German literature has been the principal cause both of its imperfections and of the enthusiasm of its warmer admirers.[19]

This sort of thing was obviously liable to give rise to all sorts of misconceptions. Thirdly, Goethe's first success in England, *Werther*, was of a peculiar and ambiguous kind, not unlike that of Rousseau with *La Nouvelle Héloise*. On its appearance in an English translation in 1779 *Werther* became extremely popular, but it also engendered a considerable amount of moral protest. Looking back in 1830, Scott saw the reception of *Werther* as a hindrance not merely to Goethe's acceptance, but that of German literature in general:

The names of Lessing, Klopstock, Schiller and other German poets of eminence were only known in Britain very imperfectly. *The Sorrows of Werther* was the only composition that had attained any degree of popularity, and the success of that remarkable novel, notwithstanding the distinguished genius of the author, was retarded by the nature of its incidents. To the other compositions of Goethe whose talents were destined to illuminate the age in which he flourished, the English remained strange.[20]

The famous suicide of 1784 did not help Goethe's reputation.[21] Apart from the moral outcry it provoked, *Werther* also hampered Goethe's reception in England by burdening him with an image of the writer that was inappropriate to his later works. Those English critics who fostered this image were liable to misinterpret his subsequent productions in order to preserve it. Thus *The Speculator*, in 1790, dealing with the dramas, made much of Goethe's 'high originality' and 'the fiery spirit of enthusiasm and overflowing sensibility which pervades the Sorrows of Werther . . . the same nervous energy, the same flow of passion, and beautiful simplicity which distinguish that singular production are visible in his dramatic compositions'.[22] On the other hand, those critics who disapproved of the image of Goethe which *Werther* had created were prone to saddle his subsequent works with it. The *Quarterly* reviewer of *De l'Allemagne*, as late as 1814, whilst not dismissing *Faust, Hermann and Dorothea*, and even *Werther* itself, formed his comments on Goethe around what one suspects was a habitual moral aggression that dated back many years:

As a writer for the theatre, indeed, except in the single play of Clavigo, Goethe has lamentably failed. His Egmont, which Madame de Staël would gladly praise, is, even setting aside its immorality, so dull as to defy a second reading. Stella our amiable author will give up, we think, without regret, as too harmlessly absurd to effect the mischief for which it seems intended; and Iphigenia, though it contains many passages of rare merit, is as a whole even more ponderous and long-drawn than the generality of imitations of the ancient tragedy.

His smaller poems, numerous as the sands of the sea, we have neither time nor inclination to criticise in detail. Most of them have some sort of whimsical originality, many have considerable pathos, and all are more or less immoral.[23]

This, however, comes from a period of transition, for the publication of *De l'Allemagne* in 1813 was perhaps the most influential single event in the history of Goethe's reputation in England. It was this enormously successful book which was to wear down the stock responses that had survived since the days of *Werther*. In the words of a German scholar, *De l'Allemagne* 'unveiled an idealised picture of an unknown fairyland to the astonished gaze of Europe'.[24] Whilst the element of idealization is not hard to detect, Madame de Staël's depiction of Goethe was not without its reservations. Goethe was described not simply as a wonderful genius, but as a peculiarly powerful and original writer whose works threatened conventional literary values:

One perceives in the writer so great an impatience of all that can be thought to bear a resemblance to affectation, that he disdains even the art that is necessary to give a durable form to his compositions. There are marks of genius scattered here and there through his drama, like the touches of Michael Angelo's pencil; but it is a work defective, or rather which makes us feel the want of many things.

The talent necessary to finish a composition of any kind, demands a sort of cleverness, and of calculation, which agrees but badly with the vague and indefinite imagination displayed by the Germans in all their works. Besides, it requires art, and a great deal of art, to find a proper denouement . . . But to combine effects seems to the Germans almost like hypocrisy, and the spirit of calculation appears to them irreconcilable with inspiration.

Certainly we must not expect to find in it [*Faust*] either taste, or measure, or the art that selects and terminates; but if the imagination could figure to itself an intellectual chaos, such as the material chaos has often been painted the 'Faustus' of Goethe should have been composed at that epoch.

If the play of 'Faustus' contained only a lively and philosophical pleasantry, an analogous spirit may be found in many of Voltaire's writings; but we perceive in this piece an imagination of a very different nature. It is not only that it displays to us the moral world, such as it is, annihilated, but that Hell itself is substituted in the room of it. There is a potency of sorcery, a poetry of wickedness, a distraction of thought, which makes us shudder, laugh, and cry, in a breath.

159

Whether it is to be considered as an offspring of the delirium of the mind, or of the satiety of reason, it is to be wished that such productions may not be multiplied; but when such a genius as that of Goethe sets itself free from all restrictions, the crowd of thoughts is so great, that on every side they break through and trample down the barriers of art.[25]

It was probably this aspect of Goethe, upon which Madame de Staël laid considerable emphasis, that resulted in the slightly nervous English conception of him as the great genius of German literature who nevertheless commanded less respect than Schiller:

Schiller presents only the genius of a great poet, and the character of a virtuous man . . . The original, singular, and rather admirable than amiable mind of Goethe – his dictatorial power over national literature – his inequality, caprice, originality, and fire in conversation – his union of a youthful imagination with exhausted sensibility, and the impartiality of a stern sagacity, neither influenced by opinions nor predelictions – are painted with extraordinary skill.

This is from Jeffrey's review of *De l'Allemagne*, and he goes on to speak of 'the terrible energy of that most odious of the works of genius, in which the whole power of imagination is employed to dispel the charms which poetry bestows on human life',[26] which he evidently sees as the characteristic feature of *Faust*.

In 1813, then, the year of *De l'Allemagne* and its reviews, the English public, including Byron, probably quite suddenly, felt themselves enlightened about a literature which they had formerly known very little about, and through Madame de Staël's lengthy quotations from Goethe's plays, and her summaries of his plots, they had reason to believe that they were fairly well acquainted with the works of the man who was commonly regarded as Germany's greatest writer. Now it is not too difficult to reconstruct the general impression of this ill-informed and badly read public. On the one hand, Madame de Staël, Jeffrey, and the *Quarterly* reviewer had encouraged them to conceive of Goethe as a great poetic genius. On the other, they were informed in *De l'Allemagne* that this genius was unrestricted and intellectually chaotic; in the *Edinburgh* that it was 'odious'; and in the *Quarterly* that it was immoral. A closer examination of these sources yields one common and important factor. All three writers take a certain delight in favourably patronizing the poet as rebel. To Madame de Staël, this was one means of proclaiming her cosmopolitan and liberal tastes. The *Edinburgh* and the

Quarterly swiftly and vigorously sanctioned her judgement, perhaps because they were all too ready to praise a work that had been censored in France (both reviews expound at some length upon the French ignorance of German literature), perhaps because they were intoxicated by novelty, or recognized that they were too badly qualified to venture any contradictions, but almost certainly also because they recognized in this assent the opportunity to profess a generous breadth of taste and tolerance which they did not in fact own. It was necessary therefore to stress Goethe's faults in order that this magnanimity might be appreciated. The English public probably felt similarly pleased with themselves. Here was an author they could talk about in tones of scandalized awe without having to read his works. This game was a safe one to reviewers and readers alike, for the place of German literature in relation to English culture was sufficiently ill defined to render any threat which Goethe posed to conventional literary values a distant or unlikely one.

Before 1822, when Shelley assisted Byron in reading *Faust*, Byron's interest in Goethe, like that of the majority of the reading public, did not amount to a serious critical concern with his works. Rather, it was probably confined to a curiosity incited by the ambivalent representation of Goethe in *De l'Allemagne* and its reviews, and by the fact that the evolution of the figure of Goethe the poet in England was remarkably similar to the public's conception of himself. The relish with which Jeffrey had spoken of Goethe in 1813 anticipated the self-indulgent deference of his reviews of Byron in 1816 to which I have drawn attention. In both instances Jeffrey could afford to be generous and play the game of the liberal critic. Goethe was far away and hardly read, and what Jeffrey was pleased to call Byron's inspiration, as I have explained, in actuality left the boundaries of art intact. It was *Cain*, finally, which transformed Byron's threatening game into a serious one as far as the reviewers and public were concerned. Goethe's metamorphosis, however, had occurred earlier: in 1816 and 1817. After three years of English ambivalence, Jeffrey published two lengthy reviews of *Dichtung und Wahrheit*, the unfavourable tones of which began a controversy over Goethe involving the *Literary Gazette* and *Blackwood's*. Jeffrey's articles are of considerable significance in the history of Goethe's reputation in England, since they were the first documents of any weight or influence to be put before the public since *De l'Allemagne*. Byron found them memorable,[27] but also, I believe, he recognized in

Jeffrey's irritation the possibilities of the figure of the poet he was discussing, and subsequently drew upon this and his rather eclectic knowledge of Goethe in his writing of *Cain*. For, looking back on these reviews in 1821, Byron would have been able to recognize in them an image of the poet which had advanced one stage beyond his own, with which formerly it had shared so much. He may also have recognized in Jeffrey's discomfort that this new image of the poet was capable of fracturing the veneer of critical cant.

For Jeffrey's change of tone is remarkable. In 1813 he spoke of the 'metaphysical passion' and 'unfixed style' of the Germans which endowed their literature with its freedom and originality. At that time, Jeffrey did not exactly present this as a virtue, but he was not disposed to suggest that it was a vice, since it allowed him to consolidate his own conservatism by setting up a decoy:

In Germany, Style, and even language, are not yet fixed. In France, rules are despotic – 'the reader will not be amused at the expense of his literary conscience; there alone he is scrupulous.' A German writer is above his Public, and firms it. A French writer dreads a Public already enlightened and severe. He constantly thinks of immediate effect. He is in society, even while he is composing; and never loses sight of the effect of his writings on those whose opinions and pleasantries he is accustomed to fear. The German writers have, in a higher degree, the first requisite for writing – the power of feeling with vivacity and force. In France, a book is read to be spoken of, and must therefore catch the spirit of society.[28]

Jeffrey could just as easily have been writing about England as France, but, through writers such as Goethe (at this stage) and Byron, he could pretend that English tastes were not so over-refined that they could not appreciate a genius that was in any way original or revolutionary. By 1816, however, Jeffrey was showing something more like his true colours:

Bolder heads, however, aspired to the merits of originality; and as they were free from those salutary restraints by which the rash absurdity of wit is kept within due limits, they soon became outrageously original. There was no general feeling which it was necessary to conciliate by avoiding too wide a departure from habitual modes of thinking: – a restraint, as useful in the world of literature, as the rules of politeness are in common life. They addressed themselves to readers who had no fixed opinions of their own, and few of whom would dare object to anything which they saw in print . . . These gross and palpable deformities are diminishing; but the era of good taste and sound judgement has not yet arrived.[29]

Clearly this is a shift of ground, and the reasons for this are not easy to determine. Perhaps, in the interim, Jeffrey had read some more Goethe, or possibly he had read him for the first time. Perhaps, after all, he was afraid that Goethe did constitute a real threat to the tenets of literature of which he was the self-appointed protector. Whatever the reason, the German writer's position 'above his public' was no longer tolerated, and the 'habitual modes of thinking' to which Jeffrey had shown such apparent indifference in 1813 were now regarded as an essential aspect of literary propriety. Although Jeffrey's attitude to Goethe does mellow a little over the course of his two articles, it is clear that the 'fairyland' effect of *De l'Allemagne* had worn off. Goethe is described as the 'faithful representative of the general character of his country',[30] about which Jeffrey is far from flattering. Whereas formerly the philosophical disposition and versatility of the German writer were to be brandished in the face of French conservatism, the typical German writer, as exemplified by Goethe, was now to be held up as an illustration of literary bad manners:

The candidate for fame is at liberty to follow the doctrines of the Academy or the Portico, he may grasp the crown of roses, or aspire to the wreath of immortal bays. But when he has elected his province, he must be content to keep within it: he must not be an Epicurean whilst he bears the staff and wallet of the cynic; nor philosophize with Plato, whilst his brows are encircled with the voluptuous garland. The Germans are perpetually sinning against this plain and obvious precept; each individual labours out of his own vocation . . . The quality which Madame de Staël has termed the poetry of the soul, contributes in seducing them to disobey the warning voice of sober reason; it gives a morbid vivacity to their faculties; it turns them into day-dreamers and visionaries and mystics; and is the chief ingredient of those lamentable characteristics – the mingled rant and sickliness of German literature.[31]

This portentous concentration of love of scribbling and of scribbling vanity, distinguishes little minds, – and little minds too who move only in little circles; and it is therefore with surprise that we find that such a man as M. Goethe should so often betray an approximation to the weaknesses which ought to be confined wholly to the *roturiers* of literature, and that he seems to retain so many of the recollections of the parvenu. He appears to us to be always deficient in literary good-breeding – in literary decorum – in short, he does not display a real aristocratic feeling in his mind and habits.[32]

The first part of this particularly strongly recalls Jeffrey's criticism of *Cain* quoted above. Byron's transgressions were obviously greater and closer to home than Goethe's, but what is important is that both writers bring out the worst aspects of Jeffrey's conservatism. Jeffrey believed that poets should not be philosophers, that they should avoid the seductive and unreasonable 'poetry of the soul' (which he rather weakly attempts to associate with parvenu writing) and represent themselves as gentlemen of 'aristocratic feelings'. These 'rules' are based on the same fundamental maxim; that 'poets ought to be confined to the established creed and morality of their country', and that they should not deviate far from 'habitual modes of thinking: – a restraint, as useful in the world of literature, as the rules of politeness are in common life'. Neither Goethe nor Byron in *Cain* had written with a proper regard of his audience, or with an appreciation of his being a part of the public. They were poets of 'feverish fancies' and exhibited a public indifference that was both dangerous and indecorous.

As well as its association with Goethe, *Cain* broadly and somewhat frivolously lays claim to another literary relationship. Byron's object in calling *Cain* 'A Mystery' may be seen as another example of his ability to amuse himself whilst provoking or even offending his audience, as his Preface suggests:

The following scenes are entitled 'A Mystery', in conformity with the ancient title annexed to dramas upon similar subjects, which were styled 'Mysteries, or Moralities.' The author has by no means taken the same liberties with his subject which were common formerly, as may be seen by any reader curious enough to refer to these very profane productions, whether in English, French, Italian, or Spanish . . . With regard to the language of Lucifer, it was difficult for me to make him talk like a clergyman upon the same subjects; but I have done what I could to restrain him within the bounds of spiritual politeness.[33]

It is extremely unlikely that Byron ever read a mystery play, but his concept of one, and that in currency in his society, would have been fairly well defined, deriving largely from Dodsley's commentary in *A Select Collection of Old Plays* and from Warton's *History of English Poetry*. Neither Warton nor Dodsley represented the Mysteries in a particularly respectable light. Warton emphasizes their comic profanity:

It may also be observed, that many licentious pleasantries were sometimes introduced in these religious representations. This might imperceptibly lead

164

the way to subjects entirely profane and to comedy, and perhaps earlier than is imagined. In a Mystery of *The Massacre of the Holy Innocents* . . . tragical business is treated with the most ridiculous levity . . . It is in an enlightened age only that such subjects of scriptural history would be supported with proper dignity. But then an enlightened age would not have chosen such subjects for theatrical exhibition. It is certain that our ancestors intended no sort of impiety by these monstrous and unnatural mixtures. Neither the writers nor the spectators saw the impropriety, nor paid a separate attention to the comic and serious part of these motley scenes; at least they were persuaded that the solemnity of the subject covered or excused all incongruities. They had no just idea of decorum, consequently but little sense of the ridiculous: what appears to us to be the highest burlesque, on them would have made no sort of impression.[34]

Warton's discussion gives the distinct impression that the most signal aspect of the Mysteries was their tone of frivolous jocularity, which occasionally degenerated into 'obscenities'. Dodsley confirms this, but also states that the Mysteries were morally pernicious, and that the Moralities (Byron makes no distinction between the two in his Preface) to some extent were used as a public arena for theological controversies:

'Tis true the *Mysteries* of *Religion* were soon after this period made very free with all over Europe, being represented in so stupid and ridiculous a manner, that the stories of the New Testament in particular were thought to encourage Libertinism and Infidelity.[35]

For religion then was every one's concern and it was no wonder if each party employed all arts to promote it. Had they been in use now, they would doubtless have turned as much upon politics . . . in the more early days of the Reformation, it was so common for the partizans of the old doctrines (and perhaps also of the new) to defend and illustrate their tenets in this way, that in the 24th year of Henry VIII in an Act of Parliament made for the promoting of true Religion, I find a clause restraining all rimors or players from singing in songs, or playing in interludes, or anything that should contradict the established doctrines.[36]

To the average literary man of Byron's day, therefore, a Mystery play invoked connotations of immorality, profanity, comic bad taste, and possibly theological controversy. Yet the year before *Cain*'s publication, 1820, had seen the printing of a work which brought the subject of Mystery plays into contemporary literary, theological, and moral debate. This was William Hone's *The Apocry-*

phal New Testament. His *Ancient Mysteries Described* followed in 1823, and in the Introduction, most conveniently for our purposes, Hone outlines the effect of *The Apocryphal New Testament* on the public:

A memorable period in my humble existence is the occasion of the ensuing sheets. On the 19th of December 1817, the late Lord Chief Justice Ellenborough observed, that 'the first scenic performances were Mysteries or representations of incidents in Sacred Writ.' This remark induced me, about three years ago, to inquire somewhat on this subject; and in consequence of a perusal, accidentally simultaneous, of the religious Coventry Plays or Mysteries in the British Museum, and certain of the Apocryphal Gospels, together with the possession of engravings by old masters, from scenes common to each, I hastily compiled and published the volume entitled 'The Apocryphal New Testament.' Though my main purpose in producing it was, that for which I stated it to be of use, namely, to explain the subjects of pictures and prints that 'are without explanation from any other source,' and notwithstanding I conceived that, so far as the Gospels were concerned, it would be regarded as a work of mere curiosity, yet it was dexterously construed into a course of attack. The fierceness of the *Quarterly* in October 1821, roused me to answer the assailant.[37]

Hone's reply was eventually transformed into *Ancient Mysteries Described*. The *Quarterly*'s attack on Hone was indeed severe, and may help us form an impression of the climate into which *Cain* was projected: 'But in an age and country in which the great aim is to inspire juster and sounder views of religion, no motive but a mischievous one could have suggested the introduction of such impure and noxious matter to those who would never otherwise have heard of its existence.'[38]

Cain was written between July and September 1821, and therefore after *The Apocryphal New Testament*, but before the *Quarterly*'s assault and *Ancient Mysteries Described*. However, it is likely that Byron would have been aware of the reputation and substance of *The Apocryphal New Testament* (although he may not have read it) before the writing of *Cain*, and it would certainly have been no difficult task for him to have predicted the nature of its reception. For Hone's trials in 1817, for publishing blasphemous parodies against the Tory government, had made him a celebrity of the radical press. His acquittal had led Richard Carlile to reprint the parodies and an edition of the works of Paine, for which he was found guilty on six charges in November 1819. Byron also had other reasons for keeping a watchful eye on Hone. In 1816 Hone's pirated edition of *Lord Byron's Poems on His Domestic Circumstances* ran through fifteen editions, and he is the suspected author too of *A Sketch from Private Life*, a parody of Byron's invective upon Mrs Clermont. In 1817 he wrote and published a prose version of *The Corsair* entitled *Conrad, the Corsair*, and in 1819 he published (and perhaps wrote) *Don John or Don Juan Unmasked*. He also figures in later continuations of *Don Juan*. Before *Cain* was published, Byron's name had also been allied to Hone's in a pamphlet entitled *The Radical Triumvirate* by 'Oxonian' (1820).[39]

Whatever the extent of Byron's acquaintance with *The Apocryphal New Testament*, Hone's dealing in the Mysteries invested his subtitle for *Cain* with an even greater degree of perfidy. The *Quarterly*, still hot from its encounter with Hone, was not impressed:

The drama of 'Cain,' Lord Byron himself has thought proper to call a 'Mystery,' – the name which, as is well known, was given in our own country, before the reformation, to those scenic representations of the mysterious events of our religion, which, indecent and unedifying as they seem to ourselves, were perhaps, the principal means by which a knowledge of those events was conveyed to our rude and uninstructed ancestors. But except in the topics on which it is employed, Lord Byron's Mystery has no resemblance to those which it claims as its prototypes. These last, however absurd and indecorous in their execution, were, at least, intended reverently.[40]

The potential political threat of the drama did not go unnoticed, although ultimately the reviewer concluded that despite its atheism and Jacobinism ('the terms are convertible') *Cain* was unlikely to prove really damaging. Murray, too, apparently took fright at the word 'Mystery', according to a conversation recorded by Medwin:

'Heaven and Earth' was commenced at Ravenna on 9th October last . . . Douglas Kinnaird tells me that he can get no bookseller to publish it. It was offered to Murray; but he is the most timid of God's booksellers, and starts at the title. He has taken a dislike to that three syllabled word *Mystery*, and says, I know not why, that it is another 'Cain.'[41]

Byron's motive in entitling *Cain* 'A Mystery' was partly to scandalize his reader before he had even begun. There is reason, however, to consider *Cain*'s subtitle as stemming from Byron's confused use of *Faust* as a model. In a conversation of 1821 recorded by Medwin, Byron allegedly compared *Cain* to *Faust*, and remarked, 'Faust itself is not so fine a subject as Cain. It is a grand mystery.'[42]

Both this peculiar description and *Cain*'s unprecedented subtitle suggest that whilst attempting to imagine what *Faust* was like, Byron was recalling the first review of Goethe's drama published in this country, an article which appeared in the *Monthly Review* in 1810. The author, probably William Taylor,[43] took exception to *Faust*'s blend of levity and tragic gravity, and accounted for Goethe's lack of decorum by suggesting that he had used as his model a Mystery play popular in the sixteenth century entitled *Doctor Faustus*. He continued:

In what degree GOETHE has availed himself of the antient mystery in the composition of the comic tragedy before us, we know not; probably, he has adhered very closely to the general disposition of the scenes and incidents, but has almost wholly re-written the dialogue. At least, this would be the most plausible and charitable way of accounting for the uncouth though fanciful mixture of farce and tragedy, of profaneness and morality, of vulgarity and beauty, of obscenity and feeling, which alternately checquer this wild production of the *insanity*, shall we say, or of the *genius*, of its celebrated author?[44]

At a time when Byron was evidently deriving considerable enjoyment from shocking the reading public, it would appear to be a strong possibility that he recalled Taylor's 'charitable' hypothesis and affixed the subtitle to *Cain* as a somewhat tongue-in-cheek apology for its impropriety. Yet wherever the inspiration for *Cain*'s subtitle is to be found, it is clear that the reputation of the Mystery plays was such that it could be allied easily to the reputation of Goethe's *Faust*. Both were indecorous, and both, as far as the average English reader was concerned, were addressed to an unrefined audience. Both were offensive, too, in their peculiar and ambiguous blend of comedy and gravity. Indeed, it was this most conspicuous oddity that led William Taylor into proposing his rather eccentric hypothesis.

One more of *Cain*'s provocations remains to be discussed: Byron's use of Cuvier. The Preface suggests that the 'notion of Cuvier' was included merely as a caprice:

The reader will perceive that the author has partly adopted in this poem the notion of Cuvier, that the world had been destroyed several times before the creation of man. This speculation, derived from the different strata and the bones of enormous and unknown animals found in them, is not contrary to the Mosaic account, but rather confirms it.

Placed against the poem's image of mammoth-like spectres inhabiting Hell, it is clear that this whim afforded Byron some sport, and this is confirmed by his elaboration in the Preface: 'The assertion of Lucifer, that the Pre-Adamite world was also peopled by rational beings much more intelligent than man, and proportionally powerful to the mammoth etc., etc., is, of course, a poetical fiction to help him make out his case.'

The use of Cuvier may have been a whim, but it was by no means an idle one, for Byron was touching on an issue that was a particularly sensitive one in the early 1820s. A letter from Moore to Byron on the subject gives some idea of this sensitivity:

I could only pity – knowing from experience, how dreary are the doubts with which even the bright, poetic view I am myself inclined to take of mankind and their destiny is now and then clouded. I look upon Cuvier's book to be a most desolating one in the conclusions to which it may lead some minds. But the young, the simple – all those whose hearts one would like to keep unwithered, trouble their heads but little about Cuvier. You, however, have embodied him in poetry which every one reads; and, like the wind, blowing 'where you list,' carry this deadly chill, mixed up with your own fragrance into hearts that should be visited only by the latter. This is what I regret, and what, with all my influence, I would deprecate a repetition of. *Now*, do you understand me?[45]

Cuvier's book had first appeared in England in 1813 under the title *Theory of the Earth*, and was probably the most widely circulated book on diluvial theory in Britain at this time. The Preface was written by Robert Jameson, professor of natural history at Edinburgh, who elaborated upon the coincidence of Cuvier's theory of the deluge and the Mosaic account. This began a controversy of some length which caused Jameson to discard his references to Moses in the third edition of 1817.[46] The controversy was revived, however, after the inaugural lecture given by the Reverend William Buckland on his appointment as reader in geology at Oxford in 1819, and his simultaneous appointment to the newly created chair in geology at the Royal Society. The lecture was entitled *Vindiciae Geologicae, or, the Connexion of Geology with Religion Explained*, and Buckland stated that his objective was 'to show that the study of geology has a tendency to confirm the evidences of natural religion; and that the facts developed by it are consistent with the accounts of the creation and deluge recorded in the Mosaic writings'.[47] It has been suggested that Buckland got his chair under an unwritten agreement that he would support the Church if in turn it would encourage the study of geology, which at the time, of course, was a suspect science.[48] Nevertheless, there was a rising interest in geology and natural history in the third decade of the nineteenth century, and the leading reviews gave more space to natural history than to any other science during these ten years, despite its contentious reputation.[49] Other geologists of the time were apparently not so ready to sacrifice their academic integrity as was Buckland, and, once again, the subject of the coincidence of catastrophist theories of geological deposits and the Mosaic accounts of the flood became an issue for debate.

The relative novelty of this area of study allowed the ensuing debate to be a democratized one, and the subject attracted any number of laymen. Coleridge's notebooks, for example, reflect his interest in the two major controversies.[50] Byron's use of Cuvier, therefore, was far from esoteric. He was deliberately employing one of the most widely disputed theories of his time, and in doing so he made no effort to avoid the awkward questions it raised. *Cain* takes the central aspect of Cuvier's theory – that there had been at least one flood before the creation of man (a part of Cuvier's argument which Buckland disputed, incidentally) – and, with the gravity of the innocent artist, places it in a ridiculous light. Those who were engaged in the arguments which Buckland had instigated would have been forced to accept the spectacle of the pre-Adamite inhabitants of Hades, even to the extent of disputing its veracity.

In 1814, when he found himself accused of scheming to overthrow 'all religion and government', Byron was surprised – and secretly pleased, one suspects – at being thought 'a little Voltaire',[51] and shortly afterwards he is to be found deep in Bayle.[52] Although one or two of the notes to *Cain* refer to Bayle, Byron's interest in the tradition of radical thinking associated with the names of Bayle and Voltaire is not clearly reflected in the drama. Nevertheless, the fact that shortly before its composition Byron was complaining about the difficulties of getting a set of Bayle sent out to him[53] suggests that in his drama he was planning mischief of this rather old-fashioned kind. It is the mode of *Cain* that announces it to be of the nineteenth century, and Byron's dependence on his notion of Goethe in creating this mode may be seen as one means by which he attempted to modernize what he understood to be radical thinking. His introduction of Cuvier may be regarded as another. It is perhaps not surprising, in view of the ease of these assimilations, that Byron slips into negligent habits of writing and trivial habits of thinking. He has felt the powerful attraction of his contemporaries' confused conception of Goethe as a poet whose genius was demonstrated in the neglect of convention and decorum, and in doing so he may be seen as following a path pointed out to him by his early reviewers.

Matthew Arnold wrote that a poet

ought to know life and the world before dealing with them in poetry; and life and the world being in modern times very complex things, the creation of a modern poet, to be worth much, implies a great critical effort behind it . . . This is why Byron's poetry had so little endurance in it, and Goethe's so much.[54]

According to Arnold, Byron (and even Wordsworth) 'had their source in a great movement of feeling, not in a great movement of mind'.[55] Certainly, no great critical effort produced *Cain*: the use of Goethe and Cuvier and the gesture in the subtitle constitute clear negative evidence. The will to be modern is manifestly half-hearted and therefore incapable of stimulating a new critical awareness. Thus far Arnold is right, but *Cain* cannot be regarded as the product of a 'great movement of feeling'. The drama's method betrays Byron's awareness of the fact that he was providing poetry in which his public could recognize such a movement: it does not confirm his identification with it. The significant fact is that it claims to represent such a movement while revealing Byron to be no more than desultorily speculative about its nature. *Cain* shows him recognizing that his poetry could meet his contemporaries' demands without springing from any inner conviction. The extent to which the drama constitutes a critique of those demands, however, is extremely limited. The awareness that they could be met so easily may have induced cynicism, but the concession itself testifies to Byron's inability – or perhaps even his underlying reluctance – to reform the values which had supported his verse so well. Whilst a similar disregard for inner conviction can be detected in the Turkish Tales and *Manfred*, there is no sustained equivalent in *Childe Harold's Pilgrimage* and the three historical tragedies, where there is ample evidence of an effort to induce conviction in himself as well as his readers. *Cain* thus lies in the line of descent which runs through the Turkish Tales and *Manfred*, but here there is a much stronger sense of the poet's boredom with his poetry and with the character his society has given him. The obvious absence of 'critical effort' in the drama is not so much due to the inertia that the pretence of being the embodiment of such a movement induced. It is a tired run for the old style in which Byron finds a temporary antidote for his boredom in a willingness to risk the discovery of the triviality and abandon that lie behind the veneer of modernism. Yet because he knows that such a discovery is extremely unlikely, even this must be regarded as a self-deluding game.

8

Don Juan

Few have difficulty in reading *Don Juan*: the critical evidence suggests that the pleasurable act of reading is sufficient to stimulate useful commentary. In common with the rest of Byron's verse, however, *Don Juan* has been summarized and introduced by statements that sit very uneasily upon it. Bernard Blackstone, for example, begins by placing Byron in the company of Caesar and Napoleon, Shakespeare and Rabelais, in order to demonstrate how he 'clearly has the edge over even such brilliant reductions as Homer's, Dante's, or Milton's'.[1] Such claims and comparisons (Blackstone's chapter on *Don Juan* has many more) are liable to deflect the reader's interest away from the many useful suggestions he has to offer (the notion of the poem as dream, 'a series of dream situations', or the importance of 'eating and being eaten . . . buying and selling', for instance).[2] Robert Gleckner, on the other hand, insists on the schematic value of the poem, and follows George Ridenour in seeing *Don Juan* as being structured around 'endless repetitions of the Fall', claiming that it represents a coherent vision 'written from the point of view of the fallen, and this central fact determines both the form and style of the entire work'.[3]

On this kind of evidence, writing a commentary on *Don Juan* is a risky business: apparently the critic, sensing that he is in the presence of a masterpiece, often finds himself perplexed as to how he may provide a suitably substantial discussion. Seeing that the poetry needs no explication as such, he projects into it themes and concepts that do. There is a real difficulty here, for *Don Juan* certainly upsets habitual critical practices. To borrow a phrase of Eliot's, the poetry is 'of the surface . . . unconscious does not respond to unconscious; no swarms of inarticulate feelings are aroused',[4] and therefore, perhaps, the modern critic finds himself unassisted. When he turns his attention to Byron, Eliot is harsh but penetrating:

All things worked together to make *Don Juan* the greatest of Byron's poems. The stanza that he borrowed from the Italian was admirably suited to enhance his merits and conceal his defects, just as on a horse or in the water he was more at ease than on foot. His ear was imperfect, and capable only of crude effects; and in this easygoing stanza, with its habitually feminine and occasionally triple endings, he seems always to be reminding us that he is not really trying very hard and yet producing something as good as or better than that of the solemn poets who take their verse making more seriously . . . The continual banter and mockery, which his stanza and Italian model serve to keep constantly in his mind, serve as an admirable antacid to the high-falutin which in the earlier romances tends to upset the reader's stomach.[5]

This may be hard for most Byron scholars to accept (and perhaps that is why few have chosen to recognize the validity of Eliot's commentary), but it provides us with a sound introduction to *Don Juan*. In common with W. W. Robson, Eliot sees the correlation between the poet's weaknesses and strengths in his handling of *ottava rima*, and both critics also recognize that the poem is best seen not as a vehicle for conveying theories, attitudes, or themes, but as the result of Byron's discovery of a stanza. Perhaps it is possible to go further, and suggest that the stanza discovered Byron, or at least allowed him to discover himself, for it is not that he chanced upon a form that was perfect for his purposes. The mode in part determined those purposes, demonstrating to him even as he wrote where his strengths really were located. Just as the farcical rhyming and the stanza's movement guided him away from the compulsion to present himself as an emotional participant in the poem's events (as Eliot suggests), so the attitude that it dictated to him married happily with the latent attitudes of the early verse. *Don Juan* set Byron at ease with his art, not simply because it accommodated the ambivalence to which I have drawn attention throughout this book, nor just because it allowed him to affect an enjoyable insouciance, but because its genesis had nothing to do with appeasement. It was not written for Shelley, nor for the reviewers, nor for the public taste, but it allowed Byron to find that for which he had covetously sought in the illusions prompted by all these sources of inspiration – his independence. This makes way for the establishment of an authentic relationship between Byron and his verse, which here, uniquely, is his property, the fiction under complete control. The poetry created under these conditions exhilarates in the denial of its public's expectations and demands, and shows Byron's confidence in his powers of manipulation. The new-found assurance proceeds from the poet's delight in the new stanza form, but this in turn derives from the circumstances of its discovery.

The poem in its Italian context

At the time of *Beppo*'s composition, Byron's grasp of the history of Italian prosody was limited. As late as March 1818, we find him claiming that his poem's style is Italian, and that 'Berni is the original of all.'[6] Berni's work in *ottava rima*, however, was limited to his revision of Boiardo. By 1820, Byron had realized his error, writing in the Preface to his translation of Pulci that 'Pulci may be considered as the precursor and model of Berni altogether, as he has partly been to Ariosto, however inferior to both his copyists.' Both this and the preceding judgement that Boiardo in the original was 'too harsh' do not necessarily imply that Byron had made a study of the Italian poets by 1820. They are conventional opinions which probably derive from an article published in the *Quarterly Review* in 1819: a review of Frere's *Whistlecraft* and Rose's translation of Casti by Ugo Foscolo, which offered a historical survey of the Italian narrative poets.[7] Despite the unsatisfactory nature of Byron's comments on his Italian models, it would be a mistake to conclude that Italian poetry and society were lesser influences on the style of *Don Juan* than Frere. Frere undoubtedly alerted Byron to the possibilities of *ottava rima*, but his recognition of this potential originated in his acquaintance with the stanza in the context of his life in Italy.

We can be fairly certain that Byron learnt little from the literati, of whom Goethe has provided a useful description:

Conversations with them were wearisome. The moment one started talking about their national poetry, hoping for information on some point or other one could count on being asked which poet one considered the greatest – Ariosto or Tasso. If one gave the sensible answer and said that we should be grateful to God and Nature for having granted to one nation two such great men who have both in their different ways, given us such beautiful moments of comfort and delight, one satisfied nobody. Whichever of the two they had decided to prefer, they extolled to the skies and dismissed the other as being beneath contempt. At first I would try to defend the rejected one by pointing out his merits, but this had not the slightest effect. They had taken sides and therefore they stuck to their opinion . . . I realised that they had no real interest in poetry and that their pronouncements were mere empty phrases.[8]

Byron offers us nothing so detailed, but the Preface to *Childe Harold IV*, wherein he observes that 'The state of literary, as well as political party, appears to run, or *have* run, so high, that for a stranger to steer impartially between them is next to impossible', suggests that the literary milieu he found at Venice bore no essential difference from that which Goethe had encountered at Rome some years previously. His dismay at a rumoured Italian version of *Manfred* confirms this: 'I confess I wish that they would leave me alone, and not drag me into their arena as one of the gladiators, in a silly contest which I neither understand nor have ever interfered with, having kept clear of all their literary parties, both here and at Milan, and elsewhere.'[9] This makes it clear that whatever Byron learnt about Italian narrative in *ottava rima* owed nothing to contemporary Italian sophistication.

Outside of the context of the *conversazione*, however, Byron was subject to the same kind of attractions as many of his contemporary tourists. Although he tells us in *Childe Harold IV* that 'In Venice Tasso's echoes are no more, / And silent rows the songless gondolier' (iii), Hobhouse's note to these lines gives a full account of how he and Byron rowed to the Lido with two singers (a carpenter and a gondolier) chanting from Tasso. Similar accounts are offered by Goethe, Stendhal, and D'Israeli.[10] The facts that some tourists of this period were led to believe that they had found the last singers in Venice (see for instance D'Israeli's account and Rogers's *Italy*)[11] and that most reports of this period imply that these performances were extremely rare suggest that the singing of the gondoliers was tightly controlled by the strategies of a localized tourist trade. Goethe tells us that the performance 'has to be ordered in advance',[12] and whilst Hobhouse delicately avoids explaining how he and Byron arranged theirs, it is transparently clear that payment was involved:

The carpenter, however, who was the cleverer of the two, and was frequently obliged to prompt his companion, told us that he could *translate* the original. He added that he could sing almost three hundred stanzas, and he had not spirits (morbin was the word he used) to learn any more, or to sing what he already knew: a man must have idle time on his hands to acquire, or to repeat, and, said the poor fellow, 'look at my clothes and at me; I am starving.' This speech was more affecting than his performance.

Hobhouse adds that the chanting was not restricted to the gondoliers, and that 'several amongst the lower classes' knew a few stanzas, although these were hardly ever rendered voluntarily.[13]

Hearing Tasso in this way was perhaps not that important for Byron, but we know that Ariosto, no less than Tasso, was also chanted. It also seems likely that he would have heard both poets in different circumstances: Smollett was impressed by the ability of the Italians to memorize large pieces of Ariosto and Tasso, and to offer them, with musical accompaniment, as entertainment for guests.[14]

To attempt to discover what Byron read and when, therefore, might be a misleading strategy, for the impressions he received of Italian literature almost certainly filtered primarily through these living, oral contexts where poetry was offered as an entertainment, and applauded, no doubt, for the virtuosity of its rendering and its display of the powers of memory, or sold as a commodity to tourists, a given number of stanzas at a time. Even when confronted by the literati, Byron would probably have noticed a similar disregard for text and author, in the emphasis upon the emotional conviction and verbal dexterity of the speaker – that which Forsyth had described as the literati's 'well-managed talent of display and evasion'.[15] All of these things were liable to make more acute Byron's awareness of the fact that he had arrived in the culture of the *improvvisatore*, with its emphasis on performance and its shameless affectation of spontaneity and style. They bear a rather obvious approximate relation to the mode of *Don Juan*, and although none of them taken singly may have been to Byron's taste, they were nevertheless prominent features of a culture in which *ottava rima* enjoyed a peculiar ahistorical currency, proclaimed no less by the recitations of Ariosto than by the allusions to the old style in the reduced six-lined stanza of Casti.[16] This currency of Byron's verse form, its coming to him as an integral part of his Italian experience, is all-important.

At this point it is also worth hypothesizing how Byron would have conceived of the comic modes of Pulci and Ariosto, and to what extent this conception determines the mode and technique of *Don Juan*. Characterizing the comedy of Italian narrative verse was, and is, a challenging task: Foscolo's article on the subject makes it clear that the difficulty of defining the comedy of this tradition was one important reason why it was not accepted outside Italy as part of a classic European tradition,[17] and the academic debate on the subject continues.[18] Assuming that Byron found the style unfamiliar, at least in the first instance, and remembering that he lived in an era when the gradus was an important part of every gentleman's education, and when Bysshe's *Art of English Poetry* was liable to be found in that same gentleman's library, it is probable that the normal Italian rhyme of two syllables (*rima piana*) and the far less common rhyme of three syllables (*rima sdrucciola*), neither of which is intrinsically comic, could sound so to his ears. Byron's fluency in Italian may have allowed him to know better, and the comic effects of these rhymes therefore would have demanded conscious refutation, and this, I suggest, may have been sufficient to introduce into his reading (or his listening or recitation) an element of facetious detachment. This does not mean of course, that he would have found Petrarch or Dante comic. It means that when encountering verse that he knew to be comic, yet where the precise location of the comedy was unclear, the rhymes peculiar to his English ear were likely to receive an exaggerated comic emphasis. And where the comic effects of Pulci, Ariosto, Boiardo, or Berni were more obvious, they were likely to have been heightened by his reception of the rhymes.

This is perhaps the source of the games played with polysyllabic rhyming in *Don Juan*, and Byron may not differ much in this respect from Frere or Rose, who, we may assume, followed a similar path. But Byron produced something far more memorable than a clever *jeu d'esprit* because of his own historical circumstances. It is not difficult to see how such lines as Ariosto's 'Non piú, Signor, non piú di questo Canto; / ch'io son già rauco, e vo' posarmi alquanto'[19] would have sounded both quaint and facetious in an age when massive printings had made the manuscript and oral traditions extinct, whereas in fact it was written as a recognized form of leave-taking. And if we imagine such lines to have been recited by a ragged carpenter who is using them as a convenient means of requesting payment for a further fifty stanzas, to a poet who cannot help but see in this a crazy paradigm of his own relationship to his verse, then the comic effects and attractions are multiplied. Under such circumstances Byron would have been amused by the speaker's utter indifference to his material, but he would also have sensed in that material something of which the speaker remained oblivious – the versification of aristocratic table-talk:

> Ben furo avventurosi i cavallieri
> ch'erano a quella età, che nei valloni,
> ne le scure spelonche e boschi fieri,
> tane di serpi, d'orsi e di leoni,
> trovanan quel che nei palazzi altieri
> a pena or trovar puon giudici buoni;

donne, che ne la lor piú fresca etade
sien degne d'aver titol di beltade.[20]

Ariosto's verse, like Pulci's, necessarily embraced the spoken idiom, but, more important, it incorporated the exclusive intimacy in which it was read. The attraction of this quality to a poet so ill at ease with his public, so anxious to preserve illusions of his independence, is easily realized.

Any transposition of this mode into nineteenth-century English necessitated a radical transformation, and Byron had the experience of writing the early stanzas of *Childe Harold* to remind him of this. The citation of Ariosto as a precedent in the Preface to *Childe Harold I & II* (a precedent for the 'full scope' granted to 'inclination' and 'humour') is by no means sleight-of-hand: it demonstrates Byron's awareness of the common element in the styles of Thomson and Ariosto – that which proceeds from the poet's consciousness of his limited audience, its tastes, and its familiarity with certain poetic models. Looking back upon *Childe Harold I & II*, Byron must have seen it as a most ironic failure, or an equally ironic success. The attempt in the early parts to produce a quasi-comic mode that was perfectly suited to a limited audience and a privileged poet he would recognize to have been totally ignored by the massive readership which the poem's publication discovered. Writing *Beppo* and *Don Juan* for this massive readership, Byron is therefore not going to be seduced by the same illusions about his audience: the Lyttelton circle is as dead for him as that of Lorenzo de' Medici or Cardinal Hippolytus. When attempting to translate Pulci in 1820, however, Byron is forced to return to something approximating to the Thomsonian manner:

> The abbot said, 'The steeple may do well,
> But, for the bells, you've broken them, I wot.'
> Morgante answer'd, 'Let them pay in hell
> The penalty who lie dead in yon grot;'
> And hoisting up the horse from where he fell,
> He said, 'Now look if I the gout have got,
> Orlando, in the legs – or if I have force,' –
> And then he made two gambols with the horse.
>
> (*Morgante Maggiore*, I, lxxiii)

The reversion to the archaic 'I wot' and its quaint rhyme with 'grot' remind us far more of *Childe Harold I* than of *Don Juan*, and seem mysteriously unprecedented at this point in Byron's translation. It is to be explained by his recognition that the style of the facetious eighteenth-century Spenserians was the nearest familiar English equivalent to Pulci's self-conscious sophisticated humour:

> Disse l'abate: – Il campanil v'è bene,
> ma le campane voi l'avete rotte. –
> Dicea Morgante: – E' ne porton le pene
> color che morti son là in quelle grotte. –
> E levossi il cavallo in su le schiene,
> e disse: – Guarda s'io sento di gotte,
> Orlando, nelle gambe, o s'io lo posso. –
> E fe' duo salti col cavallo addosso.

(Pulci, *Morgante Maggiore*, I, lxxiii)[21]

'Grotte' and 'rotte' were acceptable Italian rhymes; Dante uses them, for instance, rhyming with 'notte' (*Purgatorio*, I, 44, 46, 48). Pulci's use of 'gotte' (gout), therefore, is to be seen as a sophisticated piece of indecorum, introduced for the enjoyment of his cultivated audience, in a similar manner to his rhyming of 'l'uova' (eggs) with 'pruova' and 'ritruova' (I, lxviii) (see Petrarch 154 and Dante, *Paradiso*, VIII, 139, 141, XXVI, 32, 36, and *Inferno*, VIII, 122, 126).[22] Obviously, Byron can make nothing of this in English, but his reversion to a mode that is reminiscent of his emulation of Thomson is symptomatic of his frustration at the lack of a contemporary equivalent for Pulci's circle of readers.

Don Juan nevertheless testifies that Byron found a way to capitalize on the potential of Pulci's farcical rhyming, by avoiding the temptation to find an equivalent for Pulci's literary jokes, exaggerating instead the comic effects of polysyllabic rhyming, and transforming gestures belonging to an oral tradition by placing them in a new context. The making of this new context, Byron's distinctive handling of *ottava rima*, is achieved through his conviction that the stanza is his own, his sense of real possession. *Don Juan* may have been suggested to Byron by his reading of Frere, but ultimately this had little to do with it: the conviction with which the poem was written derived from Byron's placing of the stanza within his day-to-day life in Italy. Having heard *ottava rima* in streets, in gondolas, after dinner, extempore or memorized, it must have been impossible for him to dislocate it from these living associations.

The setting of *Beppo* in the Venetian carnival testifies to this. Byron continually alludes to the carnival in the letters from Venice, and it seems reasonable to conjecture that it is given such prominence because it signified the strong sense of liberation which he found in his Venetian existence. Here Byron thought he had found 'life', emancipated from the stifling conventions and habits of thinking that predominated over the rest of Europe:

Their moral is not your moral – their life is not your life – you would not understand it – it is not English nor French – nor German – which you would all understand – the Conventual education – the Cavalier Servitude – the habits of thought and living are so entirely different – and the difference becomes so much more striking the more you live intimately with them – that I know not how to make you comprehend a people – who are at once temperate and profligate – serious in their character and buffoons in their amusements . . . They go to the theatre to talk – and into company to hold their tongues . . . Their best things are the Carnival balls – and masquerades – when everybody runs mad for six weeks. – After their dinners and suppers they make extempore verses – and buffoon one another – but it is in a humour which you would not enter into – ye of the North.

This comes from a letter in which Byron is refusing Murray's request to write something on the manners of Italy: having lived in the Italians' houses, he says, he will not 'make a book of them'.[23] This is one piece of evidence through which we can perceive Byron's resistance to the conventional English curiosity about men and manners. Clearly, he has no wish to assist those who aspired to affect a cosmopolitan liberalism, or to reinforce evangelical prejudices, and neither has he any desire to produce a book for those who merely want to be amused. To Byron, Italy was far more than a pleasant distraction; his life in Venice offered him an important liberation. For the first time he found himself in a position where his social life was not directed by his literary reputation. Here the invitations he received were primarily the consequence of a recognition of his rank and residence, whereas in London his eminence and access to fashionable society had depended, not upon the recognition of his aristocratic peers, but upon the recognition of those people who had purchased the first two cantos of *Childe Harold*. His place in society was the result of his appeasing the tastes of the upper-middle classes, and his exile the result of their moral righteousness.

In Venice Byron found himself liberated into what seemed to him to be the richness of life, typified by the liberation of the carnival, 'when everybody runs mad for six weeks'.[24] Bakhtin, who writes interestingly on Goethe's response to the Roman carnival, sees a special use for the word 'carnivalesque' which is of relevance here:

Carnival is a well-known festivity that has often been described throughout many centuries. Even during its later development in the eighteenth and nineteenth centuries it still preserved certain fundamental traits in a quite clear, though reduced, form. Carnival discloses those traits as the best preserved fragments of an immense, infinitely rich world. This permits us to use precisely the epithet 'carnivalesque' in that broad sense of the word. We interpret it not only as carnival per se in its limited form, but also as the varied popular-festive life of the Middle Ages and the Renaissance; all the peculiarities of this life have been preserved in carnival, while the other forms have deteriorated.[25]

Although this is of especial pertinence to Goethe, given his interest in popular-festive forms, and although moving from the *Italian Journey* to Byron's documentation of his Italian experience we can only be disappointed by the relative superficiality of the response, Bakhtin provides a perspective analysis of a case which, however different, is analogous to Byron's.[26] We are not likely to find Byron articulating it, but the life of the carnival which was evidently of such importance to him was recognizably 'the best preserved fragments of an immense, infinitely rich world'. For his Italian experience owed many of its positive attractions to Venice's cultural insularity, an insularity which preserved not only the social order of the close of the sixteenth century, but also customs and conventions (including the carnival, the *improvvisatore*, and the oral traditions of poetry) that stretched back to the early Renaissance and beyond. Most important, the metre of Ariosto, Pulci, Boiardo, and Berni was the metre which embodied the vestiges of that world, and, like the carnival, it was woven into the fabric of Byron's everyday Venetian existence, presenting itself therefore as his means of incorporating this experience into a poetic world view. Bakhtin suggests of Goethe's response to the Roman carnival that

Beyond the isolated, apparently unrelated foolish pranks, obscenities, and coarse familiarity of carnival, and also in its complete lack of seriousness the poet sensed a single viewpoint on the world and a single style. He discovered this unity, even though he did not find a clear, theoretic expression for it in his concluding lines.[27]

Although we have from Byron no such carefully documented analysis of his 'carnivalesque' Venetian life as Goethe's description of the Roman carnival, we do have the relatively sudden appearance of *Beppo* and *Don Juan*; poems which announce more boldly than Goethe's reflections that their poet has discovered in an ostensibly non-serious mode 'a single viewpoint on the world and a single style', even though that viewpoint may not make explicit the kind of profundity that Goethe offers.

Because of its insularity, Venice had been preserved from the social divisions that had denied Byron his aristocratic independence in England. With its major social division firmly established between the lower and middle classes, nineteenth-century England not only precluded a specifically aristocratic culture, but the vestiges of that cultural milieu (in which Byron doubtlessly placed himself) found itself dictated to by the tenets of middle-class seriousness, that which Byron chose to call 'cant'. In one sense, the history of his poetry may be understood as a series of unhappy attempts to come to terms with this seriousness through a strange mixture of reaction and compliance. In Venice, as the exuberance of the letters demonstrates, Byron was able to assert a new-found independence in his daily conduct, this freedom manifesting itself most obviously in his relationships with women. It is not the sexual freedom itself which is of significance, but the fact that to Byron it confirmed his position as a privileged gentleman who was directly accountable to no one:

I have a world of other harlotry – besides an offer of the daughter of the Arlechino of St Luke's theatre – so that my hands are full – whatever my Seminal vessels may be – With regard to Arpelice Terucelli (the Madcap above mentioned) – recollect there is no *liaison* only *fuff-fuff* and passades – & fair fucking – you may easily suppose I did not much heed her Austrian Dragon – who may do as he likes and be damned. – I have taken part of the Mocenigo Palace for three years (on the Grand Canal) and have been much among the Natives since you went – particularly at the *Benzona's* – who is a kind of Venetian (late) Lady Melbourne. – Recollect my demands – *money* – *monies* – tooth powder – Magnesia – Soda powders – Spooney's papers – & good news of you & yours always and ever.[28]

Most important, this confidence informs *Beppo*, the subject of which is the storyteller and the storyteller's new attitude: the manner of his narration compels us to attend not to its events, but to his allusions to his own behaviour and his virtuosity in handling the stanza. What has happened in the poem is partly the result of Byron's transposition of the effects of the Italian oral performance, with its inevitable focus on manner rather than matter, on to the printed page, but primarily *Beppo* draws on the carnival atmosphere, with its masks and anonymity (Byron's name, we remember, was not put to the poem when first published) permitting new kinds of freedom, and demanding conduct that is consciously the inverse of conventional behaviour. This allows Byron, albeit anonymously, to do all that is not expected of him: the poet of passionate tales is transformed into the raconteur preoccupied with his own mannerisms, happy to postpone the narrative in favour of the rehearsal of his gestures; the most celebrated poet of the day finds room to expose his habit of frivolous rhyming, and to sneer at the kind of production which had made him famous – 'those pretty poems never known to fail . . . samples of the finest Orientalism' (li). It is the atmosphere of the Venetian carnival which offers Byron the opportunity to don this mask, but what we have seen in the Turkish Tales particularly (and Byron's reference to them in the poem can hardly be regarded as accidental) might cause us to prefer a reversal of the metaphor, and recognize in *Beppo* an unmasking rather than the adoption of a disguise.

The bad conscience that is evident in *Beppo*'s allusion to the history of Byron's popularity marks the emergence of his independence not only as an aristocrat, but also as a producer of verse. Indeed, ultimately the two cannot be separated. This independence is not wholly asserted until *Don Juan*, where we can appreciate the penetration of Leavis's observation that 'the very essence of his manner is a contemptuous defiance of decorum and propriety'.[29] *Beppo* retains an apologetic decorum, albeit facetiously:

> But I am but a nameless sort of person,
> (A broken Dandy lately on my travels)
> And take for Rhyme, to hook my rambling verse on,
> The first that Walker's Lexicon unravels

(lii)

The 'defiance of decorum and propriety' that emerges with the adoption of *ottava rima* does not mean that we can regard *Beppo* as the point at which Byron simply takes stock of his former poetic performance and revokes its pretensions and compromises in the light of a new freedom discovered in a new culture. The new form dictates the new attitude; the 'single viewpoint' proceeds from the 'single style', which to Byron was essentially non-serious and, moreover, non-English. In this sense the stanza is the means by which Byron discovers a new way of looking at the world, or rather a new way of presenting his relationship to the world and his audience without compromising his independence. It must be stressed that the attitudes rehearsed in *Beppo* and developed in *Don Juan* are defined partly by the stanza's movement. Outside the *ottava rima* poems the attempts to reproduce them result in something quite different. Here in *The Island*, for instance, written in 1823, Byron is obviously attempting to reproduce the kind of digression that characterized the mode of *Don Juan*:

> Sublime tobacco! which from east to west
> Cheers the tar's labour or the Turkman's rest;
> Which on the Moslem's ottoman divides
> His hours, and rivals opium and his brides;
> Magnificent in Stamboul, but less grand,
> Though not less loved, in Wapping or the Strand
>
> (II, 448–53)

The movement of the couplet is tyrannical, demanding something that sounds more like the parodies of Hawkins Browne than *Don Juan*. Something similar can be found in *Mazeppa*:

> It was a court of jousts and mimes,
> Where every courtier tried at rhymes;
> Even I for once produced some verses,
> And sign'd my odes 'Despairing Thyrsis.'
>
> (151–4)

But the impossibility of continuing in this vein leads Byron to produce verse of another kind, wherein the symptoms of his indifference are equally obvious:

> With glossy skin, and dripping mane,
> And reeling limbs, and reeking flank,
> The wild steed's sinewy nerves still strain
> Up the repelling bank.
>
> (601–4)

> Onwards we went – but slack and slow;
> His savage force at length o'erspent,
> The drooping courser, faint and low,
> All feebly foaming went.
>
> (625–8)

It is significant that the attempt to capitalize on the experience of writing *Beppo* in *Mazeppa* places Byron finally in a position where the most obvious means of doing so is by reviving the games of the Turkish Tales. A glance at *Mazeppa* and *The Island* confirms the importance of *ottava rima* in preventing Byron from falling back upon old models. Indecorum and impropriety may come fairly readily to a man with a propensity to aristocratic insouciance, but successfully transferring this attitude through the medium of English poetic models, as almost the whole of Byron's *oeuvre* outside of the *ottava rima* poems testifies, inevitably results in compromise.

Don Juan and the contemporary reader

If Hazlitt's distressed and emotional response to *Don Juan* is typical of a contemporary reaction (as the evidence of the reviews suggests), then Byron succeeded in creating a poem that assaulted its predominantly middle-class audience with a display of aristocratic irresponsibility. *Beppo* was innocuous, apologetic even, but *Don Juan* is not so polite; from its very beginning the reader is aware of the claim Byron makes upon the poem's voice as his own, a voice that not only announces a languid indifference to the epic task in hand, but also carefully reminds the reader of its social and educational qualifications. The pieces of Greek and Latin and the allusions to classical writers are not to be seen as Byron's anxious declaration of his credentials. They are facetiously handled, reminders to the reader that this is a poem by Lord Byron of Newstead, Harrow, and Cambridge, whose education and rank allow him to treat the writers of antiquity with exclusive familiarity ('Most epic poets plunge *in medias res* / (Horace makes this the heroic turnpike road)' (I, 6)). This kind of treatment, however much it derives from an extension of public schoolboy humour, alienates and disconcerts the average reader of Byron's period (who is neither a poet nor a lord nor from a public school), and is markedly different from the non-excluding classical references in *Childe Harold III & IV*, points of information offered almost patronizingly, with peculiarly pedantic annotations. Hazlitt, with typical shrewdness, noted the analogy between the manner of *Don Juan* ('the satire of a person of birth and quality') and the 'coarse facetious familiarity' of the letters to Bowles and Roberts.[30] These indeed are the terms established between Byron and his reader in *Don Juan*. The poem's garrulousness soon sheds the *Beppo*-like air of gossip occasionally seen in the first canto, and becomes far more of a display of the kind of conversational talent – sometimes risqué, sometimes obscene, sometimes offered in a spirit of mock sagacity, but always supremely confident – that is to be associated with the table-talk of an elitist minority. Its *bon mots* are not necessarily clever –

> I said the smallpox had gone out of late;
> Perhaps it may be followed by the great.
>
> (I, 130)

– but they are pronounced with an after-dinner hauteur that is not acceptable in a predominantly bourgeois culture.

To suggest that *Don Juan* 'shows us life as viewed by a brilliant exponent of worldly commonsense'[31] is extremely misleading: what may have been mistakenly recognized as 'commonsense' is in fact a flaunting of a deliberately facetious and essentially non-serious way of coming to terms with the world. Those who believe Byron's claim that the 'illusion' of his youthful emotion has been replaced by a 'deal of judgement' (I, 215) are mercilessly teased by its apparent application:

> Oh ye who teach the ingenuous youth of nations,
> Holland, France, England, Germany or Spain,
> I pray ye flog them upon all occasions;
> It mends the morals, never mind the pain.
>
> (II, 1)

Similarly, there is nothing 'sensible' about

> for she was one
> Fit for the model of a statuary
> (A race of mere imposters, when all's done;
> I've seen much finer women, ripe and real,
> Than all the nonsense of their stone ideal).
>
> (II, 118)

Like so many of the interposed remarks of *Don Juan*, this is not a considered statement, but primarily a swaggering allusion to Byron's experience, made in the face of an audience whose first inclination is towards solemnity and the defence of proper behaviour. It is a gesture that announces the poet's aristocratic independence, that which allows him a kind of licence from which the middle classes are excluded, proclaimed here as surely as it is in the occasional pieces of bad taste masquerading as satire:

> Timbuctoo travels, voyages to the poles
> Are ways to benefit mankind, as true
> Perhaps as shooting them at Waterloo.
>
> (I, 132)

The parenthetical placing of this is Byron's means of defining his relationship to its sentiment: rather than being conceived of as a piece of satire, therefore, it must be seen as a demonstration of his expansiveness, a piece of provocative irresponsibility.

Byron himself claimed that 'the soul' of *Don Juan* was its licence, and his qualification of this famous remark helps us to define precisely how this licence is exercised: 'at least the liberty of that licence if one likes – not that one should abuse it – it is like trial by jury and Peerage – and the Habeas Corpus – a very fine thing – but chiefly in the *reversion* – because no one wishes to be tried for the mere pleasure of proving his possession of the privilege'.[32] And *Don Juan* is not an indulgent poem. Its success derives partly from its restraint in demonstrating Byron's rights of access without ever exploiting them to excess. His confidence in his restraint, no doubt, is that which supplies his defences of the poem with their characteristic vigour. For *Don Juan* includes nothing like this:

> Now, I'll put out my taper
> (I've finished my paper
> For these stanzas you see on the *brink* stand)
> There's a whore on my right
> For I rhyme best at Night
> When a C—t is tied close to *my Inkstand*.[33]

Just as *Beppo* avoids a gratuitous description of the events of the Venetian carnival, so *Don Juan* succeeds in conveying the sense of its poet's worldly experience without ever describing it. Thus Byron's famous defence of the poem based upon the benefit of his experience ('Could any man have written it – who has not lived in the world? – and tooled in a post-chaise? in a hackney coach? in a Gondola?')[34] and his repeated protests that Prior, Pope, and Little (Moore) were more explicitly immoral amount to a serious insistence that we recognize *Don Juan*'s skilful employment of gestures alluding to his experience. These may be of a blatant nature:

> but never was there planned
> A dress through which the eyes give such a volley,
> Excepting the Venetian *fazzioli*.
>
> (II, 7)

or rather subtle:

> Think you, if Laura had been Petrarch's wife,
> He would have written sonnets all his life?

(III, 8)

or delivered in the form of a mock aphorism:

> You will find
> Though sages may pour out their wisdom's treasure,
> There is no sterner moralist than pleasure.

(III, 65)

But whatever their form they are always restrained: the marks of an aristocrat demonstrating his gentlemanly relationship to his fund of worldly experience by his refusal to attempt anything approximating to its recreation.

In this sense *Don Juan* anticipates and plays provocatively upon the evangelical piety that resided in a significant proportion of its readers. The mad and bad Lord Byron that they wanted to see cannot be secured for the accusations and inquisitions: he struts somewhere beyond the poem, parading his misdeeds and his blasphemies, and we are constantly made aware of his presence, but he rarely, if ever, commits his cardinal sins within the poem itself. Hence the mischievous delight, the supreme confidence, of such adopted stances as these:

> And Julia sate with Juan, half embraced
> And half retiring from the glowing arm,
> Which trembled like the bosom where 'twas placed.
> Yet still she must have thought there was no harm,
> Or else 'twere easy to withdraw her waist.
> But then the situation had its charm,
> And then – God knows what next – I can't go on;
> I'm almost sorry that I e'er begun.

(I, 115)

> Haidée and Juan were not married, but
> The fault was theirs, not mine. It is not fair,
> Chaste reader, then in any way to put
> The blame on me, unless you wish they were.
> Then if you'd have them wedded, please to shut
> The book which treats of this erroneous pair,
> Before the consequences grow too awful;
> 'Tis dangerous to read of loves unlawful.

(III, 12)

Hence too the fact that Don Juan is always seduced, never the seducer. Contrary to all expectations, the poem does not celebrate a libertine hero. It is provocative but not outrageous, suggestive rather than explicit, the art of allusion rather than that of ostentation. Through almost the whole poem, Byron maintains his equanimity and restraint, refusing to be drawn into a position wherein he would be forced to defend himself against his moralistic adversaries in a combat fought on their own terms.

Don Juan consistently denied the demands and expectations of the contemporary reader. It did not give them what they really wanted to disapprove of (hence the poem's misrepresentation) any more than it provided them with what was dictated by contemporary tastes. Its gentlest denials perhaps are its habitual digressions and its employment of bathos; its harshest, possibly, the savage destruction of the Haidée episode. But its most consistent means of disturbing the reader's preconceptions are Byron's proclamations of indifference, most commonly declared in his representation of the creative act as being governed by his whimsy. Our full appreciation of this manifestation of Byron's independent control depends upon a recognition of the continuity between the newly declared attitude and the conditions under which the earlier verse was written. Thus the characteristic leave-taking of Ariosto, perhaps transformed and given a new emphasis by the manner and circumstances of a recitation in nineteenth-century Venice, is transformed once again by the poet of the Turkish Tales:

> In the meantime, without proceeding more
> In this anatomy, I've finished now
> Two hundred and odd stanzas as before,
> That being about the number I'll allow
> Each canto of the twelve or twenty-four;
> And laying down my pen, I make my bow
>
> (II, 216)

> I feel this tediousness will never do;
> 'Tis being too epic, and I must cut down
> (In copying) this long canto into two.
> They'll never find it out, unless I own
> The fact, excepting some experienced few,
> And then as an improvement 'twill be shown.
>
> (III, 111)

The adaptation of the mannerism pleases Byron because it is so

appropriate to his unique circumstances. This is the root of his
confidence, by which the gesture expands into the pervasive characteristic attitude given free rein in the poem:

> A fourth as marble, statue-like and still,
> Lay in a breathless, hushed, and stony sleep,
> White, cold and pure, as looks a frozen rill,
> Or the snow minaret on an Alpine steep,
> Or Lot's wife done in salt – or what you will.
> My similes are gathered in a heap,
> So pick and choose; perhaps you'll be content
> With a carved lady on a monument.
>
> (VI, 68)

We know from a reading of *Childe Harold* and the Turkish Tales that
Byron's habits of composition have undergone no radical transformation, but the new stanza allows him to move beyond his trivial
games, and in permitting the proclamation of this attitude demands
so much more of him technically.

This aspect of *Don Juan* has received ample attention elsewhere,
and it is not my purpose here to document it, therefore, but to point
to the continuity between the poem's affected attitudes and the 'real'
attitudes of the early verse – the tales in particular. Yet the burlesque treatment of poetic conventions is not an end in itself, nor a
by-product of a prevalent attitude, but an essential part of the relationship established between Byron and the events of his narrative,
in which the reader's tastes and expectations are only considered
antithetically. The poem was not concerned with what its contemporary reader wanted, but it consistently, although not wholly, provided what was not wanted. Ostensibly, Byron writes what he will
and the reader must take it as he pleases, but in effect the events of
the narrative itself and Byron's method of presenting it frequently
allow him little choice. In this sense the real strengths of *Don Juan*
are to be found in its narrative.

Don Juan as narrative

If we are to restrict our claims for *Don Juan* to its burlesque, its
impropriety, or its shock value, then it is hard to see how it can be
represented as anything other than a piece of glorious tomfoolery.
Leavis is right to characterize Byron's *ottava rima* manner as 'a con-

temptuous defiance of decorum and propriety' in his discussion of
The Vision of Judgement, but when we are confronted with *Don Juan*,
we are confronted with a narrative about which we have to say much
more. Byron has been given scant credit for the narrative successes of
his poem: too frequently it is described as a satire and the emphases
placed accordingly on the English cantos and the satiric interpolations elsewhere. The intermittent attacks on Wordsworth and
Coleridge may be well presented, but they represent only a very mild
form of cleverness (the cleverness in fact depends on the affectation
of crassness, and the ability to make room for this within the artefact). To one critic, apparently, they are instrumental in suggesting that 'the whole point of *Don Juan* was to attack the "Romantic"
position especially'.[35] The implications do the poem no credit. By
1818, its 'Romantic' jokes were up to twenty years old, so standardized, in fact, that Peacock had no difficulty in cataloguing them
when discussing the common techniques of the reviewers:

Yet on examination these excellent jokes reduce themselves to some half
dozen, which have been repeated through every number of every review of
the bulk of periodical criticism to the present day . . . One of these is the
profundity of the Bathos. There is in the lowest deep a lower still, and the
author in question (be he who he may) has plunged lower than anyone before
him. Another is that the work in question is a narcotic, and sets the unfor-
tunate critic to sleep. A third is that it is unintelligible, and that true no-
meaning puzzles more than wit. A fourth, that the author is insane. It cannot
be denied that this is super-excellent wit which can bear so much repetition
without palling, for there is not any number of any review which does not
contain them all at least once, and sometimes six or seven times.[36]

The reader of *Don Juan* will be familiar with most of these
witticisms. Even the highly enjoyable Preface to Cantos I and II,
wherein Byron parodies Wordsworth's Preface to 'The Thorn',
derives directly from Jeffrey's ridiculing of the same poem and its
prefatory apparatus in a well-known review of Crabbe.[37] The fact is
that in the attacks on his contemporaries Byron depends heavily on
stock material, and the limited resources betray a very limited
viewpoint, and suggest that the animosity was affected rather than
deeply felt. Moving from here to that part of the poem's satire that
has received ample attention, the English cantos, an increased
sophistication is immediately obvious:

> Smart uniforms and sparkling coronets
> Are spurned in turn, until her turn arrives,

> After male loss of time and hearts and bets
> Upon the sweepstakes for substantial wives.
> And when at last the pretty creature gets
> Some gentleman who fights or writes or drives,
> It soothes the awkward squad of the rejected
> To find how very badly she selected.

(XII, 36)

Undoubtedly these cantos offer many localized successes of a similar nature, but from Canto XIII the poem begins to decline. Cantos X and XI show the traces of Byron's relief at extricating Juan from Catherine's court (where clearly he could do little with him) in the exhilaration of the ride into London, the expertly rendered highwayman episode, and the *ubi sunt* passage, fed with nostalgia, yet restrained by the awareness that, however disturbing the changes may be, what has passed is not to be seen as a race of heroes. Thus Castlereagh finds himself alongside Napoleon, Romilly alongside Whitbread, and even Johanna Southcote has a place here. Byron is evidently moved, even perplexed, by the passage of events in his day, but he never degenerates into sentimentality, finding instead the independently conceived voice of cynical detachment:

> But how shall I relate in other cantos
> Of what befell our hero in the land,
> Which 'tis the common cry and lie to vaunt as
> A moral country? but I hold my hand,
> For I disdain to write an *Atlantis*.
> But 'tis well at once to understand:
> You are not a moral people, and you know it
> Without the aid of too sincere a poet.

(XI, 87)

This anticipates the tone of the canto which follows, in which Byron declines to moralize upon the state of the marriage market, wryly accepting and facetiously condoning the prevalence of commercialism, and concentrating on the absurdity of its rituals and pettymindedness. It also adequately summarizes the extent of his satiric animus, which, in the context of what follows, must be taken completely seriously. For the Peacockian framework which Byron adopts for his house party suggests once again an unimaginative dependence upon a stock model. He arranges his crotcheteers for the kill only to discover that the mode of his poem allows him to do nothing with them, a fact that has enabled Howard Mills to make a claim for Peacock's supremacy over Byron as a satirist.[38] The loss of narrative impulse in these later cantos weakens the poem, and is hardly compensated for by the recourse to farce:

> Back fell the sable frock and dreary cowl
> And they revealed, alas, that ere they should,
> In full, voluptuous, but not o'ergrown bulk,
> The phantom of her frolic Grace – Fitz-Fulke!

(XVI, 123)

Placing Juan in England deprives Byron of the scope which his poem had previously exploited so successfully, and the damaging consequences of his boredom with his subject have been astutely summarized:

great art cannot be made out of a boredom with oneself, which is expressed as a boredom with one's subject-matter; and the later cantos of *Don Juan*, which are the finest and most mature parts of the poem, are also, significantly, the parts in which that distaste, that boredom, is becoming a settled attitude.[39]

But the later cantos of *Don Juan* are not the finest precisely because of the reasons here stipulated. The achievement of *Don Juan* is to be recognized in the first eight cantos, where the digressions are not really made because of the poet's inability to conceive of his narrative's direction, whatever he may claim, and where Byron consistently establishes his right not to express the kind of feelings that his readers might expect. Thus disburdened, Byron's narrative skills are able to create the peculiarly fascinating and unique world of *Don Juan*, a world viewed through Italianate, ostensibly non-serious eyes, a world purged of its emotional complexities, and yet capable of fully evoking its events. The affectation of acceptable or legitimized emotional responses to events within real experience or otherwise is avoided. In *Don Juan* the avoidance of conventional models and subjects is an abjuration of stock responses, and the world which emerges out of the poet's apparent nonchalance is a transfigured one, thrown into new relief by his new approach.

It is relatively easy to recognize in the whole of Byron's *oeuvre* an attempt to recreate a world of real sensations and events, and relatively easy also to discern an element of desperation in his failure to do so. We may suppose that his frustration is intensified by his belief that the experience of life to which he repeatedly laid claim gave him an exclusive qualification for fulfilling this aim. Only in *Don Juan*, however, is the sense of deprivation made moving. The confession itself may not be so:

> No more – no more – oh never more on me
> The freshness of the heart can fall like dew,
> Which out of all the lovely things we see
> Extracts emotions beautiful and new
>
> (I, 214)

But the pathos of the poem's constant recourse to dismissing the significance of its events as a means of coming to terms with this impasse can hardly be missed. Indeed, the poem's incorrigible restlessness suggests a sensibility that has tired of life itself. The image of Byron writing *Don Juan* through the lonely nights to arise the following afternoon and fritter the time away with Shelley and Hunt is a telling one when placed against the manner of its narration. Life was 'lived' alone by night, by the evocation of events and episodes which possessed a sequence that life itself seemed to lack, and offered a texture therefore through which Byron's imagination could freely percolate without suffering the impediments of reflection and emotional response. Paradoxically perhaps, it is this which makes *Don Juan* such a moving poem.

Yet we cannot simply rest the case there: the poem may repeatedly evoke the pathos of the man who claims that he has tired of life itself, and startle us also by its apparent indifference, but the narrative itself is anything but tired. The manner in which *Don Juan* presents its events is new and vital. Whether or not its poet has tired of life, the evidence before our eyes is that he has only just discovered his art, and is delighting in it. Byron's detachment here, for instance, allows him to discover a vocabulary of detail that results in a polished and economical piece of characterization:

> This note was written upon gilt-edged paper
> With a neat crow quill, rather hard but new.
> Her small white fingers scarce could reach the taper,
> But trembled as magnetic needles do,
> And yet she did not let one tear escape her.
> The seal a sunflower; *Elle vous suit partout,*
> The motto, cut upon a white cornelian;
> The wax was superfine, its hue vermilion.
>
> (I, 198)

Perhaps he never made better use of his reading of Pope. At last

Byron has made room within his poetry for the telling literal detail, the concern with facts, that manifests itself so frequently (although differently of course) in the letters. This is more casual:

> but at intervals there gushed,
> Accompanied with a convulsive splash,
> A solitary shriek, the bubbling cry
> Of some strong swimmer in his agony.

(II, 53)

In fact it is almost itemizing, but it succeeds where the verse tales fail, by its deliberate renunciation of the kind of excitement that the younger Byron felt compelled to supply. Instead we have that unpoetic word 'bubbling', uncomfortable amidst the rhetoric of *Childe Harold*, and here, again, issuing from the kind of literal-mindedness that is Byron's forte. In this respect, the following must surely rate as one of the most extraordinary passages in the poem:

> The other evening ('twas on Friday last) –
> This is a fact and no poetic fable –
> Just as my greatcoat was about me cast,
> My hat and gloves still lying on the table,
> I heard a shot – 'twas eight o'clock scarce past –
> And running out as fast as I was able,
> I found the military commandant
> Stretched in the street and scarce able to pant.
>
> Poor fellow! For some reason, surely bad,
> They had slain him with five slugs and left him there
> To perish on the pavement; so I had
> Him borne into the house and up the stair
> And stripped and looked to. But why should I add
> More circumstances? Vain was every care;
> The man was gone; in some Italian quarrel
> Killed by five bullets from an old gun barrel.
>
> I gazed upon him, for I knew him well;
> And though I have seen many corpses, never
> Saw one, whom such an accident befell,
> So calm. Though pierced through stomach, heart, and liver,
> He seemed to sleep, for you could scarcely tell
> (As he bled inwardly, no hideous river
> Of gore divulged the cause) that he was dead;
> So as I gazed on him, I thought or said,

196

'Can this be death? then what is life or death?
Speak!' but he spoke not. 'Wake!' but still he slept.
'But yesterday and who had mightier breath?
A thousand warriors by his word were kept
In awe. He said as the centurion saith,
"Go," and he goeth; "come," and forth he stepped.
The trump and bugle till he spake were dumb,
And now nought left him but the muffled drum.'

And they who waited once and worshipped, they
With their rough faces thronged about the bed
To gaze once more on the commanding clay,
Which for the last though not the first time bled.
And such an end! That he who many a day
Had faced Napoleon's foes until they fled,
The foremost in the charge or in the sally,
Should now be butchered in a civic alley.

The scars of his old wounds were near his new,
Those honourable scars which brought him fame;
And horrid was the contrast to the view.
But let me quit the theme; as such things claim
Perhaps even more attention than is due
From me. I gazed (as oft I have gazed the same)
To try if I could wrench aught out of death
Which should confirm or shake or make a faith

(V, 33–8)

The tone is not quite casual, but deliberate; the deliberation registering the depth to which the experience has penetrated, as well as a
significant hint of Byron's perplexity. With no literary models before
him, and now well practised in exploiting his stanza's easy accommo-
dation of anecdotal mannerisms, he finds himself able to render the
details of the scene with admirable directness ('Just as my greatcoat
was about me cast, / My hat and gloves still lying on the table') and
with a literal, but not pedantic, attention to the facts ('twas eight
o'clock scarce past', 'pierced through stomach, heart, and liver').
Here too is that peculiar curiosity of the letters, that seemingly satis-
fies itself with scientific explanations ('As he bled inwardly, no hid-
eous river / Of gore divulged the cause'). A more surprising presence,
perhaps, is Childe Harold, insistently breaking in because of his
sensing of the kind of ironies that lend themselves to his rhetorical
procedures (see stanza 36). The whole context and tone, however, do

not allow the stock procedures to be evolved; the temptation only is registered. The ironies are observed rather than elaborated, and what we perceive here is that they stem from the same kind of literal-mindedness that gives the passage its strength. The common source may be clearly seen in the pleasingly unpretentious stanza which follows:

> But it was all a mystery. Here we are,
> And there we go, but where? Five bits of lead,
> Or three or two or one send very far!
> And is this blood then formed but to be shed?
> Can every element our elements mar?
> And air – earth – water – fire live – and we dead?
> We, whose minds comprehend all things? No more;
> But let us to the story as before.

(V, 39)

The speculations are conventional but not conventionally rendered. Childe Harold, though still a strong presence, is controlled by *Don Juan*'s characteristic nonchalance, here epitomized in 'Here we are, / And there we go, but where?' This oscillates between the attraction of apparent superficiality and a dissatisfaction with its inadequacy, both stemming from the same propensity which forms the basis of the rhetoric of the sixth line – the tendency to weigh heavily the data of experience. Here this is manifested as an almost obsessive concern with factual evidence, and in the context of this, the nature of the irony of 'We, whose minds comprehend all things?' is questionable. Is this a fully conscious undermining of the previous lines, or delivered as part of the whole rhetorical pattern? Ultimately it does not matter very much. The significance of the passage depends upon the controlled rendering of its events, and in the wholeness of Byron's response. The issue is finally closed by a Childe Harold-like 'No more', yet all of *Childe Harold* can offer nothing so authentic.

What has happened here is the successful transposition of the world of the letters into the world of the poem:

Dear Murray – I intended to have written to you at some length by this post, – but as the Military Commandment is now lying dead in my house – on Fletcher's bed – I have other things to think of. – – He was shot at 8 o Clock this evening about two hundred paces from our door. – – I was putting on my great Coat to pay a visit to the Countess Guiccioli – when I heard a shot – and in going to the hall – found all my servants on the balcony – exclaiming that 'a Man was murdered'. – – As it is the custom here to let people fight it through – they wanted to hinder me from going out – but I ran down into the Street – Tita the bravest of them followed me – and we made our way to the Commandant who was lying on his back with five wounds – of which three in the body – one in the heart . . . I made my Servant & one of the mob take up the body – sent off Diego crying to the Cardinal – the Soldiers for the Guard – & had the Commandment carried upstairs to my own quarters. – But he was quite gone. – I made the Surgeon examine him & examined him myself. – He bled inwardly, & very little external blood was apparent. – One of the Slugs had gone quite through – all but the Skin, I felt it myself. – Two more shots in the body – one in a finger – and another in the arm. – His face not at all disfigured – he seems asleep – but is growing livid. – The Assassin has not been taken – but the gun was found – a gun filed down to half the barrel.[40]

Here the curiosity, the passion for determining and presenting the facts, proceeds further ('I made the Surgeon examine him & examined him myself . . . One of the Slugs had gone quite through – all but the Skin, I felt it myself'). This is the Byron who demanded Williams's skull of Trelawney so that he might satisfactorily identify it 'by the teeth',[41] the Byron who wrote the persistently detailed and carefully documented letter to Murray describing the public execution of three criminals in May 1817, observed through an opera glass ('I was close – but was determined to see – as one should see everything once – with attention').[42] It is the insistently inquisitive Byron, whose curiosity is nevertheless not simply a matter of wanting to see or examine, but also a controlled performance, in which he publicly declares the nature of his relation to the incident. It is this quality, perhaps above all others, that gives the letters (many of which were read to an audience at Murray's) their vital interest.

It is essential to see that the authenticity of *Don Juan* inheres not in the accuracy of the facts described, but in Byron's establishment of his relation to them. To speak of the poem's 'realism' or its 'accurate truthful picture of human life'[43] is to misplace the emphasis. It may be that Byron sometimes receives his conviction from the knowledge that he is dealing with events that have really happened (such as in the episode dealt with above and in the shipwreck scene), and certainly he was prone to defend his verse by emphasizing its literal accuracy, but, consciously or otherwise, *Don Juan* is concerned with the presentation of events through its narrator, not with the recreation of those events for the sake of verisimilitude. One only has to consider some of the more startling stanzas in Cantos II, VII, and VIII:

8   James Gillray, *The High German method of destroying Vermin at Rat-Stadt, 1799*

> The surgeon, as there was no other fee,
> Had his first choice of morsels for his pains,
> But being thirstiest at the moment, he
> Preferred a draught from the fast-flowing veins.
> Part was divided, part thrown in the sea,
> And such things as the entrails and the brains
> Regaled two sharks who followed o'er the billow.
> The sailors ate the rest of poor Pedrillo.
>
> (II, 70)

This may be realistic in the very crudest sense of the word, but one is struck most forcefully by the huge gulf between the poet and the events of his poetry. By no means is Byron attempting to recreate a world of 'reality'. In effect, he is emphasizing just how distant it is, and offering for our scrutiny the means by which he chooses to establish his relationship to it, a relationship that makes it clear that the emotional complexities of the real world lie beyond the scenes of his poetry. The world of *Don Juan* may be factual ('But then the fact's a fact, and 'tis the part / Of a true poet to escape from fiction' (VIII, 86)) but it is not realistic.

If we regard *Don Juan* primarily as a satire, then it is perhaps inevitable that Cantos VII and VIII will be represented as 'an attack on war' and that the skills and point of the shipwreck scene will be missed. Commenting on the style of the Siege of Ismail, Byron wrote, 'There is a deal of war – a siege, and all that, in the style, graphical and technical, of the shipwreck in Canto Second.'[44] His use of the word 'graphical' here provides an important clue as to the derivation and definition of the narrative style of these episodes. For in both instances the quasi-comic manner combining with the grotesquerie strongly recalls the graphic language of the caricaturists, that which is evident in Gillray's *The High German method of destroying Vermin at Rat-stadt*, for instance (see fig. 8). The peculiar metaphor employed to describe the beginning of the siege, with its reference to bodily functions, marks the point at which he actually assumes the vocabulary of this graphic tradition:

> Three hundred cannon threw up their emetic,
> And thirty thousand muskets flung their pills
> Like hail to make a bloody diuretic.
>
> (VIII, 12)

This surely makes it clear that the tradition to which the depiction

9 Isaac Cruikshank, *Genl. Swallow Destroying the French Army*

of war in *Don Juan* belongs is far closer to that of Gillray than that of Goya. It is significant that this vocabulary and style find their way into the poem through two possible sources, both of them deriving ultimately from the popular culture of Italy. The style is as much the equivalent of Pulci's culinary imagery in his battle scenes as it is the equivalent of the techniques of the caricaturists of Gillray's era, who inherited their style from the surviving tradition of Italian popular graphic art. The common source of the two traditions can be clearly seen in Isaac Cruikshank's caricature of Suwarrow (*Genl. Swallow Destroying the French Army*), wherein he is depicted as a giant impaling tiny French soldiers on forks before stuffing them into an already overfull mouth (see fig. 9). With only the slightest of alterations this picture might equally be taken as an illustration from the *Morgante Maggiore*. It is important to recognize that the ready access of Cruikshank and Byron to the grotesque depiction of Suwarrow's battle scenes is determined by their common acceptance of what is ultimately an Italian way of looking at the world. Indeed, in all probability it is the presence of the graphic tradition of Gillray and Cruikshank within Byron that aids his reading of Pulci, his understanding of the Italian mode, and his successful deployment of it.

The non-serious narration of *Don Juan* does not result in the trivialization of the poem's events, however. Whilst Byron's facetiousness is clearly defined in such passages as Juan's brawl with Don Alfonso, his farewell to Julia, or even intermittently in the shipwreck scene ('there was one / That begged Pedrillo for an absolution, / Who told him to be damned – in his confusion' (II, 44)), he is not always so ready to exploit the comic potential of his poem's situations in this knockabout manner. The grotesque passages in Cantos II and VIII are for the most part devoid of this element, and this may be one reason why they have attracted the epithet 'realistic'. Both sections demand a different kind of attention from that which the rest of the poem elicits, and their significance derives partly from their relation to those parts of Byron's earlier verse that made emphatic claims upon sensational effect:

> From a Tartar's skull they had stripp'd the flesh;
> As ye peel the fig when its fruit is fresh;
> And their white tusks crunch'd o'er the whiter skull,
> As it slipp'd through their jaws, when their edge grew dull
> (*The Siege of Corinth*, 458–61)

Turning from here to the shipwreck scene, one is immediately conscious of a vast improvement:

> And when his comrade's thought each sufferer knew,
> 'Twas but his own, suppressed till now, he found.
> And out they spoke of lots for flesh and blood,
> And who should die to be his fellow's food.
>
> (II, 73)

It seems quite probable that the calm modulation of this may owe something to Byron's recognition of the understated conviction of the narrative of the *Inferno*. The attempt to reproduce a Dantesque effect in *The Siege of Corinth* (deriving probably from the Ugolino passage) registers no awareness of Dante's avoidance of melodrama or the laconic energy of his verse's movement. Byron's adoption of an Italian mode which, although different from Dante's, nevertheless inherited some of these elements in its detachment permits him to produce a marvellously convincing and compelling narrative that evokes the horror of its situation in an essentially restrained manner. Because the movement of the stanza in no sense attempts to supplement the range of emotions evoked by the events it is describing (unlike the metre of the Turkish Tales) its effects are peculiarly dream-like:

> He but requested to be bled to death.
> The surgeon had his instruments and bled
> Pedrillo, and so gently ebbed his breath
> You hardly could perceive when he was dead.
> He died as born, a Catholic in faith,
> Like most in the belief in which they're bred,
> And first a little crucifix he kissed,
> And then held out his jugular and wrist.
>
> (II, 76)

The unfamiliar documentary nature of this, so surprising in its context, may lead the reader to believe that he senses elements of realism here. The authenticity, however, derives primarily from the relationship achieved between the poet and the events of his verse, wherein he makes no demands upon his metre or his rhetoric to transport his emotional empathy with its events. Whether this new control comes directly from an improved reading of Dante, or whether Byron achieves an insight into Dante's method whilst conceding to the demands of *ottava rima*, the reference to Dante at verse 83 makes it clear that he played some role here:

204

> And if Pedrillo's fate should shocking be,
> Remember Ugolino condescends
> To eat the head of his archenemy,
> The moment after he politely ends
> His tale. If foes be food in hell, at sea
> 'Tis surely fair to dine upon our friends
> When shipwreck's short allowance grows too scanty
> Without being much more horrible than Dante.
>
> (II, 83)

That 'politely' may be facetious, but it also testifies to Byron's recognition of Dante's unselfconscious terse precision, a precision surprising to the average reader of Byron's period, who felt that poets were obliged to express correct feelings. Byron's own subjection to these expectations in his previous poetry perhaps renders Dante all the more peculiar to him, and it seems possible, therefore, that he may have subconsciously identified the unfamiliarity of Dante with the unfamiliarity of Pulci's comic savagery, both being defined against his rhetorical norm.

Whilst Dante may figure largely in the creation of the shipwreck episode, it seems unlikely that he played a part in the making of Cantos VII and VIII. The stylistic similarity depends instead on the strongly conveyed sense that what is being described is also being subjected to the poet's sardonically inclined humour, and yet at the same time is being fully engaged. The simultaneity is nowhere better realized than in the final couplet of II, 76 quoted above. The movement of these lines combines Byron's declaration that he is dispatching poetic formalities with a sense of inevitability that complements Pedrillo's religious resignation. The conflation is a peculiar one: the couplet is at once glib and moving, signifying the poet's prevalent attitude of indifference and also his imaginative engagement of the events in the narrative. In the war cantos the affectation of flippancy takes many forms, ranging from the assumption of the idiom belonging to the officer and the gentleman to the schoolboy weakness for word-play, even within a single stanza:

> Our friends the Turks, who with loud 'Allahs' now
> Began to signalize the Russ retreat,
> Were damnably mistaken. Few are slow
> In thinking that their enemy is beat
> (Or beaten if you insist on grammar, though

I never think about it in a heat),
But here I say the Turks were much mistaken,
Who hated hogs, yet wished to save their bacon.

(VII, 42)

Yet even amidst many stanzas of a like inclination, the reader remains firmly with the narrative, as Byron admirably deploys his imaginative reading of his source (de Castelnau's *Essai sur l'Histoire ancienne et moderne de la Nouvelle Russie*):

First one or two, then five, six, and a dozen
Came mounting quickly up, for it was now
All neck or nothing, as like pitch or rosin
Flame was showered forth above as well's below,
So that you scarce could say who best had chosen,
The gentlemen that were the first to show
Their martial faces on the parapet,
Or those who thought it brave to wait as yet.

But those who scaled found out that their advance
Was favoured by an accident or blunder.
The Greek or Turkish Cohorn's ignorance
Had palisadoed in a way you'd wonder
To see in forts of Netherlands or France
(Though these to our Gibraltar must knock under).
Right in the middle of the parapet
Just named, these palisades were primly set,

So that on either side some nine or ten
Paces were left, whereon you could contrive
To march, a great convenience to our men,
At least to all those who were left alive,
And thus could form a line and fight again.
And that which further aided them to strive
Was that they could kick down the palisades,
Which scarce rose much higher than grass blades.

(VIII, 45–7)

In no way does the nonchalance of *Don Juan* work against or detract from its narrative coherence. The internal tensions between Byron's casual manner and his detailed descriptions are strong, but they reinforce rather than threaten the narrative structure. Eliot might have said that the prevalent attitude serves to repel Byron's propensity for what he called 'high-falutin', thus preserving the poetry from melodrama and rhetorical histrionics. This may be so, yet the achievement of *Don Juan*'s potentially sensational scenes is not to be described in terms of its author's successful suppression of his bad poetic habits. The idiom does not merely inhibit, it actively encourages an economically direct presentation of factual detail:

> For having thrown himself into a ditch,
> Followed in haste by various grenadiers,
> Whose blood the puddle greatly did enrich,
> He climbed to where the parapet appears,
> But there his project reached its utmost pitch
> ('Mongst other deaths the General Ribaupierre's
> Was much regretted), for the Mussulmen
> Threw them all down into the ditch again.
>
> And had it not been for some stray troops landing
> They knew not where, being carried by the stream
> To some spot where they lost their understanding
> And wandered up and down as in a dream,
> Until they reached as daybreak was expanding
> That which a portal to their eyes did seem,
> The great and gay Koutousow might have lain
> Where three parts of his column yet remain.
>
> (VIII, 71–2)

However nonchalant this may be, its effect is not to transfer our attention from the events of the poem to its poet. Throughout these cantos a delicate balance is maintained: we are highly conscious of Byron's creative organization, of the manner of his presentation, but by no means preoccupied with his mannerisms. The lack of conventional response from the poet, the absence of rhetorical procedure, allows the reader no readily available means of assimilating the events described. The attention elicited by the poem is of an utterly new kind, and the digressions, far from relieving the tension and discomfort by diverting attention away from the narrative, frequently provide an approach for a particularly blunt delivery of the facts:

> The Kozaks, or if so you please, Cossacks
> (I don't much pique myself upon orthography,
> So that I do not grossly err in facts,
> Statistics, tactics, politics and geography),
> Having been used to serve on horses' backs,
> And no great dilettanti in topography
> Of fortresses, but fighting where it pleases
> Their chiefs to order, were all cut to pieces.
>
> (VIII, 74)

207

Here the abruptness is at once a truncation of decorum and an appropriately sudden termination of the scene.

The mode of *Don Juan* does not limit Byron's vision; it permits a new perspective, a new view of the world. It allows him to see beyond those points at which his earlier verse would have stopped, to see beyond tragic tableaux which persist even here in such forms as the shipwrecked fathers and sons (II, 87–90) and the heroic deaths of the Sultan and his sons (VIII, 104–19), to deal with scenes and events for which no conventional responses exist:

> A dying Moslem, who had felt the foot
> Of a foe o'er him, snatched at it and bit
> The very tendon which is most acute
> (That which some ancient Muse or modern wit
> Named after thee, Achilles), and quite through't
> He made the teeth meet, nor relinquished it
> Even with his life, for (but they lie) 'tis said
> To the live leg still clung the severed head.

> (VIII, 84)

The grotesque image of the body, here as elsewhere, is drily presented as a challenge to contemporary assumptions and prejudices. It is an important element in the definition of the world of the poem, a world which is incoherent in terms of the contemporary reader's mores, and therefore to be resisted. But one of *Don Juan*'s triumphs, perhaps, is its irresistibility: however much its implications may have been resented, it maintained its hold on a substantial readership.

'Cant Political'

The validity of Byron's claim that *Don Juan* was written as an attack on the cant of the day is readily appreciated, but the way in which two of the best narrative sequences, the shipwreck episode and the war cantos, relate to 'cant political' has been missed. It seems highly probable that the narrative quality of these episodes owes something to Byron's conviction that they have a specific political purpose. These parts of the poem are not concerned only with a battle that belonged to history and a shipwreck based on eighteenth-century mariners' accounts, but with issues that were particularly sensitive in the contemporary political climate: the uneasy history of the Alliance and the wreck of the *Medusa*. Each demands separate treatment.

When reading the shipwreck episode, one might be surprised to find

Byron apparently sanctioning a superstition which sorts so badly with the post-Enlightenment scepticism exhibited in this poem and elsewhere in his works:

> The sailors ate him, all save three or four,
> Who were not quite so fond of animal food.
> To these was added Juan, who, before
> Refusing his own spaniel, hardly could
> Feel now his appetite increased much more.
> 'Twas not to be expected that he should,
> Even in extremity of their disaster,
> Dine with them on his pastor and his master.
>
> 'Twas better that he did not, for in fact
> The consequence was awful in the extreme.
> For they who were most ravenous in the act
> Went raging mad. Lord! how they did blaspheme
> And foam and roll, with strange convulsions racked,
> Drinking salt water like a mountain stream,
> Tearing and grinning, howling, screeching, swearing,
> And with hyena laughter died despairing.
>
> (II, 78–9)

It might have been expected that Byron would have seized the opportunity of presenting his readers with the disconcerting possibility that the eating of human flesh had no ill consequences. Here the poem is operating on a very subtle level, however, and the account of cannibalism inducing madness, I believe, is being treated ironically. The tone of stanza 79 readily permits such a reading: Byron's assumption of a colloquial idiom denoting a scandalized and credulous response ('The consequence was awful in the extreme . . . Lord! how they did blaspheme') and his emphasis on this naivety by a clever use of rhyme may be seen as an ironic mimicry of what he imagines to be a typical contemporary reaction to the events of his narrative. But the full force of the irony cannot be appreciated without recognizing its allusion to what was probably the most notorious maritime scandal of the decade, the wreck of the *Medusa*.

The events proceeding from the *Medusa*'s wreck in 1816 were so well known by 1819 (when the first two cantos of *Don Juan* were published) that a direct allusion was unnecessary. Joseph Severn's account of Keats reading this episode of the poem demonstrates that the connection was readily made: 'Keats took up Ld Byrons *Don Juan* accidentally as one of the books he had brought from England

& singular enough he opened on the description of the Storm, which is evidently taken from the Medusa frigate & which the taste of Byron tryes to make a jest of.'[45] The news of the wreck of the *Medusa* first reached the public in September 1816, when an account written by Henri Savigny, the ship's surgeon, was published in the *Journal des Débats*. Within a week a complete translation had appeared in *The Times* (17 September 1816). In 1817, a more detailed record of the shipwreck and what followed, written by Savigny and Alexandre Corréard, another survivor, was published in Paris as *Naufrage de la Frégate la Méduse faisant partie de l'expédition du Sénégalen en 1816*. This was received in an interestingly chauvinistic way by the *Quarterly Review* (18 (October 1817)), and was quickly followed by an enlarged edition in Paris in 1818. An English translation of this enlarged version was published in London in the same year under the title *Narrative of a Voyage to Senegal in 1816*. In 1819, therefore, when Byron began *Don Juan II*, the wreck of the *Medusa* was still European news, and although there is no evidence to support the reasonable hypothesis that he read Corréard and Savigny at first hand, it would be foolhardy to suggest that he remained ignorant of the wreck of the *Medusa* and the published accounts. Most important, these accounts proved unequivocally that many, and perhaps all of those who survived, were able to do so by their consumption of human flesh. Indeed, the events aboard the raft of the *Medusa* were later considered to be amongst the most significant in the history of cannibalism at sea.[46]

It is known that Byron took certain details of his shipwreck from Sir J. G. Dalyell's *Shipwrecks and Disasters at Sea* (3 vols., London, 1812), the relevant account in this instance being the 'Sufferings of Twelve men in an open boat', the story of the survivors of the wreck of the slave ship *Thomas* in 1797. Cannibalism being the only recourse, the victim requests to be bled to death, the operation being performed by the ship's surgeon, who thereupon 'applying his own parched lips, drank the stream as it flowed'. The consequences of eating the body are given as follows: 'Those who indulged their cannibal appetite to excess, speedily perished in raging madness, teaching the survivors by an awful example their probable fate on recurring to a similar expedient. But some who had refused participation in the repast still preserved their senses.'[47] Now although it may be confidently asserted that many readers of the early nineteenth century were well aware that cannibalism did not induce madness or death, it must also have been the case that the inclination of many was to accept the effects of eating human flesh as described in this passage. Such a consequence, after all, could be interpreted as a kind of retribution, perhaps divinely ordained, for the violation of the civil and natural order. But most important, this passage from Dalyell indicates the existence of a system of unofficial censorship: the survivors of this particular wreck evidently felt compelled to exculpate themselves from any suspicion that they had eaten their comrades.

The review of *Naufrage de la Frégate la Méduse* in the *Quarterly* exemplifies a closely related piece of reactionary censorship, deliberately misrepresenting Corréard and Savigny in an ambiguous passage which suggests that the acts of cannibalism were as ineffectual as the consumption of clothing and other miscellaneous items:

The 'extreme measure' was, indeed, horrible: the unhappy men, whom death had spared in the course of the night, fell upon the carcasses of the dead and began to devour them; some tried to eat their sword-belts and cartridge-boxes; others devoured their linen, and others the leathers of their hats; but all these expedients, and others of a still more loathsome nature, were of no avail.[48]

The reviewer is clearly using Corréard and Savigny for his own purposes, and he concludes his article with a comparison between the anarchic behaviour of the *Medusa*'s crew and the disciplined conduct of recently shipwrecked British sailors.[49] The political manoeuvring is in line with the *Quarterly*'s anti-Jacobinal traditions: the *Medusa* affair is presented as an example of the chaotic consequences of French republicanism and political discontinuity. In fact, the reviewer would have experienced few difficulties in achieving this, for the account of Corréard and Savigny was primarily critical, but designed to publicize the incompetence of the ship's captain, whose appointment was one of many implemented by Royalist factions attempting to regain control of the French military. These important circumstantial details are omitted by the reviewer, who thereby deflects his readers' attention away from the democratic and pro-republican interests of Corréard and Savigny, and directs it towards the consequences of the breakdown of traditional patterns of authority. Simultaneously, he preserves the myth that cannibalism was not an effective remedy for starvation.

The transformation of the accounts of the British and French wrecks into political metaphors, the former representing a fair-minded authoritarian regime, the latter representing chaotic mob-rule, may lead us to consider the historical significance of the disappearance from early-nineteenth-century maritime accounts of the kind of mythological elements associated with cannibalism found in the extract from Dalyell. The model of a group of men equalized by circumstances, determining and organizing their own survival with no regard for conventional autocratic ethics, clearly lent itself as a political metaphor through which the complexities of a new democratic morality could be explored. It is significant that one of the other most famous published accounts of cannibalism ensuring survival from this period is American: the *Narrative of the Most Extraordinary and Distressing Shipwreck of the Whale-ship Essex, of Nantucket*, by Owen Chase and other survivors, published in New York in 1821. And it is certainly no coincidence that Charles Olsen's *Call Me Ishmael*, a remarkable study of the paradoxes of American democracy as explored in Melville's *Moby Dick*, should begin with a dramatic paraphrase of Chase's account. All this may seem a long way from *Don Juan*. But it is not so: Olsen's perception of the pertinence of Chase's narrative to his study is a perception of its historical significance, a significance which we should extend to the account of Corréard and Savigny, and to Canto II of *Don Juan*. For the publication of these accounts coincides with the evolution of relatively new political ideologies, and they raise the same contentious issues, asserting that man's fate and morality are determined by the interaction between the individual and his particular environment, not by divinely appointed authority. Such an assertion is anticipated by Voltaire's pragmatic discussion of cannibalism in the *Dictionnaire philosophique*[50] and by the entry in Diderot's *Encyclopédie* which asserts that cannibalism cannot simply be regarded as a defining characteristic of ethnic groups.[51] Here the taboos attached to the subject of cannibalism are confidently disparaged. But it is later, in the Romantic period, that we find the first positive celebration of the cannibal as a man struggling heroically with his environment, in Géricault's famous painting *The Raft of the Medusa*. Byron does not present his mariners in the same way: he has no equivalent for the sinewy vigour of Géricault's figures, although it is worth recognizing that Delacroix, in *Le Naufrage de Don Juan*, has. Nevertheless, the detailed rendering of the lot-drawing sequence, the fact that it is the gentleman's 'pastor and master' who is eaten, and the grotesquerie of the whole piece place Byron in a controversial position with regard to the tastes and ethics of his society, a position that is perhaps analogous to that occupied by Géricault. The subtle but incisive irony of stanza 79 is his own method of dealing with English cant, and this episode as a whole marks a point in English literary history when the subject of cannibalism was no longer restricted to the speculative arena of moral philosophy (as in Defoe), but had become a fact of life with the capacity to seriously disturb the political ethos of England, as the *Quarterly*'s elusive response to Corréard and Savigny testifies. The value which Byron placed upon the authenticity of the shipwreck episode must be appreciated in this context.

Bearing in mind the impact of the wreck of the *Medusa* and the published accounts, we can be fairly sure that only a minority of maritime historians (and perhaps some pedants belonging to the literary sub-culture that produced A. A. Watts's series of articles on Byron's plagiarisms in the *Literary Gazette*) saw Dalyell's book behind the shipwreck scene, and that the majority of its readers recognized an indirect and topical allusion to one of the most sensational scandals of the period. The point of Byron's ironic deployment of Dalyell is that he offers his readers an account which accords readily with their conceptions of the divine and civil order in the knowledge that their recent acquaintance with the events of the *Medusa* made these conceptions untenable. Further, he may be ironically complying with the genteel delicacy of his lady readers. Almost certainly, the narratives of Corréard and Savigny were regarded as improper reading for ladies, and Byron's avoidance of any direct allusion to the *Medusa* may be seen as a piece of disingenuous deference to this large proportion of his reading public. Whilst he guessed that many ladies had in fact been reading of the wreck of the *Medusa*, its apparent absence from his account shows him sardonically participating in the decorous game of unmentionables. Indeed, it is Byron's incisive understanding of the way in which the cant of his society operated that gives the subtle irony of the cannibalism sequence its edge.

Byron's characterization of Suwarrow – upon which so much depends in Cantos VII and VIII – has received considerable attention. Many critics have justly admired the achievement, but have failed to recognize the historical significance of its derivation. Critics such as John Jump and M. K. Joseph understand Byron's depiction of Suwarrow as a butcher to be part of his realistic exposure of the horrors of warfare,[52] and the other side of the debate may be represented by Helen Gardner's rebuking of E. Steffan for his complaint that Byron's apparent sympathy damages the force of his satire on the grounds that his 'realistic insight into the folly, wickedness and futility of war does not blind him to the facts of human nature'.[53] But Byron's presentation of Suwarrow derives from neither satiric conviction nor psychological interest. It relies heavily on the English ambivalence to the allies that was prevalent throughout the campaigns against the French: Suwarrow's famous victories over the French in Italy granted him heroic status in England, but his nationality rendered his reception less than enthusiastic. As a consequence, his renowned ruthlessness was made much of, and the field-marshal's character attracted a considerable amount of interest in early-nineteenth-century society. In 1810, a memoir, *Historie du Feld Marachel Souvarof*, by L. M. P. Laverne (first published in Paris in 1809), was imported into England, and a critic writing for the *Monthly Review* responded by commenting on the kind of interest that Suwarrow had aroused:

The character of Suwarof has been the subject of much difference of opinion. Some persons have gone so far as to deny him even the merit of military skill, and insist that he should be considered in no other light than as a headstrong champion, whose rule was to accomplish everything by dint of force and by an indiscriminate profusion of human blood.[54]

a caricature by Gillray, notably bereft of exaggeration and extraneous motifs, presents him as a decidedly barbaric figure, with a brigand-like air. Yet Suwarrow's resolute stare and the gloss reproduced beneath the print make it clear that the artist found him fascinating rather than repulsive.[55] Clearly Byron draws upon this stock notion in his portrait, and he has a purpose in doing so.

Suwarrow's reputation as an efficient military butcher originated largely in his massacre of the Turks at Ismail in 1790, the siege depicted in *Don Juan*, and in the alliances against the French this reputation was both an asset and an embarrassment to the British. The British ambivalence to her allies can be seen in Cruikshank's *Genl. Swallow* and Gillray's *High German method*, which both celebrate allied victories over the French whilst simultaneously preserving myths of British decency by suggesting that the atrocities of warfare derive exclusively from the barbarism of her allies. Thus the horrors of the battlefield are dissociated from the gentlemen of the British drawing-rooms, and the political uneasiness of the Alliance also finds expression. The presence of Johnson in *Don Juan* may perhaps be seen as Byron's reminder that however minimal Britain's involvement was in the early disputes of the 1790s, she was providing a considerable amount of financial and mercenary support to the armies on the continent (Johnson's mercenary instincts are emphasized at VIII, 101). But this is really of secondary importance, for in reviving the embarrassment of the Alliance of the 1790s through the controversial figure of Suwarrow, Byron seems to be commenting on Castlereagh's policy of non-interference in continental affairs in the 1820s, which in radical English circles amounted to compliance with the principles proclaimed by the major European powers at the Congress of Troppau in 1820. Broadly speaking, this was a proclamation made by Prussia, Austria, and Russia that it was their right to put down any resurgences in Europe that were not sanctioned by monarchy, a declaration made in response to revolutions in Spain, Portugal, and Sicily in the same year. Castlereagh objected but maintained neutrality, and in doing so provoked the Opposition to prolonged protests. He had not kept his hands sufficiently clean: a British man-of-war had taken Ferdinand of Naples to meet the European monarchs, and his representation of Austrian policy was too favourable. Whig rumours had it that the Troppau congress had discussed the possibility of a Tory defeat in Britain, and would react by invading. Despite these pressures, Castlereagh adhered to his policy of passivity, and in 1821 Austria curbed the Neapolitan revolt and also one in Piedmont with the aid of Russia. By 1822 Russia had announced an intention to march troops across Europe to restore Ferdinand of Spain, an event that was precluded by France's intervention, supported by Austria and Prussia. Throughout, Britain remained neutral, to the discontent of the radical factions in the Opposition, who, whilst they would not commit themselves to a declaration of war, felt that Castlereagh's diplomacy amounted to complicity. Indeed, these factions chose to recognize no real distinction between the Quadrupal Alliance of Britain, Russia, Prussia, and Austria (formed at Chaumont in 1814 and designed to create a balance of power), the Alliance proceeding from the Congress of Troppau, and Alexander's scheme for a Holy Alliance, a proposal for the alliance of all the European monarchs to uphold their divinely appointed rights by suppressing all anti-monarchist revolutions.

Byron's preface to Cantos VI–VIII of *Don Juan* makes it clear that we can number him amongst these factions.[56]

Byron therefore has a political motive in bringing Suwarrow and his particular brand of warfare into the public eye again in 1822. In a situation where Russia was advocating the suppression of anti-despotic revolutions across Europe and (in Byron's eyes) Britain's passivity amounted to tacit approval – in effect an alliance – he is reminding his reader of a previous alliance with Russia to put down republicanism in the wars with Napoleon. Suwarrow's notorious tactics, made famous by the victory at Ismail, sanctioned by the alliance against the French, stand as epitomizing the forces of oppressive tyranny. The reader is also reminded of Russia's claim that her expansion into Turkey was for the liberation of the Orthodox Turks, a war sanctioned by God:

> Suwarrow was now a conquerer, a match
> For Timour or for Zinghis in his trade.
> While mosques and streets beneath his eyes like thatch
> Blazed, and the cannon's roar was scarce allayed,
> With bloody hands he wrote his first dispatch,
> And here exactly follows what he said:
> 'Glory to God and to the Empress' (Powers
> Eternal, such names mingled!) 'Ismail's ours.'
>
> (VIII, 133)

In the context of the Liberal accusations about a Holy Alliance in the 1820s, this last couplet would have had particular pertinence, and the following stanzas continue to press the Republican line.

In Cantos VII and VIII Byron is not simply attacking war from a position of moralizing humanitarianism any more than he is involved in a Swiftian exposure of its absurdity. His portrait of Suwarrow as a hero of a very peculiar kind is a reminder to his public of the way in which their propaganda machine operated, and simultaneously an allusion to the kind of military oppression, with all its barbarism, to which they had been, and were continuing to be, a party. For Russia's continuing role in Europe was essentially of the same cause as that which had carried Wellington to eminence:

> Though Britain owes (and pays you too) so much,
> Yet Europe doubtless owes you greatly more.
> You have repaired Legitimacy's crutch,
> A prop not quite so certain as before.
> The Spanish and the French, as well as Dutch,

Have seen and felt how strongly you restore.
And Waterloo has made the world your debtor
(I wish your bards would sing it rather better).

You are 'the best of cutthroats'. Do not start;
The phrase is Shakespeare's and not misapplied.
War's a brain-spattering, windpipe-slitting art,
Unless her cause by right be sanctified.
If you have acted once a generous part,
The world, not the world's masters, will decide,
And I shall be delighted to learn who,
Save you and yours, have gained by Waterloo?

(IX, 3–4)

In Byron's pro-republican eyes, no distinction is to be made between
a Wellington and a Suwarrow. But it is not that this section of the
poem, any more than that alluding to the wreck of the *Medusa*,
receives its impetus from wholehearted political commitment. Byron
attempts to disconcert rather than convince his audience, and that is
why the allusions are oblique and not direct. He has no desire to use
his poetry as a means of participating in a political harangue,
preferring to absorb his reader in a narrative which discloses its full
significance only in the light of current events.

Don Juan appears to resolve the major difficulties that impaired
everything Byron had written outside of *ottava rima*: the poet of the
tales finds himself enabled to declare the nature of his relationship
with his audience, and the poet of *Childe Harold* no longer depends
upon fantasies about his readers or fantasies about his inspiration to
suppress his worries about his rhetorical routine and his arbitrary
engagement of subject. Yet *Don Juan* is not merely a deployment of
the limited technical abilities of an uncommitted poet; it is a deployment of those abilities that allows him to discover new skills and a
more profitable relationship to his art: the conscious assumption of
the guise of indifference and the subsequent release from the most
uncomfortable of his audience's demands paradoxically results in
the dissipation of the problems that stemmed from his indifference.
The 'settled attitude' of the English cantos perhaps marks the beginning of its insidious return, but until this point Byron's indifferent
role permits him to come to terms with the events of his narrative in a
remarkably mature way. The non-serious framework of the poem is
in fact much more serious than any framework he had adopted previ-

ously, because it liberates him from the compulsion to supplement the events of the poem with claims upon its emotional effects. T. S. Eliot astutely remarked that 'it was by being so thorough-going an actor that Byron arrived at a kind of knowledge: of the world outside, which he had to learn something about in order to play his role in it, and of that part of himself that was his role'.[57] *Don Juan* shows him using the knowledge that his varied poetic ventures had brought him to: the knowledge that as a surrogate context for the projection of emotions and sensations which he wished to claim for his own, his writing was inadequate. This realization carries with it the full recognition of his poetry as a performance, the dramatization of events and feelings that, whatever their roots in the real world, are defined ultimately by the actor's mode, the presentation of himself before his public. The 'thorough-going actor' or actor-poet of *Don Juan* registers his recognition of this fact by using his poetry as a structure through which the world is transformed, rather than as a means of reconstituting its episodes and feelings.

Yet whatever the considerable success of *Don Juan*, the contemporaneity of *The Island*, *The Age of Bronze*, and all the dramas apart from *Manfred* suggests that we cannot regard the poem as a full and final resolution of the kind of artistic problems to which this book has drawn attention. The poem is not to be seen as proceeding from a fully conscious reorientation, a review made by Byron of his career to date. *Ottava rima* was responsible for *Don Juan*'s stability, and whilst the experience of writing the poem may have made Byron more self-aware, his consistent retreats therein to the role of a man whose wide experience of the world has dulled his sensibility might imply the lack of a controlling self-awareness. The presence of these other works alongside *Don Juan* may even suggest a need for a diversion away from the kind of realizations that the poem was liable to elicit: the realization, for example, that his best poetry by no means entitled him to stand alongside Milton and Shakespeare (where many of his public would have him stand), or the realization that the feelings which his previous poetry had appropriated were fictitious, or even the realization that he was not the kind of modern poet that Shelley thought he was. The historical tragedies, *The Island*, and *Cain* (together with *Heaven and Earth* and *The Deformed Transformed*), respectively, may be regarded as means by which these realizations were postponed. We may detect a lack of conviction in any of these works, but they nevertheless suggest that Byron was still liable to be seduced away from *Don Juan* by habitual self-delusions. Although *Don Juan* allowed him to fantasize about his wordly experience, the illusions offered were perhaps not as stimulating as those to be found in poetry based on his earlier models, nor were they able to be so fully indulged.

Whether or not we feel that the history of Byron's poetry is a history of self-deceit, we must remember, above all, that it is a chronicle of its time. The poetry before 1817 looks backward to the eighteenth century in its implicit yearning for an exclusive audience which could be defined in terms of its shared tastes, habits, and assumptions, and forwards to the nineteenth in its blatant concessions to the demands of its public. But out of this compromise is born *Don Juan*, a poem which cannot wholly resolve Byron's unique difficulties, but one which is able to accommodate the ambivalence which stems from them in its predominant tones: the sense received when reading the poem is of a performance conducted with ironic self-regard, utterly under Byron's control. *Don Juan* impresses us with its extreme self-consciousness. One course of Byron's poetry, running from the opening stanzas of *Childe Harold* through the games of the tales, the carelessness of *Manfred*, and the abandon of *Cain*, may be seen as a series of frustrated attempts to project his self-conscious ambivalence into the verse itself, which is at once the object and source of this ambivalence. Only *Don Juan* absorbs this self-consciousness and turns it to good account. It establishes a unique relationship between the poet and the events of his narrative and, thereby, an equally novel relationship between the poet and his reader. Byron's negative response to his audience's demands results in a complete and valuable poetic triumph, the fully convincing performance of a poet before his public.

Notes

Introduction

1. T. B. Macaulay, 'Moore's Life of Lord Byron', *Critical and Historical Essays*, 2 vols. (London, 1860), I: 160.
2. W. W. Robson, 'Byron as Poet', *Proceedings of the British Academy*, 43 (1957), 25–62 (p. 62).
3. Macaulay's rapid rise to a position of eminence, and his acquaintance with circles in which Byron had previously moved, perhaps made him peculiarly well qualified to understand Byron's relation to his public. His assessment of Byron still offers much of interest.
4. *LJ*, IV: 85.
5. *The Complete Works of William Hazlitt*, ed. P. P. Howe, 21 vols. (London, 1930), XI: 77.
6. Robson, p. 58.
7. *Ibid.*, p. 30.

1. Experiment in *Childe Harold I & II*

1. *PW*, II: 39.
2. 'The "Cosmopolotite" was an acquisition abroad, I do not believe it is to be found in England, it is an amusing little vol. & full of French flippancy.' *LJ*, II: 105.
3. *PW*, II: 20.
4. *PW*, II: 38. See Matthew Prior, 'An Epistle to Fleetwood Shephard', lines 9–12, *The Literary Works of Matthew Prior*, ed. H. Bunker Wright and Monroe K. Spears, 2 vols. (Oxford, 1959), I: 86.
5. For an example of the former judgement, see Andrew Rutherford, *Byron: A Critical Study* (London, 1961), pp. 32–5. The latter response can be found in Robert F. Gleckner, *Byron and the Ruins of Paradise* (Baltimore, 1967), pp. 51–3.
6. Bernard Blackstone, *Byron: A Survey* (London, 1975), p. 89.
7. *CC*, pp. 39–40.
8. Gleckner, p. 271.
9. Leslie A. Marchand, *Byron's Poetry: A Critical Introduction* (London, 1965), p. 38.

10. *CC*, p. 320.
11. The Rev. George Gilfillan (ed.), *The Poetical Works of Beattie, Blair, and Falconer* (Edinburgh, 1854), p. 5.
12. *Ibid.*
13. *The Works in Verse and Prose of William Shenstone*, 3 vols. (London, 1764), I: 340.
14. Quoted in Alan Dugald McKillop (ed.), *'The Castle of Indolence' and Other Poems* (Lawrence, Kans., 1961), p. 62.
15. *The Poems of Alexander Pope*, ed. John Butt (London, 1963), p. 11. All subsequent quotations from Pope are from this edition. Line references are given in parentheses after each quotation.
16. See McKillop (ed.), p. 64.
17. *The Poetical Works of James Thomson*, ed. J. Logie Robertson (Oxford, 1908), p. 252. All subsequent quotations from Thomson are from this edition. Line references are given in parentheses after each quotation.
18. See Prothero, II: 418.
19. *The Poetical Works of James Thomson*, ed. Peter Cunningham, 2 vols. (London, 1862), I: cvi.
20. *The Poems of John Milton*, ed. John Carey and Alastair Fowler (London, 1968), p. 501.
21. See for instance Rutherford, *Byron: Critical Study*, pp. 28–9.
22. *Lives of the Poets, The Works of Samuel Johnson*, vols. IX–XI (London, 1792), XI: 230.
23. See *Paradise Lost*, IX, 24 (Carey and Fowler (eds.), p. 854).
24. Prothero, II: 429–30.
25. Thomas Moore, *The Life of Lord Byron* (London, 1851), p. 184. I am indebted to Howard Mills for drawing my attention to the usefulness of this passage. See Howard Mills, *Peacock: His Circle and His Age* (Cambridge, 1969), p. 194.
26. Andrew Rutherford seems to conceive of the poem in this way. See *Byron: Critical Study*, p. 31.
27. Johnson, *Poets*, IX: 155.
28. An example of such an interpretation can be found in Marchand, *Byron's Poetry*, pp. 38–41.

2. The discovery of an audience: the Turkish Tales

1. 'I have been amongst the builders of this Babel, attended by a confusion of tongues.' Prothero, V: 559.
2. 'Preface to the Second Edition of the *Lyrical Ballads*', *The Prose Works of William Wordsworth*, ed. W. J. B. Owen and J. W. Smyser, 3 vols. (Oxford, 1974), I: 128.
3. 'There has never been a period, and perhaps never will be, in which vicious poetry, of some kind or other, has not excited more zealous admiration, and been far more generally read, than good.' 'Essay Supplementary to the Preface of 1815', *ibid.*, III: 83.
4. *Ibid.*

5. *The Table-Talk and Omniana of Samuel Taylor Coleridge* (Oxford, 1917), pp. 413–14.
6. *Ibid.*, p. 414.
7. Robert Southey, *Letters from England*, ed. Jack Simmons (London, 1951), p. 342.
8. Thomas Love Peacock, *Memoirs of Shelley and Other Essays and Reviews*, ed. Howard Mills (London, 1970), p. 94.
9. *Ibid.*
10. See for example Upali Amarsinghe, *Dryden and Pope in the Early Nineteenth Century: A Study of Changing Literary Taste, 1800–1830* (Cambridge, 1962), p. 63.
11. *Ibid.*, pp. 65–6.
12. Elie Halévy, *A History of the English People in 1815*, 3 vols. (Harmondsworth, 1938), III: 134.
13. *Ibid.*
14. Samuel Smiles, *A Publisher and His Friends: Memoir and Correspondence of the Late John Murray*, 2 vols. (London, 1891), I: 204.
15. Southey, *Letters from England*, p. 342.
16. John O. Hayden, *The Romantic Reviewers 1802–1824* (Chicago, 1968), p. 39.
17. Richard D. Altick, *The English Common Reader: A Social History of the Mass Reading Public 1800–1900* (Chicago, 1967), p. 392.
18. *Edinburgh Review*, 20 (Nov. 1812), 277–303 (p. 280).
19. Samuel Taylor Coleridge, *Biographia Literaria*, 2 vols. (facs. repr., London, 1971), II: 117.
20. *Edinburgh Review*, 20 (Nov. 1812), 277–303 (p. 279).
21. W. E. K. Anderson (ed.), *The Journal of Sir Walter Scott* (Oxford, 1972), p. 308.
22. Quoted in Amy Cruse, *The Englishman and His Books in the Early Nineteenth Century* (London, 1930), p. 182. No reference is provided.
23. Coleridge, *Biographia Literaria*, II: 123.
24. Lionel Madden (ed.), *Robert Southey: The Critical Heritage* (London, 1972), p. 68.
25. Southey, *Letters from England*, pp. 345–6.
26. Peacock, *Memoirs*, p. 96.
27. *Ibid.*, p. 132.
28. Southey, *Letters from England*, p. 345.
29. *Ibid.*, p. 349.
30. *The Novels of Thomas Love Peacock*, ed. David Garnett (London, 1948), p. 348.
31. Jane Austen, *Persuasion*, ed. John Davie (London, 1971), p. 316.
32. *LJ*, II: 192.
33. Prothero, II: 413.
34. Southey, *Letters from England*, p. 348.
35. *LJ*, VI: 47.
36. It was this aspect of Sotheby's behaviour that led Byron to pillory him in *The Blues*, where he appears as Mr Botherby. After his first meeting with him in 1811, Byron described him as 'a disagreeable

dog, with rhyme written in every feature of his wrinkled Physiognomy'. *LJ*, II: 128.

37. After the publication of '*The Prisoner of Chillon*' *and Other Poems* in 1816, Byron received an anonymous note criticizing his poetry, and believed Sotheby to be the author. See *LJ*, V: 252.

38. Howard Mills makes this point about Byron's criticism forcibly. *Peacock: His Circle and His Age* (Cambridge, 1969), p. 194.

39. 'I had rather be a kitten, and cry mew! / Than one of these same metre ballad-mongers.'

40. *English Bards and Scotch Reviewers*, 174.

41. *Ibid.*, 278.

42. *Ibid.*, 919.

43. Arthur Melville Clark, *Walter Scott: The Formative Years* (London, 1969), pp. 254–5.

44. '*The Chase*', and '*William and Helen*': *Two Ballads from the German of Gottfried Augustus Bürger*, published without Scott's name in 1796.

45. Sir Walter Scott, 'Essay on Imitations of the Ancient Ballad', *Minstrelsy of the Scottish Border*, ed. T. F. Henderson, 4 vols. (London, 1932), IV: 40–1.

46. This account was by William Taylor. Further details are given in Werner W. Beyer, *The Enchanted Forest* (Oxford, 1963), p. 44.

47. *LJ*, II: 191.

48. Smiles, *A Publisher and His Friends*, I: 215.

49. *Ibid.*, I: 76.

50. *CC*, p. 47.

51. The fact that Byron frequently made gifts of his copyrights at this stage in his career is irrelevant.

52. *LJ*, III: 101.

53. Two examples will suffice: 'Gazes of wonder, fear, terror, hatred, and the like rebound from the Giaour, so that he is realized in the emotional reactions which he provokes. In this respect his position is a focal and determining one for other characters, like Hassan and Leila, who function in similar ways at various times. In scenes where a character responds to the Giaour, Byron will frequently attach a specific epithet to the sensation that is felt (e.g. "wonder" or "loathing"). We must not conclude from this that such responses are either simplified or stereotyped. These epithets are formal devices which fix the reader's attention so that Byron can complicate the dramatized emotional nuances in his characters and weave them around a variety of "objective" details about the Giaour.' Jerome J. McGann, *Fiery Dust: Byron's Poetic Development* (Chicago, 1968), pp. 150–1. 'And it is this "immutable law" which Byron seeks to dramatize for the first time in *The Giaour*, whose world is one of love and death, beauty and death, freedom and death, nature and death, man's human and heroic virtues and death . . . what I am concerned with here is Byron's "elaborately coherent" vision of the human condition and his earnest though self-deprecated efforts to achieve a form, a structure, a technique for embodying that vision of his art.' Robert F. Gleckner, *Byron and the Ruins of Paradise* (Baltimore, 1967), p. 100.

54. For suggestions of Byron's source see J. G. Robertson, 'Goethe and Byron', *Publications of the English Goethe Society*, n.s., 2 (1925), 1–132 (pp. 7–8).
55. *LJ*, IV: 321.
56. See for example *The Corsair*, I, 359, 466.
57. *Don Juan*, IV, 68.
58. This rhyme recalls that of 'knee' and 'chimney' in 'The Rebuilding', James and Horace Smith, *Rejected Addresses* (London: New Universal Library, n.d.), p. 100. A note explains that the couplet was introduced by way of bravado, 'in answer to one who alleged that the English language contained no rhyme to chimney'.
59. The nature of Pope's decorum as a translator of Homer is discussed by Harold Mason in *To Homer through Pope* (London, 1972). See for example 98–112.
60. *The Works of Alexander Pope . . . Printed Verbatim, from the Octavo Edition of Mr. Warburton*, 6 vols. (London, 1776), IV: 178.
61. *Ibid.*, IV: 178–9.
62. *The Corsair*, Preface.
63. *Don Juan*, V, 150.
64. *LJ*, V: 186.
65. *LJ*, V: 192.
66. See Leslie A. Marchand, *Byron: A Biography*, 3 vols. (London, 1957), I: 341.
67. *Quarterly Review*, 10 (Jan. 1814), 331–42 (pp. 333–4).
68. *Edinburgh Review*, 22 (July 1813), 299–309 (p. 307).
69. See n. 24 above.
70. Lord Lytton, *England and the English* (London, 1874), p. 139.
71. Compare for instance with Parnell's 'A Night Piece on Death', where there are very few pauses within the lines.
72. See Thomas Moore, *The Life of Lord Byron* (London, 1851), p. 20.
73. *Ibid.*, p. 20.
74. *The Poetical Works of Sir Walter Scott*, ed. J. L. Robertson (Oxford, 1921), p. 1.
75. See for example John O. Hayden (ed.), *Sir Walter Scott: The Critical Heritage* (London, 1970), p. 30.
76. See the early paragraphs of Jeffrey's review of the Turkish Tales for a representative sample of this kind of approval. *CH*, pp. 55–9.
77. Scott, *Works*, p. 112.
78. Medwin, p. 164. The remark is reminiscent of Gilpin and the cult of the picturesque, and the 'sharpness of outline' also recalls Reynolds, Blake, and Flaxman.

3. Shelley and the new school of poetry: *Childe Harold III* and *The Prisoner of Chillon*

1. *Poetical Works*, ed. Thomas Hutchinson, rev. Ernest de Selincourt (Oxford, 1936), p. 357. All subsequent quotations from Wordsworth are taken from this edition. Line references are given in parentheses after each quotation.

2. Medwin, pp. 293–4.
3. Certainly the relationship between Wordsworth and Byron has never been adequately discussed. Bernard Blackstone, for example, dealing with *Childe Harold III*, states that he has 'never been able to see anything Wordsworthian in Byron's view of Nature'. *Byron: A Survey* (London, 1975), p. 188. According to Blackstone, 'Byron's view is a complex one' (p. 189), and the awkwardnesses of the poetry of 1816 are comparable to the 'awkwardnesses' of Shakespeare's later plays. 'Byron's relation to Nature . . . is a true "interview", in which the being who has issued out of the earth, and will return thither, and she who is the universal mother-and-grave *look at* each other in a glance of quiet and loving recognition' (p. 194). This is an extremely speculative statement and one in which there is little evidence of a serious consideration of the verse itself.
4. See *CH*, p. 109.
5. Medwin, pp. 294–5.
6. *LJ*, IV: 324–5.
7. See Jeffrey's review of *The Corsair* and *The Bride of Abydos*, *CH*, pp. 53–64.
8. Writing on the Lake poets in 1814, Byron claimed, 'They are a set of the most despicable imposters – that is my opinion of them. They know nothing of the world; and what is poetry, but the reflection of the world? What sympathy have this people with the spirit of this stirring age?' *LJ*, IV: 85.
9. '"Tintern Abbey" the source of it all . . .' *CH*, p. 109.
10. F. R. Leavis, *Revaluation: Tradition and Development in English Poetry* (London, 1936), p. 194.
11. Evidence for Byron's recognition of Wordsworth's authenticity is to be found in 'Churchill's Grave' (also written in 1816), which included the following note on its manuscript: 'The following poem (as most that I have attempted to write) is founded on a fact; and this detail is an attempt at a serious imitation of the style of a great poet – its beauties and its defects: I say the *style* – for the thoughts I claim as my own. In this, if there be anything ridiculous, let it be attributed to me, at least as much to Mr Wordsworth: of whom there can exist few greater admirers than myself. I have blended what I would deem to be the beauties as well as defects of his style; and it ought to be remembered, that, in such things, whether there be praise or dispraise, there is always what is called a compliment, however unintentional.' *PW*, IV: 46–7. The quasi-parodic nature of the poem itself reflects Byron's insecurity and ambivalence.
12. 'Preface to the Second Edition of the *Lyrical Ballads*', *The Prose Works of William Wordsworth*, ed. W. J. B. Owen and J. W. Smyser, 3 vols. (Oxford, 1974), I: 138.
13. 'A Defence of Poetry', *The Complete Works of Percy Bysshe Shelley*, ed. R. Ingpen and Walter E. Peck, 10 vols. (London, 1926–30), VII: 112.
14. Preface to *Alastor*, *ibid.*, I: 173.
15. This and all subsequent quotations from Shelley's poetry are taken from

the *Complete Works* cited above. Line references are given in parentheses after each quotation.

16. Wordsworth, 'Preface to the Second Edition of the *Lyrical Ballads*', *Prose Works*, I: 128.
17. See Andrew Rutherford, *Byron: A Critical Study* (London, 1961), pp. 61–2; Jeffrey's review of *Childe Harold III*, *CH*, pp. 108–9; and Coleridge's annotations, *PW*, III: 261–2, 271–2.
18. A favourite compliment of Byron's. See for example *LJ*, III: 215 and Prothero, III: 131. (Prothero is cited here because his transcription is preferable to Marchand's.)
19. James Rieger, *The Mutiny Within: The Heresies of Percy Bysshe Shelley* (New York, 1967), p. 92.
20. Medwin, p. 365.
21. Listed in the sale catalogue of Byron's library was a five-volume set of the *Confessions*, dated 1796. A. N. L. Munby (ed.), *Sale Catalogues of the Libraries of Eminent Persons*, 12 vols. (London, 1971), I: 224. This would have included the *Rêveries*, the five volumes being made up of *The 'Confessions' of J.-J. Rousseau with the 'Reveries of the Solitary Walker'*, 2 vols. (London, 1783), supplemented by *The 'Confessions', Part the Second, To Which Is Added a New Collection of Letters from the Author*, 3 vols. (London [1796–1790] (1790–1796?). All quotations from the *Rêveries* which follow are given from this edition, vol. II.
22. See Frederick L. Jones (ed.), *The Letters of Percy Bysshe Shelley*, 2 vols. (Oxford, 1964), I: 480.
23. *Rêveries*, p. 145.
24. *Ibid.*, p. 273.
25. *Ibid.*, pp. 234–8.
26. Rousseau's explanation of this theory again suggests why his writings may have distorted Byron's understanding of Wordsworth: 'The more sensible the soul of a contemplative man is, the more he abandons it to the extasies this harmony excites. A reverie soft and deep invades all his senses: he sinks with delightful enebriety into the immensity of that beautiful system' (*Rêveries*, p. 243). This passage also stands as an example of the kind of attraction Rousseau may have held for Shelley.
27. *Rêveries*, p. 221.
28. *Ibid.*, p. 153.
29. but still I cannot seek paths so harsh or so savage that Love does not always come along discoursing with me and I with him.
    Petrarch's Lyric Poems, trans. and ed. Robert M. Durling (London, 1976), p. 94.
30. Jean-Jacques Rousseau, *Julie, ou la Nouvelle Héloise* (Paris, 1960), p. 52.
31. *Ibid.*, p. 212.
32. See fig. 1. The interest in scenery excited by *La Nouvelle Héloise* is demonstrated in Wheatley's deviation from the conventions of book illustration, the constraints of which are exemplified in the corresponding illustration of this scene in *Recueil d'estampes pour la Nouvelle Héloise* (1761), fig. 8, 'Les monuments des anciennes amours', reprinted

in the edition of the novel listed in the Bibliography. See also Mary Webster, *Francis Wheatley*, Studies in British Art (London, 1970), pp. 59–64.
33. *LJ*, V: 82.
34. Jones (ed.), *Letters of Shelley*, I: 486.
35. Edward Young, *The Complaint: or, Night Thoughts on Life, Death, and Immortality* (London, 1812), p. 50. All subsequent quotations from Young's poem are taken from this edition. Line references are given in parentheses after each quotation.
36. See M. K. Joseph, *Byron the Poet* (London, 1964), pp. 77–9 and Robert F. Gleckner, *Byron and the Ruins of Paradise* (Baltimore, 1967), pp. 244–60.
37. *CH*, p. 99.
38. John O. Hayden, *Romantic Bards and British Reviewers* (London, 1971), p. 228.
39. *CH*, pp. 112–13.
40. Commenting on Hunt in 1822, Byron wrote, 'I do not know what world he has lived in, but I have lived in three or four; and none of them like his Keats and Kangaroo *terra incognita*.' Prothero, VI: 157. See also *LJ*, IV: 85.
41. Wordsworth, 'Preface to the Second Edition of the *Lyrical Ballads*', *Prose Works*, I: 138.
42. In this chapter this term is always used with an implicit reference to these approximations of critical thought.
43. Wordsworth, 'Preface to the Second Edition of the *Lyrical Ballads*', *Prose Works*, I: 138.
44. See Graham McMaster (ed.), *William Wordsworth: A Critical Anthology* (Harmondsworth, 1972), pp. 89, 103 for documentation of this.
45. Samuel Taylor Coleridge, *Poetical Works*, ed. Ernest Hartley Coleridge (Oxford, 1969), p. 185. All subsequent quotations from Coleridge are taken from this edition. Line references are given in parentheses after each quotation.
46. In his review of Southey's *Thalaba*, Jeffrey admitted that Southey was less addicted to 'the perverted taste for simplicity' than Wordsworth, but at the same time he reminded his readers of the *English Eclogues*, and quoted a passage from *Thalaba* 'almost at random' which emphasized the simplicity of Southey's style. Lionel Madden (ed.), *Robert Southey: The Critical Heritage* (London, 1972), pp. 73–5.
47. *Ibid.*, p. 69.
48. See 'The Ancient Mariner', lines 117, 193, 240. The echoes of Wordsworth are less specific, but behind them there may be lines 4, 8, and 48 of 'Tintern Abbey'.
49. McMaster (ed.), *Wordsworth*, p. 95.
50. Edwin M. Everett, 'Lord Byron's Lakist Interlude', *Studies in Philology*, 55 (Jan. 1958), 62–75.
51. Laurence Sterne, *A Sentimental Journey through France and Italy*, ed. Graham Petrie (Harmondsworth, 1967), pp. 97–8.
52. For a fuller discussion of this subject see Lorenz Eitner, 'Cages, Prisons, and Captives in Eighteenth-Century Art', in Karl Kroeber and William Walling (eds.), *Images of Romanticism* (London, 1978), pp. 13–38.

53. Quoted by A. Alvarez in his Introduction to the Petrie edition, p. 11.
54. Sterne, p. 100.
55. Eitner, p. 17.
56. Frances A. Yates, 'Transformations of Dante's Ugolino', *Journal of the Warburg and Courtauld Institutes*, 14 (1951), 92–117.
57. *Ibid.*, p. 94. The list given by Frances Yates includes three translations that we might reasonably suppose Byron to have been acquainted with: Joseph Warton's (in his essay on Pope), Thomas Warton's (in his *History of English Poetry*), and one by Frederick Howard, 4th Earl of Carlisle (father of Byron's first cousin once removed and guardian).
58. Quoted by Frances Yates, p. 107. Her reference appears to be in error.
59. See fig. 3. For a brief account of the controversy surrounding this and the painting by Reynolds see Peter Tomory, *The Life and Art of Henry Fuseli* (London, 1972), pp. 121–2.
60. There may also be a conflation here with 'The Ancient Mariner'.
61. 'The last and most eminent characteristic of the Greek works is a noble simplicity and sedate grandeur in gesture and expression. The bottom of the sea lies peaceful beneath a foaming surface, a great soul lies sedate beneath the strife of passions in Greek figures. It is in the face of Laocoön [that] this soul shines with full lustre.' J. J. Winckelmann, *Writings on Art*, ed. David Irwin (New York, 1972), p. 72.
62. Gert Schiff, *Johann Heinrich Füssli: Text und Oeuvrekatalog*, 2 vols. (Zurich, n.d.), 1/1, p. 562.
63. Thomas Medwin, *The Life of Percy Bysshe Shelley*, ed. H. B. Forman (Oxford, 1913), p. 249.
64. For example his employment of David's *Oath of the Horatii* in *The Three Witches*. See Tomory, *Life and Art of Fuseli*, pls. 72, 73.

4. Tourist rhetoric: *Childe Harold IV*

1. *CH*, pp. 98–9.
2. *CH*, p. 109.
3. John O. Hayden (ed.), *Romantic Bards and British Reviewers* (London, 1971), p. 225.
4. 'History of a Six Weeks' Tour', *The Complete Works of Percy Bysshe Shelley*, ed. Roger Ingpen and Walter E. Peck, 10 vols. (London, 1926–30), VI: 87–8.
5. *LJ*, VII: 225.
6. Dedication to *Childe Harold's Pilgrimage*, Canto IV.
7. See *PW*, II: 327–8; *CH*, pp. 134–5; J. J. Winckelmann, *Writings on Art*, ed. David Irwin (London, 1972), p. 124.
8. See Alastair MacDonald, 'Gray and His Critics: Patterns of Response in the Eighteenth and Nineteenth Centuries', in James Downey and Ben Jones (eds.), *Fearful Joy: Papers from the Thomas Gray Bicentenary Conference at Carleton University* (Montreal, 1974), pp. 172–97 (p. 175).
9. Quoted by MacDonald, p. 176.
10. *Ibid.*, p. 181.
11. *Ibid.*

12. Matthew Arnold, 'Thomas Gray', *Essays in Criticism,* second series (London, 1895), pp. 70–1.
13. *Ibid.,* p. 96.
14. *CH,* p. 111.
15. *LJ,* V: 269.
16. Matthew Arnold, 'Courage', *The Poems of Matthew Arnold,* ed. K. Allott (London, 1965), p. 142.
17. W. W. Robson, 'Byron as Poet', *Proceedings of the British Academy,* 43 (1957), 25–62 (p. 34).
18. Thomas Campbell, 'Lines on the View from St. Leonard's', *The Poetical Works of Thomas Campbell,* ed. the Rev. W. A. Hall (London, 1868), pp. 306–8.
19. Samuel Rogers, 'The Descent', from *Italy,* in *The Poetical Works of Samuel Rogers* (London, 1867), p. 250.
20. *CH,* p. 136.
21. Andrew Rutherford, *Byron: A Critical Study* (London, 1961), pp. 93–7, 99–101.
22. Samuel Johnson, 'Life of Gray', *Lives of the Poets, Works,* vols. IX–XI (London, 1792), XI: 378.
23. Paul West, 'Byron and the World of Things: An Ingenious Disregard', *Keats–Shelley Memorial Bulletin,* 11 (1960), 21–32 (p. 25).

5. Modernizing the Gothic drama: *Manfred*

1. Andrew Rutherford, *Byron: A Critical Study* (London, 1961), p. 90.
2. Robert F. Gleckner, *Byron and the Ruins of Paradise* (Baltimore, 1967), pp. 256–7.
3. Samuel C. Chew, *The Dramas of Lord Byron* (Göttingen, 1915), p. 74.
4. Charles E. Robinson *Shelley and Byron: The Snake and the Eagle Wreathed in Flight* (Baltimore, 1976), pp. 41–59.
5. *Ibid.,* p. 59.
6. Robinson's method is to paraphrase Byron's verse and treat the resultant material in a highly speculative way. See for example his discussion of the 'paradox' of *Manfred* (pp. 55–6). No judgement of the quality of the verse is ever offered.
7. *LJ,* IV: 115.
8. Thomas Moore, *The Life of Lord Byron* (London, 1851), p. 252.
9. *LJ,* V: 170.
10. *Ibid.,* p. 185.
11. This reaction depended on the close relationship between the development of the acting styles of Byron's era and late-eighteenth-century Shakespearean criticism, documented in Joseph W. Donohue, Jr, *Dramatic Character in the English Romantic Age* (Princeton, N. J., 1970).
12. See *LJ,* II: 149 and IV: 115.
13. *Ibid.,* V: 188.
14. *Ibid.,* VII: 113.
15. When *Manfred* was produced in 1834, its success was due to its mechanical and scenic extravagance. See Martin Meisel, 'The Material Sublime:

John Martin, Byron, Turner, and the Theater', in Karl Kroeber and William Walling (eds.), *Images of Romanticism* (London, 1978), pp. 211–32 (p. 221).

16. See Frederick L. Jones (ed.), *The Letters of Percy Bysshe Shelley*, 2 vols. (Oxford, 1964), I: 490.

17. *The Novels of Thomas Love Peacock*, ed. David Garnett (London, 1948), p. 360.

18. *Ibid.*, p. 381.

19. *Ibid.*, p. 382.

20. *Ibid.*, pp. 391, 419.

21. *Ibid.*, p. 362.

22. *Ibid.*

23. *LJ*, V: 170.

24. 'Sorrow is knowledge' (I, i, 10) probably derives from Young's 'Knowing is suffering' (*Night Thoughts*, 'Night the Seventh', 708). This was first pointed out by A. A. Watts in one of a series of articles entitled 'Lord Byron's Plagiarisms' published in 1821. See *Literary Gazette and Journal of the Belles-Lettres*, 3 March 1821, 137–9 (p. 138). Young may also figure in Byron's 'half-dust, half-deity' (I, ii, 40). See 'Night the First', 75.

25. *The Complete Works of William Hazlitt*, ed. P. P. Howe, 21 vols. (London, 1930), XI: 74.

26. *Manfred*'s generous use of Gothic motifs probably accounts for its description as 'a consummation of Gothic evolution on the stage'. Bertrand Evans, *Gothic Drama from Walpole to Shelley* (Berkeley and Los Angeles, 1947), p. 232.

27. See *CH*, p. 118 and J. G. Robertson, 'Goethe and Byron', *Publications of the English Goethe Society*, n.s., 2 (1925), 1–132 (pp. 18–19).

28. Timothy Webb, *The Violet in the Crucible: Shelley and Translation* (Oxford, 1976), pp. 14–15. My quibbling with Timothy Webb here, is unpresentative of my response to his book, which has made such a large contribution to Shelley studies, and to which I am greatly indebted in my thinking about Byron's 'non-realistic' dramas.

29. *Ibid.*, p. 15.

30. Richard Cumberland's papers on Aeschylus in *The Observer* in 1793 (nos. 132–4) were also probably of significance. Cumberland emphasized that Aeschylus did not provide a suitable model for stage drama, and noted too the distinctly poetical and non-dramatic form of Potter's translations. *The British Essayists*, 45 vols. (London, 1823), XL: 165.

31. See Webb, pp. 147–9.

32. As well as being the only English translator of Aeschylus, Potter was liable to have come to Shelley's attention because of his popularity. By 1819 there had been five printings of his translation of Aeschylus, first published in 1777.

33. See John Flaxman, *Compositions from the Tragedies of Aeschylus* (London, 1795), pls. 9, 12, 16, which take their subjects from Potter's expansions of Aeschylus's choruses.

34. See *ibid.*, pl. 24.
35. Robert Potter (trans.), *The Plays of Aeschylus* (London, 1886), pp. 9–10.
36. *Ibid.*, pp. 45–6.
37. See Elizabeth Wheeler Manwaring, *Italian Landscape in Eighteenth Century England* (London, 1925), pp. 35–6.
38. Potter (trans.), pp. 68–9.
39. 'May my mind this rev'rence keep; / Print it strong, and grave it deep' (*Prometheus Chained*: *ibid.*, p. 26), for example, recalls the movement of 'Weave the Warp, and weave the woof'.
40. For example, 'me let him hurl, / Caught in the fiery tempest, to the gloom of deepest Tartarus'. *Prometheus Chained*: *ibid.*, p. 43.
41. Recalling the opening of Gray's 'The Bard'.
42. *The Complete Works of Percy Bysshe Shelley*, ed. Roger Ingpen and Walter E. Peck, 10 vols. (London, 1926–30), II: 174.
43. William Hazlitt, *Liber Amoris and Dramatic Criticism*, ed. Charles Morgan (London, 1948), p. 193.
44. Banquo's ghost had been a problem long before Philipsthal, however. Kemble's 1794 production of *Macbeth*, in dispensing with the ghost, was seen by some to be a solution to its dangerously ludicrous appearance. See Donohue, *Dramatic Character*, pp. 263–4.
45. For a close study of the textual relationship between *Manfred* and *Faust* see Robertson, 'Goethe and Byron', pp. 12–17.
46. *LJ*, III: 231.
47. *Don Juan*, III, 86.
48. Retzsch's *Outlines* was imported to Britain from Germany in 1818 and republished in London in 1820, with translated extracts from *Faust*. For further details see Webb, *Violet in the Crucible*, pp.148–9.
49. Baroness Staël Holstein (Madame de Staël), *Germany*, 3 vols. (London, 1813), II: 182–3.
50. Staël, II: 194.
51. *Ibid.*, II: 223, 226, 224.
52. Again, see *Nightmare Abbey*, *Novels of Peacock*, p. 382.
53. Staël, II: 193.
54. James Gillray, *Works* (London, 1851), pl. 166.
55. *PW*, IV: 111.
56. *CH*, p. 118.
57. *PW*, IV: 122–3.
58. *Gentleman's Magazine*, 87 (July 1817), 46.
59. See Robinson, *Shelley and Byron*, pp. 42–3 for the echoes of *Mont Blanc* in this song.
60. *The First Part of Goethe's Faust*, with a prose translation by Abraham Hayward, rev. C. A. Buchheim (London, 1892), pp. 184, 186.
61. *PW*, VII: 39.

6. Heroic tableaux: the three historical tragedies

1. *CH*, p. 64.
2. *LJ*, VIII: 57.

3. J. R. de J. Jackson (ed.), *Coleridge: The Critical Heritage* (London, 1970), pp. 131–4.
4. *Ibid.*, p. 135.
5. *Ibid.*
6. Potter's style as a translator is dealt with briefly in Chapter 4. His highly decorative translations would appear to have little to contribute to Byron's 'severe' ideal.
7. *LJ*, VIII: 23.
8. For a full discussion of this style, see Robert Rosenblum, *Transformations in Late Eighteenth Century Art* (Princeton, N. J., 1970), pp. 50–106.
9. See Joseph W. Donohue, Jr, *Dramatic Character in the English Romantic Age* (Princeton, N.J., 1970), pp. 243–69, where Donohue discusses the paradox of Kemble's neo-classic formality and his subjective interpretation of character.
10. *PW*, IV: 338–9.
11. Donohue argues that it is possible to conceive of an acting 'school' that centres on Garrick, Kemble, and Kean (pp. 243–4), and it has been demonstrated elsewhere that the rhetoric of Garrick's physical gestures was closely related to the French tragic style. See Kirsten Gram Holmstrom, *Monodrama, Attitudes, Tableaux Vivants: Studies on Some Trends of Theatrical Fashion 1770–1815*, Stockholm Studies in Theatrical History, 1 (Stockholm, 1967), pp. 36–9.
12. Quoted by Holmstrom, p. 24.
13. *Ibid.*, p. 26.
14. Quoted by Holmstrom, p. 37.
15. For a full account of Lady Hamilton's attitudes, see Holmstrom, pp. 110–40.
16. See *ibid.*, pp. 122–5.
17. The Rehberg illustration may be found in *ibid.*, p. 125, 45: 12, and the painting of Mrs Siddons is reproduced in Donohue, fig. 38, facing p. 243.
18. *LJ*, VIII: 27.
19. For a brief discussion of the relation of Senecan drama to the sensational Roman theatre see E. F. Watling (trans.), *Seneca: Four Tragedies and 'Octavia'* (Harmondsworth, 1966), pp. 17–21.
20. *Ibid.*, p. 201.
21. *Ibid.*, p. 102.
22. T. S. Eliot, 'Seneca in Elizabethan Translation', in *Selected Essays*, 2nd edn (London, 1934), pp. 65–105 (p. 74).
23. Rosenblum, *Transformations in Late Eighteenth Century Art*, pp. 71, 68.
24. See for example *Sardanapalus*, III, i, 384 ('her floating hair and flashing eyes'), which suggests something of the relaxed manner in which parts of the dramas were written. Similarly 'the many-twinkling feet' in *Marino Faliero*, IV, i, 59, after Johnson's criticism of the phrase in Gray and Byron's facetious employment of it in the first line of *The Waltz*, can only be regarded as symptomatic of a lack of real interest.
25. Prothero, V: 542.
26. Eliot, 'Seneca', p. 72.

7. *Cain*, the reviewers, and Byron's new form of old-fashioned mischief

1. M. K. Joseph, *Byron the Poet* (London, 1964), p. 117.
2. *CH*, p. 161.
3. *LJ*, VIII: 206.
4. *CC*, p. 342.
5. *CH*, p. 215.
6. Frederick L. Jones (ed.), *The Letters of Percy Bysshe Shelley*, 2 vols. (Oxford, 1964), II: 376.
7. Wilfred S. Dowden (ed.), *The Letters of Thomas Moore*, 2 vols. (Oxford, 1964), II: 495.
8. *CH*, pp. 234–5.
9. *Ibid.*, p. 234.
10. *Ibid.*, p. 217.
11. *Ibid.*, p. 241.
12. *PW*, V: 201.
13. *Quarterly Review*, 27 (July 1822), 513.
14. *Ibid.*, 23 (May 1820), 225.
15. *LJ*, VII: 132.
16. *PW*, V: 209.
17. See Prothero, V: 563.
18. See for instance E. H. Coleridge's observation in *PW*, V: 201; Joseph, p. 117; and J. G. Robertson, 'Goethe and Byron', *Publications of the English Goethe Society*, n.s., 2 (1925), 1–132 (p. 21).
19. *Edinburgh Review*, 26 (June 1816), 304.
20. Sir Walter Scott, 'Essay on Imitations of the Ancient Ballad', *Minstrelsy of the Scottish Border*, ed. T. F. Henderson, 4 vols. (London, 1932), IV: 24.
21. In 1784, a translation of *Werther* was found underneath the pillow of a young lady who had taken her own life.
22. Quoted by William Rose, 'Goethe's Reputation in England During his Lifetime', in Rose (ed.), *Essays on Goethe* (London, 1949), p. 154. No more specific reference is given.
23. *Quarterly Review*, 10 (Jan. 1814), 388.
24. See Rose, p. 188. No reference is given.
25. Baroness Staël Holstein (Madame de Staël), *Germany*, 3 vols. (London, 1813), II: 145, 167, 181–2, 183, 226.
26. *Edinburgh Review*, 22 (Oct. 1813), 215–16, 216.
27. See *CC*, p. 458.
28. *Edinburgh Review*, 22 (Oct. 1813), 202.
29. *Ibid.*, 26 (June 1816), 306.
30. *Ibid.*, p. 310.
31. *Ibid.*, pp. 307–8.
32. *Ibid.*, 28 (March 1817), 86.
33. *PW*, V: 207–10.
34. Thomas Warton, *History of English Poetry*, ed. W. Carew Hazlitt, 4 vols. (London, 1871), II: 222–3.
35. Robert Dodsley (ed.), *A Select Collection of Old Plays*, 12 vols. (London, 1780), I: xxxvi–xxxvii.

36. *Ibid.*, I: xli–xlii.
37. William Hone, *Ancient Mysteries Described, Especially the English Miracle Plays Founded Upon Apocryphal New Testament Story* (London, 1823), p. ii.
38. *Quarterly Review*, 27 (July 1822), 508.
39. The source for most of this information about Hone is Samuel C. Chew, *Byron in England: His Fame and After-Fame* (London, 1924), pp. 33–4.
40. *Quarterly Review*, 27 (July 1822), 508.
41. Medwin, p. 231.
42. *Ibid.*, p. 191.
43. See Hans Henning (ed.), *Faust Bibliographie*, 3 vols. in 5 (Berlin and Weimar, 1966), II/2, p. 11, where the correct reference is given and attributed to 'Arthur Taylor'. See also II/2, p. 21, where an incorrect reference is given, with the correct attribution.
44. *Monthly Review*, 62 (1810), 492.
45. Dowden, *Letters of Moore*, II: 505.
46. See Leroy E. Page, 'Diluvianism and Its Critics in Great Britain in the Early Nineteenth Century', in *The New Hampshire Inter-Disciplinary Conference on the History of Geology: Towards a History of Geology*, ed. Cecil J. Schneer (Cambridge, Mass., 1969), pp. 257–71.
47. *Vindiciae Geologicae*, repr. in D. C. Goodman (ed.), *Science and Religious Belief: A Selection of Primary Sources* (Open University, 1973), p. 352.
48. Page, p. 263.
49. See Charles Coulston Gillespie, *Genesis and Geology* (New York, 1970), p. 115.
50. See *Miscellanies, Aesthetic and Literary of Samuel Taylor Coleridge*, collected by T. Ashe (London, 1885), pp. 306–7.
51. *LJ*, IV: 93.
52. See *ibid.*, p. 106.
53. *Ibid.*, VII: 238.
54. Matthew Arnold, 'The Function of Criticism at the Present Time', *Essays in Criticism*, first series (London, 1895), p. 6.
55. *Ibid.*, p. 10.

8. *Don Juan* in its Italian context

1. Bernard Blackstone, *Byron: A Survey* (London, 1975), p. 288. Working from Eliot's essay on Dante, Blackstone is claiming that *Don Juan* is a 'convincing conflation' of high and low dream.
2. *Ibid.*, pp. 288–9, 311.
3. Robert F. Gleckner, *Byron and the Ruins of Paradise* (Baltimore, 1967), pp. 329–30.
4. T. S. Eliot, 'Ben Jonson', *Selected Essays*, 2nd edn (London, 1934), p. 148.
5. Eliot, 'Byron', *On Poetry and Poets* (London, 1957), p. 202.
6. *LJ*, VI: 24.
7. According to Foscolo, Boiardo's 'versification is harsh and abrupt; his style, though less confused than that of Pulci, is more ungrammatical'.

Berni and Ariosto, however, are represented as the most sophisticated of the Romantic narrative poets. See *Quarterly Review*, 21 (April 1819), 528, 541.

8. J. W. Goethe, *Italian Journey (1786–1788)*, trans. W. H. Auden and Elizabeth Mayer (London, 1962), p. 368.

9. *LJ*, VI: 15.

10. Goethe, pp. 76–8; I. D'Israeli, *Curiosities of Literature* (London, 1866), pp. 145–6; Stendhal; *Voyages en Italie*, ed. V. del Litto (Paris, 1973), p. 128.

11. D'Israeli, p. 145; Samuel Rogers, 'The Gondola', from *Italy*, in *The Poetical Works of Samuel Rogers* (London, 1867), pp. 294–7.

12. Goethe, p.77.

13. John Cam Hobhouse, 'Notes to *Childe Harold's Pilgrimage, Canto IV*', *PW*, II: 468.

14. Tobias Smollett, *Travels through France and Italy* (London, 1949), p. 208.

15. First quoted in a review of J. Forsyth's *Remarks on Antiquities, Arts, and Letters, During an Excursion in Italy, 1802 and 1803*, *Edinburgh Review*, 22 (Jan. 1814), 377.

16. Casti (1724–1803) was the most recent of the Italian poets writing in the style of Pulci and Ariosto in Byron's time. While he wrote in *ottava rima*, what was probably his most popular poem, the *Animali Parlanti* (1794), was written in *sesta rima*. It was translated into English, in a reduced form, by William Stewart Rose in 1816. For a discussion of the possible influence of Casti upon *Don Juan*, see John Hookham Frere, *The Monks and the Giants*, ed. R. D. Waller (Manchester, 1926), pp. 53–5.

17. See *Quarterly Review*, 21 (April 1819), 521.

18. The Society for Italian Studies advertised a colloquium on 'Humour in the Renaissance Chivalric Epic' (January 1980) by drawing attention to the lack of critical consensus over the nature of the humour of Pulci, Ariosto, Boiardo, and Berni.

19. 'My lord, this canto has now run its course, / and I must rest awhile, for I am hoarse.' Ludovico Ariosto, *Orlando Furioso*, ed. Piero Nardi (Verona, 1966), p. 301 (XIV, 134); trans. Barbara Reynolds, 2 vols. (Harmondsworth, 1975–7), I: 144.

20. How fortunate those cavaliers of yore,
Who in their venturings through deep ravines,
Through gloomy forests and in caves obscure,
In serpents' nests, in bears' and lions' dens,
Could find what in proud palaces no more
Are found, nor in the most exalted scenes:
Women who in the very bloom of youth
Can be considered beautiful in truth.
Ibid., ed. Nardi, p. 267 (XIII, 1); trans. Reynolds, I: 390.

21. This quotation is from Luigi Pulci, *Morgante e Lettere*, ed. Domenico De Robertis (Florence, 1962), p. 28. Byron's translation is from a parallel text printed in *The Poetical Works of Lord Byron*, 10 vols. (London, 1866), V: 248–9.

22. Robert M. Durling (trans. and ed.), *Petrarch's Lyric Poems* (Cambridge, Mass. and London, 1976), p. 301. Dante Alighieri, *The Divine Comedy*, trans. Charles S. Singleton, 6 vols. (Princeton, N.J., 1970–5), III: 92, 290; I: 86. I am indebted to Dr Roberto Bruni, of the Department of French and Italian, Exeter University, for this information, and for explaining to me the significance of Pulci's rhymes.

23. *LJ*, VII: 42–3, 42.

24. *Ibid.*, p. 43.

25. Mikhail Bakhtin, *Rabelais and His World*, trans. Helene Iswolsky (London, 1968), p. 218.

26. The differences are heightened by the differences between the Roman and Venetian carnivals. At Rome, the sense of liberation may have been greater, but the carnival itself was probably more tightly controlled. For comments on the regulation of the Roman carnival see Goethe, *Italian Journey*, pp. 446, 459.

27. Bakhtin, p. 252.

28. *LJ*, VI: 40.

29. F. R. Leavis, *Revaluation: Tradition and Development in English Poetry* (London, 1936), p. 149.

30. *The Complete Works of William Hazlitt*, ed. P. P. Howe, 21 vols. (London, 1930), XI: 75.

31. John D. Jump, *Byron* (London, 1972), p. 150.

32. *LJ*, VI: 208.

33. *Ibid.*, p. 5.

34. *Ibid.*, p. 232.

35. Jerome J. McGann, *'Don Juan' in Context* (London, 1976), p. 156.

36. Thomas Love Peacock, *Memoirs of Shelley and Other Essays and Reviews*, ed. Howard Mills (London, 1970), p. 104.

37. Graham McMaster (ed.), *William Wordsworth: A Critical Anthology* (Harmondsworth, 1972), p. 101.

38. Howard Mills, *Peacock: His Circle and His Age* (Cambridge, 1969), pp. 201–2.

39. W. W. Robson, 'Byron as Poet', *Proceedings of the British Academy*, 43 (1957), 25–62 (p. 61).

40. *LJ*, VII: 247.

41. Edward John Trelawney, *Records of Shelley, Byron, and the Author*, ed. David Wright (Harmondsworth, 1973), p. 170.

42. *LJ*, V: 230.

43. Andrew Rutherford, *Byron: A Critical Study* (London, 1961), p. 168. Whilst I believe Rutherford to have misplaced the emphasis here, his overall view of *Don Juan* as a successful narrative is one with which I broadly agree.

44. *LJ*, IX: 198.

45. *CH*, p.163.

46. 'The fact of men, in extreme cases, destroying each other for the sake of appeasing hunger, is but too well established – and to a great extent, on the raft of the French frigate Medusa, when wrecked off the coast of Africa.' Sir John Barrow, *The Mutiny and Piratical Seizure of H.M.S.*

Bounty (London, 1831), Oxford World's Classics, p. 127n. For most of the bibliographical information in this paragraph I am indebted to Lorenz Eitner, *Géricault's Raft of the Medusa* (London, 1972). Eitner notes the coincidence between Byron's shipwreck and events aboard the *Medusa*'s raft, but goes no further.

47. Dalyell, III: 357.
48. *Quarterly Review*, 18 (Oct. 1817), 173.
49. *Ibid*., pp. 175–6.
50. Voltaire, *Dictionnaire philosophique*, ed. Julien Benda and Raymond Naves (Paris, 1954), pp. 24–6.
51. Denis Diderot, *Encyclopédie ou Dictionnaire raisonné des sciences, des arts et des metiers* (Paris, 1751–80), I: 498.
52. Jump, *Byron*, p. 133; M. K. Joseph, *Byron the Poet* (London, 1964), p. 249.
53. Helen Gardner, '*Don Juan*', *London Magazine*, 5 (July 1958), 58–65 (p. 63).
54. *Monthly Review*, 61 (1810), 486.
55. James Gillray, *Works* (London, 1851), pl. 240.
56. For the historical details in this paragraph I have depended largely on Elie Halévy, *A History of the English People in the Nineteenth Century*, trans. E. I. Watkin, 6 vols. (London, 1961), II.
57. Eliot, *On Poetry and Poets*, p. 194.

Bibliography

I. Byron sources

Byron, Lord, *Poetical Works*, ed. Ernest Hartley Coleridge, 7 vols. (London, 1898–1904).
Works, 10 vols. (London, 1851).
Letters and Journals, ed. Rowland E. Prothero, 6 vols. (London, 1898–1901).
Letters and Journals, ed. Leslie A. Marchand, 9 vols. (London, 1973–9). (Publication continuing.)
Lovell, Ernest J., Jr (ed.), *His Very Self and Voice: Collected Conversations of Lord Byron* (New York, 1954).
Lady Blessington's Conversations of Lord Byron (Princeton, N.J., 1969).
Medwin, Thomas, *Journal of the Conversations of Lord Byron at Pisa*, 2nd edn (London, 1824).
Murray, John (ed.), *Correspondence of Lord Byron*, 2 vols. (London, 1922).
Steffan, T. G., E. Steffan, and W. W. Pratt (eds.), *Lord Byron: 'Don Juan'* (Harmondsworth, 1973).

II. Other published sources

Airlie, Countess of (M. F. E. Ogilvy), *In Whig Society, 1773–1818* (London, 1921).
Alfieri, Count Vittorio, *Tragedies*, trans. E. A. Bowring (London, 1876).
Altick, R. D., *The English Common Reader: A Social History of the Mass Reading Public 1800–1900* (Chicago, 1967).
Amarsinghe, Upali, *Dryden and Pope in the Early Nineteenth Century: A Study of Changing Literary Taste, 1800–1830* (Cambridge, 1962).
Anderson, W. E. K. (ed.), *The Journal of Sir Walter Scott* (Oxford, 1972).
Antal, Frederick, *Fuseli Studies* (London, 1956).
Ariosto, Ludovico, *Orlando Furioso*, ed. Piero Nardi (Verona, 1966); trans. Barbara Reynolds, 2 vols. (Harmondsworth, 1975–7).
Arnold, Matthew, *Essays in Criticism*, first and second series (London, 1895).

Poems, ed. K. Allott (London, 1965).

Austen, Jane, *Persuasion*, ed. John Davie (London, 1971).

Babbitt, I., *Rousseau and Romanticism* (Boston, 1919).

Bakhtin, Mikhail, *Rabelais and His World*, trans. Helene Iswolsky (London, 1968).

Ball, P. M., *The Central Self: A Study in Romantic and Victorian Imagination* (London, 1969).

Barbier, Carl Paul, *William Gilpin: His Drawings, Teaching and Theory of the Picturesque* (Oxford, 1968).

Barrell, Joseph, *Shelley and the Thought of His Time* (New Haven, Conn., 1967).

Bartholomeusz, Dennis, *'Macbeth' and the Players* (Cambridge, 1969).

Barton, A., *Byron and the Mythology of Fact* (Nottingham, 1968).

Bayle, Pierre, *Dictionary, Historical and Critical*, 5 vols. (London, 1734–8).

Bewley, M., 'The Colloquial Mode of Byron', *Scrutiny*, 16 (March 1949), 8–23.

Beyer, Werner W., *The Enchanted Forest* (Oxford, 1963).

Blackstone, Bernard, *Byron: A Survey* (London, 1975).

Blunden, E. C., *Leigh Hunt's "Examiner" Examined* (London, 1928).

Borst, W. A., *Lord Byron's First Pilgrimage, 1809–11* (New Haven, Conn., 1948).

Bostetter, E. E., *The Romantic Ventriloquists* (Seattle, Wash., 1963).

Bostetter, E. E. (ed.), *Twentieth Century Interpretations of "Don Juan": A Collection of Critical Essays* (Englewood Cliffs, N.J., 1969).

Bottrall, R., 'Byron and the Colloquial Tradition in English Poetry', *Criterion*, 18 (Jan. 1939), 204–24.

Boydell, Josiah, *The Boydell Shakespeare Gallery*, ed. A. E. Sartaniello, 2 vols. (New York, 1968).

Brailsford, H. N., *Shelley, Godwin and Their Circle* (London, 1913).

Brand, C. P., *Italy and the English Romantics* (Cambridge, 1957).

Briscoe, W. A., *Byron the Poet* (New York, 1969).

Brydges, Sir Edgerton, *Letters on the Character and Poetical Genius of Lord Byron* (London, 1824).

Butler, E. M., *Byron and Goethe* (Nottingham, 1950).

Byron and Goethe: Analysis of a Passion (London, 1956).

Buxton, John, *Byron and Shelley: The History of a Friendship* (London, 1968).

The Grecian Taste (London, 1978).

Calvert, W. J., *Byron: Romantic Paradox* (Chapel Hill, N.C., 1935).

Campbell, Thomas, *Poetical Works*, ed. the Rev. W. A. Hall (London, 1868).

Carnall, Geoffrey, *Robert Southey and His Age* (Oxford, 1960).

Chew, Samuel C., *Byron in England: His Fame and After-Fame* (London, 1924).

The Dramas of Lord Byron (Göttingen, 1915).

Churchill, K. G., 'Byron and Italy', *Literary Half-Yearly*, 15 (July 1974), 67–86.

Clark, Arthur Melville, *Walter Scott: The Formative Years* (London, 1969).

Clarke, I. C., *Shelley and Byron* (London, 1934).

Cline, C. L., *Byron, Shelley, and Their Pisan Circle* (Cambridge, Mass., 1952).

Coleridge, Samuel Taylor, *Poetical Works*, ed. Ernest Hartley Coleridge (Oxford, 1969).

Table-Talk and Omniana (Oxford, 1917).

Miscellanies, Aesthetic and Literary, collected by T. Ashe (London, 1885).

Biographia Literaria, 2 vols. (facs. repr., London, 1971).

Conant, Martha Pike, *The Oriental Tale in England in the Eighteenth Century* (New York, 1966).

Cooke, M. G., *The Blind Man Traces the Circle: On the Patterns and Philosophy of Byron's Poetry* (Princeton, N.J., 1969).

'The Restoration Ethos of Byron's Classical Plays', *PMLA*, 79 (Dec. 1964), 569–78.

Cruse, Amy, *The Englishman and His Books in the Early Nineteenth Century* (London, 1930).

Cumberland, Richard, *The Observer*, nos. 132–4, in *The British Essayists*, 45 vols. (London, 1823), XL: 165.

Dallas, R. C., *Recollections of the Life of Lord Byron 1808–1814* (London, 1824).

Dalyell, Sir J. G., *Shipwrecks and Disasters at Sea*, 3 vols. (London, 1812).

Dante Alighieri, *The Divine Comedy*, trans. Charles S. Singleton, 6 vols. (Princeton, N.J., 1970–5).

Davie, Donald, *Purity of Diction in English Verse* (London, 1967).

Davies, Hugh Sykes, *The Poets and Their Critics*, 2 vols. (Harmondsworth, 1943).

Diderot, Denis, *Encyclopédie ou Dictionnaire raisonné des sciences, des arts et des métiers* (Paris, 1751–80), vol. I.

D'Israeli, I., *Curiosities of Literature* (London, 1866).

Dodsley, Robert (ed.), *A Select Collection of Old Plays*, 12 vols. (London, 1780), vol. I.

Donohue, Joseph W., Jr, *Dramatic Character in the English Romantic Age* (Princetown, N.J., 1970).

Dowden, Wilfred S. (ed.), *The Letters of Thomas Moore*, 2 vols. (Oxford, 1964).

Downey, James and Ben Jones (eds.), *Fearful Joy: Papers from the Thomas Gray Bicentenary Conference at Carleton University* (Montreal, 1974).

Drinkwater, J., *The Pilgrim of Eternity: Byron – A Conflict* (London, 1925).

Du Bos, Charles, *Byron and the Need of Fatality*, trans. E. C. Mayne (London, 1932).

Durling, Robert M. (trans. and ed.), *Petrarch's Lyric Poems* (Cambridge, Mass. and London, 1976).

Edinburgh Review, 20 (Nov. 1812), '*Tales*: by the Rev. George Crabbe', 277–305 [Francis Jeffrey].

22 (July 1813), '*The Giaour . . . The Bride of Abydos . . .* by Lord Byron', 299–309 [Francis Jeffrey].

22 (Oct. 1813), '*De l'Allemagne*. Par Madame la Baronne de Staël-Holstein', 195–238.

22 (Jan. 1814), '*Remarks on Antiquities, Arts, and Letters, During an Excursion in Italy . . .* by Joseph Forsyth', 376–85.

26 (June 1816), '*Aus Meinem Leben, Dichtung und Wahrheit*, von Goethe', 304–37 [Francis Jeffrey].

28 (March 1817), '*Aus Meinem Leben*, von Goethe', 83–105 [Francis Jeffrey].

Eggenschwiler, D., 'The Tragic and Comic Rhythms of *Manfred*', *Studies in Romanticism*, 13 (Winter 1974), 63–77.

Eitner, Lorenz, *Neo-Classicism and Romanticism 1750–1850: Sources and Documents*, 2 vols. (London, 1971).

Eliot, T. S., *On Poetry and Poets* (London, 1957).

Selected Essays, 2nd edn (London, 1934).

Elledge, W. Paul, 'Imagery and Theme in Byron's *Cain*', *Keats–Shelley Journal*, 15 (Winter 1966), 49–57.

Elliot, G. R., 'Byron and the Comic Spirit', *PMLA*, 39 (Dec. 1924), 897–909.

Erdman, D. V., 'Byron's Stage-Fright: The History of His Ambition and Fear of Writing for the Stage', *English Literary History*, 6 (Sept. 1939), 219–43.

'Byron and the Genteel Reformers', *PMLA*, 56 (Dec. 1941), 1065–94.

'Byron and Revolt in England', *Science and Society*, 11 (1947), 234–48.

Evans, Bertrand, *Gothic Drama from Walpole to Shelley* (Berkeley and Los Angeles, 1947).

'Manfred's Remorse and Dramatic Tradition', *PMLA*, 42 (Sept. 1947), 752–73.

Everett, Edwin M., 'Lord Byron's Lakist Interlude', *Studies in Philology*, 55 (Jan. 1958), 62–75.

Flaxman, John, *Compositions from the Tragedies of Aeschylus* (London, 1795).

Flower, R. E. W., *Byron and Ossian* (Nottingham, 1959).

Foakes, R. A., *The Romantic Assertion* (London, 1958).

Frere, John Hookham, *The Monks and the Giants*, ed. R. D. Waller (Manchester, 1926).

Fuess, Claude M., *Lord Byron as a Satirist in Verse* (New York, 1912).

Gardner, Helen, '*Don Juan*', *London Magazine*, 5 (July 1958), 58–65.

Gentleman's Magazine, 87 (July 1817), '*Manfred* . . . by Lord Byron', 45–7.

George, M. Dorothy, *English Political Caricature to 1792: A Study of Opinion and Propaganda* (Oxford, 1959).

English Political Caricature 1793–1832: A Study of Opinion and Propaganda (Oxford, 1959).

Hogarth to Cruikshank: Social Change in Graphic Satire (London, 1967).

Gilfillan, the Rev. George (ed.), *The Poetical Works of Beattie, Blair, and Falconer* (Edinburgh, 1854).

Gillespie, Charles Coulston, *Genesis and Geology* (New York, 1970).

Gillray, James, *Works* (London, 1851).

Gleckner, Robert F., *Byron and the Ruins of Paradise* (Baltimore, 1967).

Goethe, J. W., *The First Part of Faust*, with a prose trans. by Abraham Hayward, rev. C. A. Buchheim (London, 1892).

Italian Journey (1786–1788), trans. W. H. Auden and Elizabeth Mayer (London, 1962).

Gombrich, E. J. H., *Meditations on a Hobby-Horse and Other Essays on the Theory of Art* (London, 1963).

Goode, Clement T., *Byron as Critic* (Weimar, 1923).

Bibliography

Goodman, D. C. (ed.), *Science and Religious Belief: A Selection of Primary Sources* (Open University, 1973).

Green, Clarence C., *The Neo-Classic Theory of Tragedy in England During the Eighteenth Century* (Cambridge, Mass., 1934).

Gregory, H., *The Shield of Achilles* (New York, 1944).

Griggs, E. L., 'Coleridge and Byron', *PMLA*, 45 (Dec. 1930), 1085–97.

Gurr, A., '*Don Juan* and the Moral North', *Ariel*, 3 (July 1972), 32–41.

Halévy, Elie, *A History of the English People in 1815*, 3 vols. (Harmondsworth, 1938).

Haughart, William F., *The Reception of Goethe's "Faust" in England in the First Half of the Nineteenth Century* (New York, 1909).

Hayden, John O., *The Romantic Reviewers, 1802–1824* (Chicago, 1968).

Romantic Bards and British Reviewers (London, 1971).

Hayden, John O. (ed.), *Sir Walter Scott: The Critical Heritage* (London, 1970).

Hazlitt, William, *Liber Amoris and Dramatic Criticism*, ed. Charles Morgan (London, 1948).

The Complete Works, ed. P. P. Howe, 21 vols. (London, 1930).

Henning, Hans (ed.), *Faust Bibliographie*, 3 vols. in 5 (Berlin and Weimar, 1966).

Hill, Draper, *Mr. Gillray the Caricaturist* (London, 1965).

Hilles, F. W. and Harold Bloom (eds.), *From Sensibility to Romanticism: Essays Presented to Frederick A. Pottle* (New York, 1965).

[Hobhouse, John Cam] Broughton, Lord, *Recollections of a Long Life*, ed. Lady Dorchester, vols. I–IV (London, 1909).

A Journey through Albania and Other Provinces of Turkey (London, 1813).

Holmstrom, Kirsten Gram, *Monodrama, Attitudes, Tableaux Vivants: Studies on Some Trends of Theatrical Fashion 1770–1815*, Stockholm Studies in Theatrical History, 1 (Stockholm, 1967).

Holstein, Baroness Staël (Madame de Staël), *Germany*, 3 vols. (London, 1813).

Hone, William, *The Apocryphal New Testament* (London, 1820).

Ancient Mysteries Described, Especially the English Miracle Plays Founded Upon Apocryphal New Testament Story (London, 1823).

Honour, Hugh, *Neo-Classicism* (Harmondsworth, 1968).

Hough, G. G., *The Romantic Poets* (London, 1953).

Hunt, J. H. Leigh, *The Town* (Oxford, 1907).

Autobiography, ed. J. E. Morpurgo (London, 1948).

Hussey, Christopher, *The Picturesque* (London, 1967).

Irwin, David, *English Neo-Classical Art: Studies in Inspiration and Taste* (London, 1966).

Jackson, J. R. de J. (ed.), *Coleridge: The Critical Heritage* (London, 1970).

James, D. G., *Byron and Shelley* (Nottingham, 1951).

Johnson, E. D. H., '*Don Juan* in England', *English Literary History*, 11 (June 1944), 135–53.

Johnson, Edgar, *Sir Walter Scott: The Great Unknown*, 2 vols. (London, 1970).

Johnson, Samuel, *Lives of the Poets*, *Works*, vols. IX–XI (London, 1792).

242

Jones, Frederick L. (ed.), *The Letters of Percy Bysshe Shelley*, 2 vols. (Oxford, 1964).

Joseph, M. K., *Byron the Poet* (London, 1964).

Jump, John D., *Byron* (London, 1972).

Jump, John D. (ed.), *Byron: 'Childe Harold's Pilgrimage' and 'Don Juan': A Casebook* (London, 1973).

Byron: A Symposium (London, 1975).

Klapper, M. Roxana, *The German Literary Influence on Byron* (Salzburg, 1974).

Klingender, F. D. (ed.), *Hogarth and English Caricature* (London, 1944).

Knight, G. Wilson, *The Burning Oracle* (London, 1939).

Lord Byron: Christian Virtues (London, 1953).

Byron's Dramatic Prose (Nottingham, 1953).

Laureate of Peace: On the Genius of Alexander Pope (London, 1954).

Byron and Shakespeare (London, 1966).

Kroeber, Karl, *Romantic Narrative Art* (London, 1966).

Kroeber, Karl and William Walling (eds.), *Images of Romanticism* (London, 1978).

Langbaum, Robert, *The Poetry of Experience* (London, 1957).

Leavis, F. R., *Revaluation: Tradition and Development in English Poetry* (London, 1936).

English Literature in Our Time and the University (London, 1969).

Levin, H., *The Broken Column: A Study in Romantic Hellenism* (Cambridge, Mass., 1931).

Literary Gazette and Journal of the Belles-Lettres (1821), 'Lord Byron's Plagiarisms', 122–4, 137–9, 150–2, 168–70, 201–3, 282 [A. A. Watts].

Lovell, Ernest J., Jr, *Byron: The Record of a Quest* (Austin, Texas, 1949).

Lytton, Lord, *England and the English* (London, 1874).

Macaulay, T. B., 'Moore's Life of Lord Byron', *Critical and Historical Essays*, 2 vols. (London, 1860), vol. I.

McGann, Jerome J., *Fiery Dust: Byron's Poetic Development* (Chicago, 1968).

'Don Juan' in Context (London, 1976).

McKillop, Alan Dugald (ed.), *'The Castle of Indolence' and Other Poems* (Lawrence, Kans., 1961).

McMaster, Graham (ed.), *William Wordsworth: A Critical Anthology* (Harmondsworth, 1972).

Madden, Lionel (ed.), *Robert Southey: The Critical Heritage* (London, 1972).

Manning, P. J., 'Edmund Kean and Byron's Plays', *Keats–Shelley Journal*, 21–2 (1972–3), 188–206.

Manwaring, Elizabeth Wheeler, *Italian Landscape in Eighteenth Century England* (London, 1925).

Marchand, Leslie A., *Byron: A Biography*, 3 vols. (London, 1957).

Byron's Poetry: A Critical Introduction (London, 1965).

Marjarum, E. W., *Byron as Sceptic and Believer* (Princeton, N.J., 1938).

Marshall, William H., *Byron, Shelley, Hunt and "The Liberal"* (Philadelphia, 1960).

The Structure of Byron's Major Poems (Philadelphia, 1962).

Martin, L. C., *Byron's Lyrics* (Nottingham, 1948).

Mason, H. A., *To Homer through Pope* (London, 1972).

Medwin, Thomas, *The Life of Percy Bysshe Shelley*, ed. H. B. Forman (Oxford, 1913).

Melchiori, G., *Byron and Italy* (Nottingham, 1958).

Merchant, W. M., *Shakespeare and the Artist* (Oxford, 1959).

Creed and Drama: An Essay in Religious Drama (London, 1965).

Miller, B., *Leigh Hunt's Relations with Byron, Shelley and Keats* (New York, 1910).

Mills, Howard, *Peacock: His Circle and His Age* (Cambridge, 1969).

Milton, John, *The Poems*, ed. John Carey and Alastair Fowler (London, 1968).

Monthly Review, 62 (Appendix), 'Faust . . . by Goethe', 491–5 [William Taylor].

Moore, Thomas, *The Life of Lord Byron* (London, 1851).

Munby, A. N. L. (ed.), *Sale Catalogues of the Libraries of Eminent Persons*, 12 vols. (London, 1971), vol. I.

Nichol, John, *Byron* (London, 1880).

Nicolson, Benedict, *Joseph Wright of Derby*, 2 vols. (London, 1968).

Notopoulos, James A., *The Platonism of Shelley* (New York, 1969).

Orel, H. and G. J. Worth (eds.), *The Nineteenth Century Writer and His Audience* (Lawrence, Kans., 1969).

Origo, Iris, *The Last Attachment* (London, 1949).

Pafford, Ward, 'Byron and the Mind of Man: *Childe Harold III and IV*, and *Manfred*', *Studies in Romanticism*, 1 (Winter 1962), 105–27.

Page, Leroy E., 'Diluvianism and Its Critics in Great Britain in the Early Nineteenth Century', in *The New Hampshire Interdisciplinary Conference on the History of Geology: Towards a History of Geology*, ed. Cecil J. Schneer (Cambridge, Mass., 1969).

Parker, D., 'The Narrator of *Don Juan*', *Ariel*, 5 (April 1974), 49–58.

Partridge, A. C., 'Byron and Italy', *English Studies in Africa*, 7 (March 1964), 1–12.

Peacock, Thomas Love, *Novels*, ed. David Garnett (London, 1948).

Memoirs of Shelley and Other Essays and Reviews, ed. Howard Mills (London, 1970).

Pierce, F. E., *Currents and Eddies in the English Romantic Generation* (Oxford, 1918).

Piper, W. B., *The Heroic Couplet* (London, 1969).

Pope, Alexander, *Works . . . Printed Verbatim from the Octavo Edition of Mr. Warburton*, 6 vols. (London, 1776).

Poems, ed. John Butt (London, 1963).

Potter, Robert (trans.), *The Plays of Aeschylus* (London, 1886).

Praz, Mario, *The Romantic Agony* (London, 1933).

'Byron and Foscolo', in *Renaissance and Modern Essays Presented to Vivian de Sola Pinto*, ed. George A. Panichas and Allan Rodway (London, 1966), pp. 101–18.

Prior, Matthew, *Literary Works*, ed. H. Bunker Wright and Monroe K. Spears, 2 vols. (Oxford, 1959).

Pulci, Luigi, *Morgante e Lettere*, ed. Domenico De Robertis (Florence, 1962).

Quarterly Review, 10 (Jan. 1814), 'The Giaour . . . by Lord Byron . . . The Bride of Abydos . . . by Lord Byron', 331–54.

10 (Jan. 1814), 'De l'Allemagne. Par Madame La Baronne De Staël Holstein', 355–409.

21 (April 1819), 'Prospectus and Specimen of an intended National Work, by William and Robert Whistlecraft . . . The Court of Beasts . . . by William Stewart Rose', 486–556 [Ugo Foscolo].

23 (May 1820), 'The Fall of Jerusalem . . . by the Rev. W. H. Milman', 198–225.

27 (July 1822), 'Marino Faliero, Sardanapalus, The Two Foscari, Cain . . . by Lord Byron', 476–524.

Quennell, Peter, *Byron: The Years of Fame* (London, 1935).

Byron in Italy (London, 1941).

Read, Herbert, *In Defence of Shelley and Other Essays* (London, 1936).

The True Voice of Feeling: Studies in English Romantic Poetry (London, 1953).

Redpath, T., *The Young Romantics and Critical Opinion, 1807–1824* (London, 1973).

Reynolds, Sir Joshua, *Discourses on Art*, ed. Robert R. Wark (London, 1975).

Rickwood, Edgell (ed.), *Radical Squibs and Loyal Ripostes* (London, 1971).

Ridenour, G. M., *The Style of "Don Juan"* (New Haven, Conn., 1960).

'The Mode of Byron's *Don Juan*', *PMLA*, 89 (Sept. 1964), 442–6.

Rieger, James, *The Mutiny Within: The Heresies of Percy Bysshe Shelley* (New York, 1967).

Robertson, J. G., 'Goethe and Byron', *Publications of the English Goethe Society*, n.s., 2 (1925), 1–132.

Robinson, Charles E., 'The Devil as Doppelgänger in *The Deformed Transformed*: The Sources and Meaning of Byron's Unfinished Drama', *Bulletin of the New York Public Library*, 76 (March 1970), 117–202.

Shelley and Byron: The Snake and the Eagle Wreathed in Flight (Baltimore, 1976).

Robson, W. W., 'Byron as Poet', *Proceedings of the British Academy*, 43 (1957), 25–62.

Rodway, Allan E., *The Romantic Conflict* (London, 1963).

Rogers, Neville, *Shelley at Work* (Oxford, 1967).

Rogers, Samuel, *Poetical Works* (London, 1867).

Recollections of the Table-Talk of Samuel Rogers, by A. Dyce, ed. M. Bishop (London, 1952).

Rose, William (ed.), *Essays on Goethe* (London, 1949).

Rosenblum, Robert, *Transformations in Late Eighteenth Century Art* (Princeton, N.J., 1970).

Rousseau, Jean-Jacques, *The 'Confessions' . . . with the 'Reveries of the Solitary Walker'*, 2 vols. (London, 1783).

Julie, ou la Nouvelle Héloïse (Paris, 1960).

Rutherford, Andrew, *Byron: A Critical Study* (London, 1961).

Rutherford, Andrew (ed.), *Byron: The Critical Heritage* (London, 1970).

Schiff, Gert, *Johann Heinrich Füssli 1741–1825: Text und Oeuvrekatalog*, 2 vols. (Zurich, n.d.).

Scott, Sir Walter, *The Poetical Works*, ed. J. L. Robertson (Oxford, 1921).
Minstrelsy of the Scottish Border, ed. T. F. Henderson, 4 vols. (London, 1932).

Shelley, Percy Bysshe, *The Complete Works*, ed. Roger Ingpen and Walter E. Peck, 10 vols. (London, 1926–30).

Shenstone, William, *Works in Verse and Prose*, 3 vols. (London, 1764).

Siddons, Henry, *Practical Illustrations of Rhetorical Gesture and Action*, 2nd edn (London, 1822).

Smiles, Samuel, *A Publisher and His Friends: Memoir and Correspondence of the Late John Murray*, 2 vols. (London, 1891).

Smith, James and Horace Smith, *Rejected Addresses*, The New Universal Library (London, n.d.).

Smollett, Tobias, *Travels through France and Italy* (London, 1949).

Southey, Robert, *Letters from England*, ed. Jack Simmons (London, 1951).

Speirs, John, *Poetry Towards Novel* (London, 1971).

Spencer, T. J. B., *Fair Greece, Sad Relic: Literary Philhellenism from Shakespeare to Byron* (London, 1954).
Byron and the Greek Tradition (Nottingham, 1960).

Staël, Madame de, *see* Holstein, Baroness Staël.

Stendhal, *Voyages en Italie*, ed. V. del Litto (Paris, 1973).

Stern, Bernard Herbert, *The Rise of Romantic Hellenism in English Literature 1732–1786* (New York, 1969).

Sterne, Laurence, *A Sentimental Journey through France and Italy*, ed. Graham Petrie (Harmondsworth, 1967).

Stokoe, F. W., *German Influence in the English Romantic Period 1788–1818* (Cambridge, 1926).

Stone, P. W. K., *The Art of Poetry 1750–1820* (London, 1967).

Sutherland, James, *English Satire* (Cambridge, 1958).

Symon, J. D., *Byron in Perspective* (London, 1924).

Thompson, L. C., *More Magic Dethroned* (London, 1935).

Thomson, James, *Poetical Works*, ed. Peter Cunningham, 2 vols. (London, 1862).
Poetical Works, ed. J. Logie Robertson (Oxford, 1908).

Thomson, P. W., 'Byron and Edmund Kean – A Comment', *Theatre Research/Recherches Théâtrales*, 8 (1966), 17–19.

Thorslev, P. L., Jr, *The Byronic Hero: Types and Prototypes* (Minneapolis, Minn., 1962).

Toynbee, Paget, *Dante in English Literature* (London, 1909).

Trelawney, Edward J., *Recollections of the Last Days of Shelley and Byron* (London, 1858).
Records of Shelley, Byron and the Author, ed. David Wright (Harmondsworth, 1973).

Trewin, J. C., 'The Romantic Poets in the Theatre', *Keats–Shelley Memorial Bulletin*, 20 (1969), 21–30.

Trilling, Lionel, *Matthew Arnold* (New York, 1939).
Sincerity and Authenticity (London, 1972).

Villiers, H., *The Grand Whiggery* (London, 1939).

Voltaire, François-Marie Arouet de, *Dictionnaire philosophique*, ed. Julien Benda and Raymond Naves (Paris, 1954).

Wallis, B., *Byron: The Critical Voice*, 2 vols. (Salzburg, 1973).

Warton, Thomas, *History of English Poetry*, ed. W. Carew Hazlitt, 4 vols. (London, 1871).

Watling, E. F. (trans.), *Seneca: Four Tragedies and 'Octavia'* (Harmondsworth, 1966).

Webb, Timothy, *The Violet in the Crucible: Shelley and Translation* (Oxford, 1976).

Webster, Mary, *Francis Wheatley*, Studies in British Art (London, 1970).

West, Paul, *Byron and the Spoiler's Art* (London, 1960).

'Byron and the World of Things: An Ingenious Disregard', *Keats–Shelley Memorial Bulletin*, 11 (1960), 21–32.

West, Paul (ed.), *Byron: A Collection of Critical Essays* (Englewood Cliffs, N.J., 1963).

White, Newman Ivey, 'The English Romantic Writers as Dramatists', *Sewanee Review*, 30 (April–June 1922), 206–15.

The Unextinguished Hearth: Shelley and His Contemporary Critics (New York, 1966).

Winckelmann, J. J., *Writings on Art*, ed. David Irwin (New York, 1972).

Wordsworth, William, *Poetical Works*, ed. Thomas Hutchinson, rev. Ernest de Selincourt (Oxford, 1936).

Prose Works, ed. W. J. B. Owen and J. W. Smyser, 3 vols. (Oxford, 1974).

Wright, Thomas, *A History of Caricature and the Grotesque in Literature and Art* (London, 1875).

Yates, Frances A., 'Transformations of Dante's Ugolino', *Journal of the Warburg and Courtauld Institutes*, 14 (1951), 92–117.

Young, Edward, *The Complaint; or, Night Thoughts on Life, Death, and Immortality* (London, 1812).

III. Unpublished theses

Anderson, G. R., 'The form and content of Byron's historical tragedies' (B.Litt., Oxford), 1957.

Herakly, T. G., 'Francis Jeffrey as a literary critic with special reference to his criticism of Byron and Keats' (M.A., London), 1963.

Ingleby, B., 'Byron's poetic theory: its development and application' (M.Phil., London), 1967.

Jones, L. M., 'A re-examination of the Byronic Hero: a study in alienation' (Ph.D., Exeter), 1973.

Mellown, M. J., 'The development of Lord Byron's literary criticism and of the literary attitudes revealed in his poetry and prose' (Ph.D., London), 1964.

Taborski, B., 'Lord Byron and the theatre' (M.A., Bristol), 1952.

Index

Italic page numbers denote references in quoted matter.

Index